D1553484

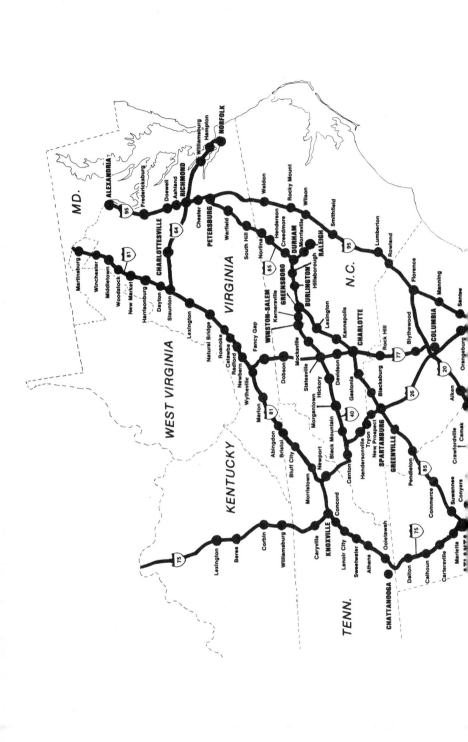

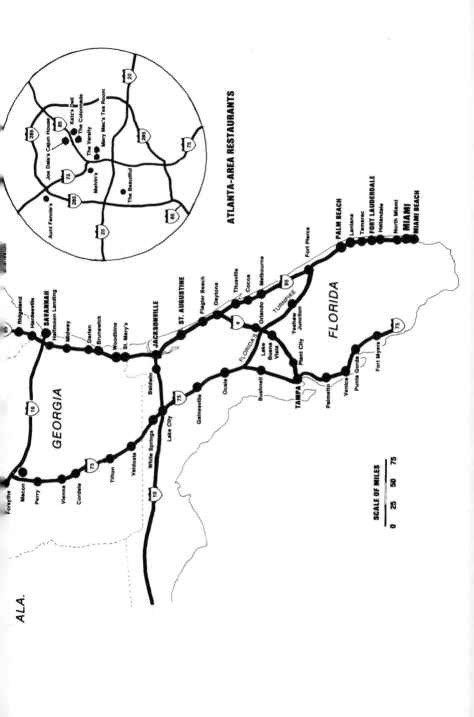

ALA.

GEORGIA

Forsythe
Macon
Perry
Vienna
Cordele
Tifton
Valdosta
White Springs
Lake City
16
75
10

Ridgeland
Hardeeville
SAVANNAH
Halfmoon Landing
Midway
Darien
Brunswick
Woodbine
St. Mary's
95
JACKSONVILLE
Baldwin
Gainesville
Ocala
75

ST. AUGUSTINE
Flagler Beach
Daytone
Titusville
Cocoa
Melbourne
Orlando
4
FLORIDA'S TURNPIKE
Lake Buena Vista
Plant City
Bushnell
TAMPA
Palmetto
Venice
Punta Gorda
Fort Myers
Yeehaw Junction
95
Fort Pierce
PALM BEACH
Lantana
Tamarac
FORT LAUDERDALE
Hallandale
North Miami
MIAMI
MIAMI BEACH
FLORIDA
75

SCALE OF MILES

0   25   50   75

ATLANTA-AREA RESTAURANTS

20
Katz's Deli
The Colonnade
85
Mary Mac's Tea Room
285
Joe Dale's Cajun House
The Varsity
75
285
The Beautiful
Melvin's
75
Aunt Fannie's
285
85
20

BY THE SAME AUTHORS

The Interstate Gourmet—New England
The Interstate Gourmet—Mid-Atlantic
The Interstate Gourmet—California and the Pacific Northwest

THE INTERSTATE
GOURMET

Southeast

Neal O. Weiner and
David M. Schwartz

SUMMIT BOOKS
NEW YORK

The reader should be aware that the restaurant business is unpredictable. Restaurants change their menus, prices and hours; some even change their names or addresses. While we have made every effort to update this book over the past year, we would be most grateful to hear about any changes you have encountered in your travels so that we may keep future editions up to date.

Copyright © 1985 by The Interstate Gourmet, Inc.
All rights reserved
including the right of reproduction
in whole or in part in any form
Published by SUMMIT BOOKS
A Division of Simon & Schuster, Inc.
Simon & Schuster Building
1230 Avenue of the Americas
New York, New York 10020
SUMMIT BOOKS and colophon are trademarks of
Simon & Schuster, Inc.
Designed by Eve Kirch
Illustrations by Kristin Funkhauser
Map by Robert MacLean
Manufactured in the United States of America
First Edition

10   9   8   7   6   5   4   3   2   1

Library of Congress Cataloging in Publication Data
Weiner, Neal O.
    The interstate gourmet—Southeast.

    Includes index.
    1. Restaurants, lunch rooms, etc.—Southeastern
States—Directories.   I. Schwartz, David M.   II. Title.
TX907.W45   1985   647'.9574   84-24108
ISBN 0-671-52336-8

ACKNOWLEDGMENTS

Two of us wrote this book, but about 200 others made it possible. We didn't want to inflict an exhaustive list on our forbearing editor, Elizabeth Kaplan, and our publisher, Jim Silberman (foremost among the 200), but some names should not go without mention.

Our eating odyssey through the Southeast was made infinitely more pleasurable by the warmth and hospitality of Tony and Rosemary Brozena, Greg Fabian, Mark and Linda Fisher, Mike and Rene Gold, Tom and Hilde Harkins, Lucille and Peter Jansen, Frank and Pat Johnson, Paul Kallina, Richard and Dorien Lancia, Jeff Lessne, Jim and Dotty Lloyd, Joan Lewis, Bob and June Morgan, Victor and Lee Remisiewicz, Robert and Carol Remisiewicz and family, Joan and R. O. Rushton, Sonny and Joan Sachs, Claire and Harold Schiesser, Rick Sebak, Doris Tennant, and Julian Toporek.

Of the many people who took the time to help us locate the kinds of restaurants we were looking for, we especially wish to thank Carol Anderson, Tina Annas, Sherie Beers, Elizabeth Bennet, Priscilla Brown, Toni Burk, Tom Carter, Deborah Clark, Tom Clarke, Elizabeth Cochran, Joe Cray, Pam Danz, Ruth Dickson, Karen Edmiston, Clara Eschmann, Jim Ezzell, Linda Fields, Connie Fiest, Karen Fitzgerald, Terry Hawthorne, Rosemary Heffernan, Edna Herman, Frank Jarrell, Valdine Keller, Joe Kennedy, David Loomis, Rennie Lumm, Jann Malone, Elizabeth Mooney, Helen Moore, Gail Nardi, David Nicholson, Andy Perry, Martin Register, Denise Richbourg, Jonathan Rogers, Dannye Romine, Seymour Rosenburg, Deborah Sansabaugh, Carlos Santos, Mary Scourtes, Yvonne Shaheen, Harold Shumacher, Carole Sugar-

Acknowledgments

man, Tom Sweeten, Joyce Taylor, Andy Thornton, Cindy Wells, Vince Wheeler, and Jennifer Woods.

Back up north, Charlotte Sheedy always answered the phone when counsel was needed; the many good people on the tenth floor of the Simon and Schuster Building oversaw the operation from start to finish; Jessica and Marcus Weiner and Mary Lou Brozena gave us good reasons to come back home.

CONTENTS

Map		2–3
Introduction		11
I-4		
	Florida	17
I-10		
	Florida	27
I-20		
	Georgia	29
	South Carolina	37
I-26		
	North Carolina	43
	South Carolina	48
I-40		
	Tennessee	60
	North Carolina	63
I-64		
	Virginia	80
I-75		
	Florida	90
	Georgia	109
	Tennessee	137
	Kentucky	148
I-77		
	South Carolina	159
	North Carolina	161
	Virginia	168

Contents

I-81

	Tennessee	170
	Virginia	173
	West Virginia	203

I-85

	Georgia	205
	South Carolina	212
	North Carolina	221
	Virginia	238

I-95

	Florida	242
	Georgia	274
	South Carolina	287
	North Carolina	292
	Virginia	302

Florida's Turnpike

	Florida	317

Index of restaurants and towns   323

INTRODUCTION

Maine to Miami without a single stop at a soulless service area or a monotonous chain restaurant—that was our goal when we launched the *Interstate Gourmet* series, and now this Southeast volume makes it possible. Whether you're driving to Florida from the Northeast or the Midwest, or just touring the Southland, this book will point you to good food and local color within minutes of the interstate highways.

Interstate 75 is the great funnel down which Midwesterners pour in search of sunshine, and here we've got it covered from northern Kentucky to South Florida. The coastal route is I-95, and this book locates good restaurants every 30 miles or so, starting in the suburbs of Washington, D.C. Combine this *Interstate Gourmet* volume with those for New England and the Mid-Atlantic, and there you have it—hundreds of interesting, worthwhile stops lining the road from Maine to Miami.

We haven't limited ourselves to I-95 and I-75. This book also visits dozens of stopoffs on I-81 in Virginia's Shenandoah Valley, I-40 across North Carolina, I-85 from Atlanta to Richmond, and more. See the map (front page) for details. It all adds up to local restaurants along 7,000 miles of interstate highways throughout Virginia, the Carolinas, Georgia, and Florida, as well as eastern Kentucky and Tennessee. There aren't many long-distance routes left in the Southeast where you'll have to get stuck at Stuckey's.

Every traveler is familiar with the dilemma we are trying to solve. There you are, locked onto that concrete ribbon at fifty-

11

five-plus miles per hour, totally insulated from local life. You're in a hurry (somehow, you're *always* in a hurry on an interstate) and you're bored (somehow, all interstates look the same). It's time to eat, if for no other reason than to break the monotony, but you don't look forward to another assembly-line meal where you will get processed as much as the food. As the exits fly by, you crane your neck in search of an inviting possibility, but all you can see are the huge signs of the chain restaurants clamoring for your dollars. For a while you hold out, but in the end you give in and resign yourself to whatever plastic food and outrageous prices turn up at the bottom of the exit ramp.

You know there's got to be something better nearby—at least a local café where color comes as a side order, or maybe even a really good restaurant in which to forget for an hour the rigors of the road. But where? Who has the time to go poking around in search of Ma's Real Home Cooking? And who wants to risk terminal heartburn in case Ma turns out to be more of a butcher than a cook?

We've done the poking (and suffered the heartburn) for you. Since beginning the *Interstate Gourmet* series two years ago, we've traveled over 50,000 miles of interstate highways and intersecting byways in search of convenient, high-quality restaurants that would take some of the tedium out of long-distance driving. We've eaten in restaurants of every type (and quality), culling the best of the lot for inclusion in these guides.

For us, an ideal restaurant would be about thirty seconds from the exit ramp, its kitchen would produce outstanding food from one cuisine or another, and its prices would be about ten years behind the times. Further, it would have a decor that we'd find unself-consciously lovely, and its tables would be occupied by local people who'd provide a charm of their own. Of course, it's rare to find all these virtues in one place, so we have had to balance one feature against another to find restaurants that came as close as possible to our vision.

Convenience was the first consideration. In compact New England we didn't even consider an eatery that was more than two minutes from an interstate exit ramp. In other parts of the country we've had to go further afield to get beyond Fast Food Alley. But with a few exceptions, a five- or six-minute detour is the most you can expect. Many of our selections are much closer. A few are more than ten minutes out of your way, included because they are so outstanding that they're worth the trouble, or because absolutely nothing bearable exists any closer to the highway. (No matter where they are, we tell you how to find all of these restaurants from the interstate using clear, easy-to-follow directions.)

Aside from relative accessibility, all these restaurants have one thing in common: we like them. We enjoy restaurants for many reasons. First, of course, there's the food. Be it burger, bagel, or bouillabaisse, what we include here must be better than what you'd find in chain restaurants; of course, it's usually *much* better. And local color counts for us too. The interstate system has so homogenized highway travel that you can't tell from typical roadhouse food (or decor) whether you're in Saint Augustine or Santa Fe.

And then there's cost. Here you'll find descriptions of places that serve everything from eighty-cent hamburgers to eighteen-dollar chateaubriand. There are some very fine restaurants herein, and if you've got the time and the purse you ought to discover how truly refreshing it can be to break up a long drive with a wonderful meal. But most people aren't looking for pricey dining on the road (especially with a backseat full of kids), so we focus on low- and medium-priced restaurants. We hasten to add that pinching pennies doesn't necessarily mean sacrificing quality. In fact, we've found that outside major cities expensive restaurants tend to be overrated and overstuffed. We're happiest when we find small, owner-operated places, the kind that everybody in town—and nobody on the nearby highway—knows about.

Within these bounds, we have searched always for variety so that you could choose between lasagna, litchi nuts, or liver and onions. All that we've ruled out categorically are bad restaurants, overpriced restaurants, chain restaurants, and the monotonous steak and seafood joints that look as if they're trying to be a chain.

For whatever reason a restaurant is included here, we try to tell it like it is and let you decide if it's worth your while. You may or may not be enthralled by the well-worn booths and excellent chili burgers described at Exit 23, but read on—perhaps the subdued tones and seafood salads to be found half an hour up the road at Exit 28 hold greater appeal. It's always easy to see what lies ahead because this book is organized according to the route you are driving: each chapter covers a different highway, and the entries are arranged geographically, not alphabetically, from south to north or west to east. (Of course, you may be driving in the opposite direction, so you'll just have to learn to read backwards.)

There's little question that sampling regional cuisine is—or should be—one of the pleasures of travel. You can find boiled scrod in Boston; schnitz und knepp in Pennsylvania; steamed crabs in Maryland; and, on the West Coast, that innovative blend of *nouvelle* and *naturel* that they call California cuisine. But in no part of the country is a distinctive regional cuisine so much a part of daily life as in the South. Our Yankee palates developed an appreciation for the much derided grits and a true love for sweet-potato pie (pages 31 and 163), peanut soup (pages 195 and 199), liver mush (page 224), turnip greens, and black-eyed peas. In almost every county we found wonderful versions of fried chicken, catfish, and country ham with red-èye gravy (see pages 108, 281, and 207 for our favorites of each); and we couldn't help but get caught up in the great barbecue cult debates (our candidates for top honors are found on pages 83, 120, and 225, although we've written about many others that are also very fine). From South Carolina to the tip of Florida, interstate highways skirt the coast, and fresh seafood is the order of the day. Expect native preparations like she-crab soup (page 57 and others) and conch chowder (page 261), along with indigenous species like rock shrimp, stone crabs, red snapper, pompano, and Spanish mackerel. We even tell you where you can order—quite legally—alligator, turtle, and Florida wild pig. No matter where you happen to be in the South when hunger strikes, you'll find delicious regional fare without straying far from your route.

We will admit, however, that on more than one occasion we wearied of the choices available. While the South is long on home-cooked food, in some areas it runs short on variety. Two explanations come to mind. Until recently, eating out simply was not a southern custom; consequently, fine dining was slower to develop here than elsewhere. Further, the South never saw the influx of ethnic groups that turned so many northern cities into adventures in eclectic eating. An exception is Florida, which has played host to its own wave of immigrants and now reflects the culinary diversity of the Northeast and Midwest.

This doesn't mean you're going to be stuck with fried chicken, like it or not, from Alexandria to Saint Augustine. Though usually confined to the larger cities, ethnic restaurants do dot the South—Harold's Kosher Deli in Knoxville, for example; or Joe Dale's Cajun House in Atlanta; or La Casita in Richmond. (We left it out if the place made too many concessions to local taste— the Chinese restaurant, for example, that served its smoked duck with a mound of ketchup-soaked french fries.)

And let it be said that, clichéd as it may sound, southern hospitality is no myth. In the humblest of southern restaurants we found some of the warmest, most trusting, wonderfully helpful people we've ever met—people who charmed us with their food and their character. We hope you'll be charmed too.

Florida

LINCOLN RESTAURANT, *Exit 23A (I-275), West Tampa*

West Tampa has become this city's Little Havana, and Columbus Drive is its Restaurant Row. In fact, the street is far more widely known as "Boliche Boulevard," a reference to the Cuban dish that can be found, along with many others, at half a dozen restaurants where menu prices look as if they predate Castro's rise to power. According to most of the people we asked, the Lincoln is *numero uno*, the King of Boliche Boulevard.

If you order boliche, the boulevard's namesake, you'll find eye round stuffed with bacon or sausage, served *au jus*. Just as popular in Cuban restaurants on the boulevard is Russian trout (or, to be more precise, *trucha a la Rusa*). Nobody seemed to know if it's a traditional Cuban dish or a culinary outgrowth of political handholding; whatever its origin, Russian trout has Tampa's Cubans hooked, and in one nibble we were hooked too. The fresh fish is lightly breaded and pan-fried to perfect crispness, then garnished with parsley butter and chopped egg, an unusual but irresistible combination. For vegetables, you've a choice of two from an enticing list that includes yellow rice, black beans, plantains, and yucca.

The portion of fish was more than ample, and its accompanying mound of rice and beans was so immense it had to be served on a separate plate. Our vivacious waitress, who called us

"Papa" (she was young, but not *that* young!), plunked the meal down on the table and said, "OK, pig out!" That was easy enough.

We also had *carnero a la Cantalana*, lamb shank in an aromatic tomato sauce. The lamb came tender and delicious, but somewhat fatty; what it lacked in leanness was compensated for by a multiplicity of flavors that exploded with every bite. There was garlic, vinegar, and the aroma of bay, along with other pungent spices and herbs.

At dinner time, when things get "expensive," the trout dinner, including its mountain of vegetables, a salad, and high-octane Cuban coffee, costs only $4.50; lamb shank is all of $4.00. They're less at lunch, of course.

The Lincoln is known also for its paella, baked eggs Malaguena, roast pork Cuban style, and baked red snapper Spanish style. There are at least fifteen other dishes, each more captivating than the last.

For dessert, we again went native, ordering guava shells. The bright red, syrup-drenched fruit (canned) comes in a bowl alongside crackers and cream cheese. Our waitress explained: first spread cream cheese on a cracker, and then lay a piece of guava on top. "Like bagels and lox," she said. Clearly, we weren't the first Anglos to have eaten here.

HOURS Mon.–Fri. 11 am–2:30 pm and 5–9 pm; Sat. noon–9 pm; closed Sun.

SPECS 3247 W. Columbus Drive; (813) 877-4205; major cards ($10 minimum); beer and wine.

DIRECTIONS Stay on I-4 West until it ends. (If you intend to enter I-75 South, this will require a detour that you may not wish to undertake; consult a map. If you are headed for I-75 North or I-275 South, there's very little detour.) I-4 ends at the junction of I-275. At this point, enter I-275 South for 2 miles to Exit 23A. From Exit 23A, bear right onto Dale Mabry Highway North (Route 92 East). Go about ¾ mile to the light at Columbus. Turn right and go about ½ mile; it's on the left at the corner of Lincoln Ave.

Note: After eating, if you are heading to Saint Petersburg or Tampa, continue along I-275 South. If you are heading to I-75 (North *or* South), take I-275 *North* and watch for signs.

YBOR CITY RESTAURANTS, *Exit 1, Tampa*

Ybor City is Tampa's cobblestoned historic district, once home to a flourishing Latin community that has since moved to West Tampa in search of more affordable real estate. We followed them there for our Latin meal (see Lincoln Restaurant, above), but the traveler who wants nostalgia as a side order will still find the streets of Ybor City paved with restaurants and cafés.

Numero uno on most lists of Tampa eateries, and in fact *numero uno* on any chronological listing of Florida restaurants, is the **Columbia,** a full block of Iberian opulence containing 11 rooms, 1,500 seats, and Lord knows how many paintings, arches, porticoes, fountains, and decorative tiles. Expect valet parking, strolling musicians, high prices, and dishes like Columbia shrimp supreme (deep-fried jumbos wrapped in bacon), red snapper Alicante (poached in sauterne, topped with almonds), and paella Valenciana (a little bit of almost everything that ever swam, crawled, or walked, on rice).

Of course the Columbia isn't Ybor City's only hot spot. Almost as classy and every bit as Latin is **Spanish Park,** where fresh Gulf seafood reigns supreme. **Café Pepe** is one rung down the price ladder, but the food is still high-caliber.

DIRECTIONS If eastbound, turn right at the bottom of ramp. If westbound, make first allowable left. Either way, you'll be on 21st St., which will take you straight to the **Columbia** in ½ mile (21st and Broadway). **Café Pepe** (2006 W. Kennedy Blvd.), **Spanish Park** (3517 E. 7th Ave.), and others are near at hand.

BUDDY FREDDY'S, *Exit 11, Plant City*

Walk into this steak-housey restaurant and you might think you've found nothing but another soporific AAA-style salad-bar affair. But take a minute to look more closely and you'll notice that those big, bold murals are actually something special (in fact, local artist John Briggs has works in the Smithsonian). And what are all those aged photographs of old-time string bands? Why, they're pictures of the family band, Pop Johnson and his Range Riders, who made the rounds with Hank Williams way back when. Now Buddy and Freddy Johnson, grandsons to Owen

19

"Pop" Johnson, have put aside fiddling and taken up restaurant-ing. But Uncle Red Johnson still plays "anything with strings and pegs," and can be heard often at the restaurant.

Whether or not you catch him, you'll likely be pleased with the food. The menu is mostly American, not fancy or exotic, but that didn't stop a darn good pasta salad from creeping in. Our charbroiled shrimp pilaf was meaty and delicious; other dinner choices include fresh grouper, frogs' legs, and any number of steaks. At $7.50, our meal was near the top of the menu; baby beef liver with onions and bacon is only $3.95, and half a dozen sandwiches (available all day) go much lower still. Breakfast is a big meal here, and locals swear that Buddy Freddy's grits can't be beat.

HOURS   Mon.–Sat. 6 am–9 pm; closed Sun.

SPECS   2104 W. Reynolds; (813) 754-5120; all cards; no liquor.

DIRECTIONS   From Exit 11, head south (turn right if eastbound, left if westbound) on Thonotosassa Blvd. In about ¾ mile get in the right lane and go straight through the light at W. Baker St. (even though the main road curves left). At second stop sign after light, it's on right.

ABOUT WALT DISNEY WORLD VILLAGE

If you'd like a taste of Disney without the mouse (or the admission fee), it's quite easy to get from I-4 to Disney World Village, the shopping and eating suburb of the greater Disney metropolitan area. Centerpiece of the complex is the Empress Lilly, a riverboat re-creation, motionless except for a paddlewheel that turns constantly with no effect other than churning up the waters behind it. Inside, you'll find three separate restaurants (not to mention five bars).

Plushest of the lot is the Empress Room, but if you're on the road forget it—"reservations and proper attire *required*" (empha-sis theirs), not to mention a wad of money. Considerably more accessible are Fisherman's Deck (seafood, of course) and the Steerman's Quarters (you guessed it, steaks). Though proletarian by comparison with their big sister on the top deck, even they will take a bite out of your wallet—a hamburger at Steerman's, for instance, costs $5.95, and things are no more affordable on the seafood side.

Back on shore, you'll find Heidelberger's Deli serving submarine sandwiches with names like Blue Max, Zeppelin, Lindenberg, etc. in the $3–$4 range. Sorry, no Hebrew National, but Hormel meats. The gardenlike Verandah Restaurant was closed for refurbishing when we were there, but it should be back to serving three meals a day before you arrive. The Lite Bite is really a fast-food restaurant, and the Village Ice Cream Parlour and Bakeshop is just what it says it is. Our attention was particularly drawn to the Village Spirits and Wine Shop, which had a placard, "Village Spirits is having a tasting today," permanently affixed to its door.

Like Disney World and Epcot, the Village has plenty to choose from, and the chances are good that you'll spend more than you had planned.

DIRECTIONS From Exit 27 turn right if westbound, left if eastbound. In ¼ mile turn left at the first light into the Walt Disney Village gate. A mile brings you there. Copious free parking.

ANGELO'S, *Exits 29 & 33, Orlando*

See page 320 for a description of this Italian restaurant that is highlighted by its wonderful antipasto bar.

DIRECTIONS **Westbound:** From Exit 33 (a left exit) you will be fed onto Orange Blossom Trail South. It's exactly 3 miles, on the left. Traffic can be heavy; it took us 10-plus minutes during rush hour.

Eastbound: You *can* get there as above (use Exit 33A), but you'll run into much less traffic if you use Exit 29, bearing right off the ramp onto Route 528A East (Sand Lake Rd.). Go about 4½ miles (fast-moving) and turn left at Orange Blossom Trail. In 1.2 miles, Angelo's is on the right, after the light at Lancaster.

KIM WU CHINESE RESTAURANT, *Exit 30B, Orlando*

Since it opened in 1983, Kim Wu has created such a stir among Orlando gastronomes that one reviewer suggested it might become the area's second-largest tourist attraction after you-know-what. We hope that doesn't happen to such a small and pleasant place, because we'd like to be able to get back in the door with the same relative ease we experienced our first time around.

Whether or not Kim Wu's popularity ever reaches Disney World proportions, its menu already has. There are nine soups from egg drop to wintermelon, seven chow meins, five lo meins, six egg foo youngs, and about fifteen Mandarin and Szechuan specialties. Or choose from a passel of lighter dishes they call Chinatown dinners. Several other meals are inexplicably categorized as "Happy Dinners," and half a dozen vegetarian dishes feature tofu. Not enough? The menu also lists a handful of combination platters.

Somehow, from that prodigious list, we settled upon a very creditable wonton soup, nongreasy egg rolls, and a chicken dish called Ho Yu Gai Po, in which breaded, fried pieces of breast are served with snow peas, Chinese black mushrooms, bamboo shoots, baby corn cobs, and other vegetables in "our chef's special sauce." We found it delightfully fresh and free from any chemical taste. Ho Yu Gai Po cost $6.25, which is about average for dinner entrées and combination platters. Lunches run $2.95

to $4.95. A big splurge here would be Peking Duck at $25 for two; it's a complete dinner beginning with a rich duck soup, a second course of duck skin that you wrap in delicate pancakes, and a main course of duck. Dessert, we are told, is duckless.

HOURS   Mon.–Thurs. 11:30 am–10 pm; Fri. 11:30 am–11 pm; Sat. 1–11 pm; Sun. 1–10 pm.

SPECS   Turkey Lake Village Shopping Center, 4904 S. Kirkman Rd.; (305) 293-0752; major cards; full license.

DIRECTIONS   Exit 30B puts you on Route 435 North. In about 1½ miles, turn left into Turkey Lake Village. It's at the far left end of the shopping center, all but hidden behind a hardware store.

RONNIE'S RESTAURANT, *Exit 41, Orlando*

Big, bright, brash, and fast, Ronnie's has been Orlando's answer to the New York-style deli-restaurant since 1956. Walk in and the Formica decor knocks you over; somehow, it seems delightfully *outré* in an age of natural wood and plants. Sit down and bowls of dill pickles, pickled beets, and sauerkraut will greet you. The decor and appointments have not changed since the '50s, and neither has much of the staff.

On one thing, Ronnie's regulars are in complete agreement: a better breakfast can't be found in Orlando. Although smaller appetites can be satisfied for less money, the thing to order before 11 o'clock is Ronnie's $3.85 all-you-can-eat extravaganza of eggs, potatoes, bacon, coffee, and homemade Danish pastries. We missed it and had to settle for a disappointing matzo-ball soup ($1.65); a much better combination sandwich with turkey, tongue, Swiss, and Russian dressing ($4.70); and a decent portion of better-than-decent cheesecake ($1.95). Other than that, you'll find on the two-foot-high menu everything from chopped liver and matjes herring to phosphates and borscht. If calories are no object, end your meal with the infamous "Mogambo Extravaganza": four ice creams, three sherbets, pound cake, whipped cream, chopped nuts, and five different toppings which we will do you the favor of not listing.

HOURS   Sun.–Thurs. 7 am–11 pm; Fri. & Sat. 7 am–1 am.

SPECS   2702 E. Colonial Dr.; (305) 894-2943; no cards; no liquor.

DIRECTIONS   Eastbound: Exit 41 brings you to a light at Amelia St. Go straight through it and turn right at second light (Colonial Dr.) ■. In 2 miles you'll come to the Colonial Plaza Shopping Center; Ronnie's is within.

Westbound: From Exit 41 turn left at the light onto Route 50 East (Colonial Dr.). Then, as above from ■.

BAKERSTREET SEAFOOD GRILL
BAKERSTREET RESTAURANT,
Exit 46, Orlando

Here's a clever idea. Take an already successful restaurant that's built a solid reputation on barbecue beef ribs, fancy hamburgers, and light meals, and build on a new establishment that draws on the old name but cooks up an entirely different kettle of fish. The Bakerstreet Restaurant was the daddy, and the Bakerstreet Seafood Grill is the child, and a precocious child it is. In less than a year, it has eclipsed the original Bakerstreet in gaining attention and plaudits from Orlando gastronomes. It's easy to see why.

You'll notice, as soon as you enter the Grill, that its kitchen is part of its decor. Behind a glass bubble plainly visible from every table, chef/maestro Gary Carouthers plays to his audience like a symphony conductor. Retrieving a 35-pound red snapper from the cooler, he holds it up to the customers' applause. Four swift swipes of the sharpening steel and he's turning it into fillets. Now the fish is on the grill, searing and sputtering while the cook turns his attention to an enormous hunk of yellowfin tuna.

Needless to say, the fish is all fresh. Not only that, it's all cut to order. If Bakerstreet can't buy a fish whole, they won't buy it at all—precut fillets just won't do. When served, it's seared on the outside but tender and flaky and—in the case of our tuna—still pink within. But the real trick (aside from the visual effects) is the mesquite that fuels the grill. Yes, you *can* taste the difference.

Lamb chops and filet mignon are also dropped on the grill, and an excellent spinach salad with feta cheese and marinated black beans will satisfy diners of the vegetarian persuasion. The Seafood Grill is extremely attractive, appropriately decorated right down to the hexagonal tile floor and scallop lamps—with low-level lighting it's almost romantic but by no means overly atmospheric. Expect to spend $7.50 to $13 for most seafood entrées, served with french fries or rice pilaf and a choice of seven gourmet sauces (we loved the Szechuan peanut). A full-meal salad will be $6.50, a hamburger $4.25.

Since the Bakerstreet Seafood Grill is open only for dinner, you may not connect with its schedule. In that case, you'll probably do well by the Bakerstreet Restaurant next door. There's no mesquite-grilled fish or grillside performance, but the food is varied and good: three kinds of quiche each day, potato skins, and other trendy things alongside steak-house fare. Some cleverly concocted stuffed potatoes can make a light meal of themselves. Everything—soups and salad dressings to desserts—is made from scratch. Prices at the Restaurant run $4.50–$6 for light meals, $8–$10 on the heavier end.

HOURS Bakerstreet Seafood Grill: Mon.–Sat. 5:30 pm–11 pm; Sun. 5:30 pm–10 pm. Reservations highly recommended on weekends, especially Jan.–Apr. Bakerstreet Restaurant: Every day, 11 am–1 am.

SPECS 743 Lee Rd.; (305) 644-8811; major cards (except Diners); full license.

DIRECTIONS **Eastbound:** Use Exit 46. On ramp, get in left lane (signs for Lee Rd. West). Turn left at light onto Lee Rd. Go 0.4 mile to restaurant on right.

Westbound: From Exit 46 turn right onto Lee Rd. In ¼ mile it's on your right.

KLAUS' CUISINE, *I-95 Interchange, Daytona*

See page 263 for a description of this fine restaurant with an Olympian chef.

DIRECTIONS   When I-4 ends, enter I-95 North for about 1 mile to Exit 87. Turn right onto Route 92 East. In 5 miles, turn left on US 1 North (Ridgewood Ave.). Go 1.2 miles; it's on the left (actually in Holly Hills, not Daytona).

I-10

Florida

ROBERT'S DOCK, *Route 441 Exit, Lake City*

On page 107 we describe this restaurant; it is just as accessible from I-10 as it is from I-75.

DIRECTIONS From exit marked Route 441/Lake City/Fargo, head south on Route 441 toward Lake City. Go about 3½ miles to the junction of Route 90 and turn left. In 3.3 miles, the restaurant is on the left, across from the airport. If, after eating, you are headed for I-75 South, do not return to I-10, but take Route 90 West all the way to I-75 (about 7 miles).

EVERYBODY'S RESTAURANT, *Exit 50, Baldwin*

Everybody's? Well, everybody in Baldwin, maybe, since there simply are no alternatives in town. Here we overheard a thickly accented debate on whether turnip greens cure colic, and also one of the best-ever cracks on local politics: "I don't care who wins, so long as everyone gets agitated."

No culinary surprises at all. Just a weather-beaten, yellow, cinder-block building with a few moribund cacti in the window. A U-shaped counter inside, a big menu, typical prices, and lots of joking.

HOURS Mon.–Sat. 6 am–9:30 pm; Sun. 11 am–2 pm.

DIRECTIONS From Exit 50 go north on US 301 0.9 mile to US 90. Turn right and go 0.4 mile. On the left.

BEIGNETS, *I-95 Interchange, Jacksonville*

See page 271 for a description of this marvelous little restaurant with authentic creole cooking and New Orleans's favorite breakfast pastry.

DIRECTIONS Do not use I-295, but continue east on I-10 until it ends at the junction of I-95. Head south on I-95 for about 5 miles to the University Blvd. West exit. Drive about 1 mile on University Blvd. to the light at Saint Augustine Road. Go straight through the light, and almost immediately pull into the small shopping center on your left. Return to I-95 North or South; there is no need to backtrack to I-295 (consult a map).

I-20

Georgia
South Carolina

Georgia

THE BEAUTIFUL RESTAURANT, *Exit 15, Atlanta*

See p. 123 for an excellent and inexpensive soul-food restaurant.

DIRECTIONS   From I-20 take Exit 15 onto I-285 South. Go 2.4 miles south and follow directions given.

THE VARSITY
MARY MAC'S TEA ROOM,
I-75 Junction, Atlanta

See pages 126 and 127 for descriptions of these two renowned Atlanta institutions.

DIRECTIONS   Go north on I-75 about 3 miles and follow directions given.

THE VICTORIAN HOUSE, *Exit 40, Conyers*

Antonio DaSilva began his restaurant career many, many years ago in France, Switzerland, and his native Portugal. Then came the Fairmont and Hilton hotels in this country, and now in good American fashion he's struck out on his own. The result is excellent European cooking at relatively modest prices in a comfortable and unpretentious atmosphere.

Do not imagine some grand Victorian mansion. The Victorian House is just a little old home in an industrial neighborhood. The renovation has been amateur work—heavy Victorian wallpaper, matching paint on the banged-up woodwork, some American-Oriental rugs and poshly padded chairs that match nothing in particular. With a fireplace in each of the four small rooms, the result is comfortable, cozy, and unique—a welcome relief from the clichéd Victoriana of the trendy restaurant business.

We guess that Antonio wielded the paintbrush himself. If not, then it was probably another DaSilva family member who did. This is a true family operation. Ms. DaSilva works on the pastry, a niece does the preparation, and a daughter buses tables. These collective efforts produce some of the best food we tasted—especially the perfectly cooked vegetables and the mysteriously seasoned, paper-thin sliced carrots. With four excellent lamb chops on a bed of rice, this made for a delightful meal at $13.00.

Dinners are $9.00–$13.00, lunches $3.75–$5.75. The menu changes depending on what looks best at the market, but you can always expect the likes of trout meunière, veal Oscar, crabmeat au gratin, and also just plain chopped steak.

HOURS   Mon.–Fri. 11:30 am–3 pm & 6:30 pm–11:30 pm; Sat. 6:30 pm–11:30 pm. Closed Sun., major holidays, and for two weeks in July.

SPECS   1973 Industrial Blvd.; (404) 922-5621; M/V/AE; full license.

DIRECTIONS   From Exit 40 go north one block to light and turn right onto GA 12 (Old Covington Highway). Go ½ mile, and then bear left at the fork. One block farther, on the left.

YE OLDE COLONIAL RESTAURANT, *Exit 51, Madison*

The name is hokey, but the restaurant isn't. And it comes by its colonial association honestly. It seems that Madison was the only town in northern Georgia that Sherman didn't burn on his devastating march to the sea (he had a friend who lived here). Consequently it is one of the few towns in Georgia still in possession of its colonial architecture—a delight to the eye, a lovely break from the road, and a great place for an after-dinner stroll.

Nor is the Colonial Restaurant your typical country eatery. The food, to be sure, comes from the typical southern menu, served cafeteria style ($1.69 for fried chicken, $.59 for sweet potatoes, $1.95 for two eggs with cheese). But the building is one of those handsome renovated banks with tall decorated ceilings, small-pane windows, and a floor of circular tiles in a patchwork of colors. No plants, no stained glass, and no quiche. Just a village restaurant that's been where it is for 25 years, doing what it knows how to do without pretensions.

The chicken was good; the sweet potatoes and black-eyed peas were better. The portions were large, and the people were lovely. If you haven't just filled up on Mrs. Bonner's sweet-potato pie (below) and you don't want haute cuisine, don't hesitate to give the Colonial a try. If it's shrimp Wellington you're after, drive on to Conyers.

HOURS Mon.–Sat. 6:30 am–8:30 pm. Closed Sun.

SPECS 108 E. Washington St.; (404) 342-2211; no cards; no liquor.

DIRECTIONS From Exit 51 go 2.8 miles north on US 441 to the light at the center of town. You're there, on the corner, on the right.

MRS. BONNER'S PRIVATE CLUB,
Exit 55, Crawfordville

When they enter Mrs. Bonner's, most folks walk right past the spotless, homey dining area and chat awhile in the kitchen before sitting down. Then Mrs. Bonner, a short, smiling woman in her seventies, joins them at the table, and everyone chats a little more before she takes the order. Even strangers get this country-home treatment, and if you don't fall instantly in love with this wonderful woman, your heart is harder than the hardest rock that ever broke a plow in Taliaferro County.

Should her charm, simplicity, and straightforwardness fail to win you, her sweet-potato pie surely will. It is quite simply, absolutely, and without a doubt the world's best sweet-potato pie. No one passing within 100 miles of Crawfordville should miss its light, subtle flavors. Mrs. Bonner has raised this bit of country cookin' to the level of haute cuisine. What more can we

31

say except to tell you that we bought out her entire supply of it and took it back to skeptical friends in Atlanta, who were as ecstatic over it as we. She was a bit flustered by our praise and seemed almost to blush as she hunted around behind the counter for wrapping paper.

For sixty years now Mrs. Bonner has been preparing Crawfordville's meals in this very spot. The rest of her cooking is very good, but not that good. It's plain southern fare, costing $4.00 for salad, beverage, rolls, one meat, and three vegetables. (The limas are especially recommended; the greens were bacon-flavored and ever so slightly sweetened—the best version of that dish we found.) Fifteen sandwiches run from $.85 to $3.00.

So well known is the restaurant that there's no sign out front except for the one word "café." Which brings us to the name. It seems that a while back some of the young folks were getting a mite rowdy, and she converted the place to a club so as to enforce order. "It wasn't to keep anyone out," she says with a wink, "but you had to be nice."

HOURS   Mon.–Sat. 7 am–8 pm, maybe later. Closed Sun.

SPECS   Monument St.; (404) 456-2347; no cards; no liquor.

DIRECTIONS   From Exit 55 follow GA 22 for 2 miles north to center of Crawfordville. Turn left at the light, and go half-block. On the right.

RACHEL'S CAFÉ, *Exit 58, Camak*

We've seen many a train station resurrected from decay, decked out in the latest trends, and converted to yet another quichery by day and beef bourguignonnery by night. We've really no objections to such places, but all the same it was a pleasure to find Rachel's in a real working station. The peeling fluorescent-green paint has not been replaced by some tastefully chosen, historically accurate color. There's no Mozart, nor even Muzak. Just the bang and rumble of the freight cars as the trains get made up ten feet outside the window, a display of chewing tobacco, low prices, and plain good food, assuming the accuracy of reports we heard 30 miles away. Unfortunately Rachel's was closed when we arrived, so we really can't guarantee it. But we can tell you that the restaurant is dearly loved by the men who work here. Keep your expectations appropriate and we think you won't be disappointed.

HOURS   Mon.–Fri. 5:30 am–2:30 pm.

DIRECTIONS   From Exit 58 go south on GA 80 for 3.4 miles. On the right.

MICHAEL'S RESTAURANT
NEAL'S BARBEQUE, *Exit 60, Thompson*

Michael's has, as the signs in the windows of roadside eateries used to say, "good food"—no more, no less. The restaurant's simple, honest preparation of its fare produced for us an excellent baked ham which was recommended 30 miles down the road. With the tasty, fresh creamed corn and the good-but-canned yams, it made for a more than acceptable supper at the very affordable price of $3.20 (including muffins and beverage).

Other possibilities would have been fried chicken and/or spareribs, the latter tender and tasty, if not exactly memorable. The lunch menu has the usual array of sandwiches and simple meals. Hamburgers are $1.05.

Its utter lack of external distinction is perhaps the most distinguishing thing about this absolutely local institution of 20 years' standing. From the outside it's just a brick box painted an unappealing shade of faded yellow-green, relieved only a bit by heavy drapes in the picture windows and a pair of fanciful carriage lamps over the side door. Inside, it's just a clean, rather barren combination of linoleum, paneling, pink vinyl, and Formica, pepped up with some mellow Muzak. Clean and inoffensive, with no pretensions and nothing to recommend it except the cook, who's been there since the doors opened, and the waitress, who was wonderfully helpful.

Down the road is Neal's BBQ, operating now out of a trailer and rumored to be quite good—open, unfortunately, only on Friday night and Saturday until sold out.

HOURS Mon.–Fri. 6:15 am–8:30 pm; Sat. 6:15 am–2:15 pm. Closed Sun., one week around July 4, Christmas, and New Year's.

SPECS (404) 595-1275; no cards; no liquor.

DIRECTIONS From Exit 60 go south on GA 150 for 4.5 miles to second light (GA 17). Turn left for two lights (0.6 mile) to Hill St. Left onto Hill for 0.2 mile, on the right. Go 0.5 mile farther for **Neal's,** on the left.

THE GREEN JACKET, *Exit 65, Augusta*

Every April the winner of the Masters Tournament receives, in addition to a check large enough for most folks to retire on, a humble green jacket emblazoned with the seal of the Augusta National Golf Course. The restaurant that is named for this badge of victory sits right across the street from the course, and though you won't meet Gary Player or Arnold Palmer there unless it's early April, you will get some very good food any time of the year.

You would not guess this from its looks. The Green Jacket is one of those big, windowless, suburban monstrosities with a fake mansard roof, and to make matters worse it's painted that hopeless shade of industrial green. No matter. Pull on the golf-club-shaped door handle and go boldly in. The interior is appealing enough—light, cheerful, and sort of semiposh in the way of deep-tufted booths and fancy chandeliers, but not at all intimidating. Folks are very friendly, and if you can't stand the Muzak, sit in the cool and quiet lounge.

Whatever else you do, don't miss the house salad. Seldom have we come across so much attention lavished on a salad. They mix parsley, green onions, and tiny flecks of tomato with a foundation of finely shredded lettuce; add bits of toasted pita bread; and crown it all with a lovely, light herb dressing. Real imagination and attention to detail go into this Green Jacket original, and it arrives handsomely arrayed on the plate. Best of all, at lunchtime $2.98 buys you an unlimited portion, and you don't have to keep trekking to the salad bar to get it.

Try the vegetable soup, too; a potato stuffed with cheese and onions; or a Green Jacket steak that is rubbed in olive oil, Worcestershire, and pepper before broiling. Dinners run $6.95–$11.95, luncheon about $5.50, all of it straight American stuff. Quiche and hamburgers are $3.50 at midday.

We consider it the traveler's God-given right to eavesdrop in local restaurants. How else are you supposed to imbibe the local atmosphere in just an hour? Usually we get an earful of political opinion, but at the Green Jacket we learned all about retirement programs for professional golfers.

HOURS   Lunch: Sun.–Fri. 11:30 am–2:30 pm. Dinner: Mon.–Sat. 5:30 pm–11 pm; Sun. 5 pm–10 pm.

SPECS   2563 Washington Rd.; (404) 733-2271; V/MC/AE; full bar.

DIRECTIONS   From Exit 65 turn right if eastbound, left if westbound onto GA 28 (Washington Rd.). Go 1.5 miles; on the left.

LE CAFÉ NATUREL, *Exit 65, Augusta*

If you're looking for really fine food in Augusta, the place to go *sans doute* is Le Café Naturel. As its name suggests, this restaurant began life as purveyor of tofu and bean sprouts back in the days of flower children and love-ins. By a slow series of sometimes painful steps it has evolved into a very good eclectic restaurant. (Once upon a time current owner and cook Don Du Tau had to sneak in beef behind the backs of his macrobiotic partners to flavor the onion soup.) The purists have left the business, but the do-it-yourself-and-do-it-right spirit of the early days remains. Don makes his own meat and seafood sausages, grows his own grapes, smokes his own ribs (on mesquite, no less), and uses only the freshest ingredients, making all stocks and sauces from absolute scratch.

Some of that sausage gave a fine smoky flavor to the wonderful seafood gumbo we sampled. The chicken marsala ($4.95 at lunchtime) was richly delicious, and the careful seasonings in the rice showed concern for detail. Beef Stroganoff, seafood crepes, or singing shrimp ($6.95) would also make delightful lunches, the latter a sautéed blend of the shrimp, butter, garlic, mushrooms and green onions, white wine and parsley served over rice. Other lunches start at $2.95 and go through an interesting variety of sandwiches, salads, omelettes, and croissants before reaching the $6.95 limit. Dinners run from $5.95 for crepes to $15.95 for lamp chops with Dijon mustard, honey, and garlic, and there's a lot to choose from. On the pricey side, to be sure, but weekdays there's a special that gives you dinner for two, with wine, for $17.95. You could pay that much at Howard Johnson's!

Le Café Naturel is a pleasant place to sit in—plaster walls wainscoted in barnboard; tan carpeting; here some bare wood tables, and there some tablecloths; here a bricky, woody lounge, and there a little room done up more formally than the rest. There's outdoor seating and quiet jazz or classical music. Nothing is overdone; nothing is bare or unpleasant. And we can assure you that the place is run by a man who lives to cook.

HOURS Lunch: Tues.–Sun. 11:30 am–2:30 pm. Dinner: Sun. & Tues.–Thurs. 5:30 pm–10 pm; Fri. & Sat. 5:30 pm–10:30 pm. Closed Mon.

SPECS 1855 Central Ave.; (404) 733-3505; V/MC/AE; full bar.

DIRECTIONS From Exit 65 turn right if eastbound, left if westbound onto GA 28 (Washington Rd.) and go 1.4 miles to the light at Berkman's Rd. Right onto Berkman's and follow it for 2.2 miles to Walton Way. Left onto Walton for 2 blocks, and then right onto Monte Sano Ave. Go 0.4 mile on Monte Sano, and left onto Central. Restaurant is on the left in 1.9 miles. (Yes, it's long, but it goes very quickly and it's a pretty drive.)

South Carolina

POLLY'S LUNCHEONETTE
GILBERT'S RESTAURANT, *Exit 18, Aiken*

Aiken, it seems, is not your ordinary southern town. You can tell that much the minute you see its handsome tree-lined streets. There's a touch of grandeur here, which stems from the fact that Aiken is the thoroughbred racing center of America. (Or so say its local boosters.) With the ponies comes money, and with money come handsome streets and a taste for good food. Sure enough, little Aiken has a continental restaurant.

Now although Gilbert's offers tableside salad preparation, silver service, and fine crystal for its wines, you musn't think of it as some pretentiously posh, back-country Casa de la Maison House. It's in a small converted house, and its two small rooms are as hodgepodgy plain and simple as can be. There are bare floors, plain oak chairs, and two different kinds of curtains on the windows. The only decoration is a pair of crossed polo mallets over a doorway, and all the greenery is out on a porch that is used for summer dining.

All the same, these people care. In such humble surroundings every effort is made to do things right—effort that goes into the food, not the decor. Dinners run $9.50 to $11.75, changing nightly depending on what looks good at the market. Seafood Victoria, steak Diane, lamb with capers, and seafood creole made an appearance during our visit, all of it prepared by ex-New York country club chef Gilbert Bagnell, now both chef and owner of his own establishment.

Actually there are two restaurants at this address. By day Gilbert's withdraws and Polly's Luncheonette takes over—deli sandwiches at about $3.50; four salads from $2.25 to $4.50; burgers ($3.50), crepes ($3.50, including salad), and crabmeat croissants ($5.00), not to mention homemade napoleons, linzer torte, and cheesecake.

HOURS **Gilbert's:** Mon.–Thurs. 6 pm–10 pm; Fri. & Sat. 6 pm–11 pm. Closed Sun. **Polly's:** Mon.–Sat. 10 am–2:30 pm; Closed Sun.

SPECS 233 Chesterfield St., S.E.; (803) 649-6850; major cards; full license.

DIRECTIONS From Exit 18 go 5.7 miles south on SC 19 to light in the center of Aiken. Turn left on Richland and go two blocks to Chesterfield. Right on Chesterfield, 1½ blocks, on the right, in a little house.

VARIETY RESTAURANT, *Exit 18, Aiken*

It was the folks at Gilbert's who, with the warmest recommendations, sent us over to the Variety. Clearly it was their campy, straight-American favorite, and you can be sure that there will be no silver service within the Variety's plain paneled walls. What you will find, though, is fine home cooking and something you're not likely to find anywhere else—bullisis, a preserve made from a grapelike fruit that grows locally. Most of one wall at the Variety is given over to a display of mason jars, and believe us, bullisis is good.

The home canning is done by the same woman who does the cooking, Theresa Burke, who's been at it the whole ten years since she turned fourteen. The beef stew we tried had good cuts of meat and a deep rich flavor, but we had to try the $8.00 rib eye we heard about at Gilbert's. Not the tenderest piece of meat we've ever met, but it was very flavorful and, yes, it was as enormous as they said it would be. Fresh vegetables only and fresh seafood, too. Dinners run $3.95 to $9.00, with sandwiches anywhere from $1.00 to $2.95.

For 19 years Theresa's grandmother ran the Variety. Just lately it's been bought by New Yorker Jimmy Varos (New Yorkers seem to have a penchant for Aiken restaurants), who plans no changes except possibly to add lunch hours. "But first I need time to fix things up."

Not too much, we hope.

HOURS Mon.–Sat. 5 pm–midnight; closed Sun.

SPECS 921 York Street; (803) 649-9156; no cards; beer and wine.

DIRECTIONS From Exit 18 go 5.7 miles south on SC 19 to the light in the center of Aiken (Richland). Turn left on Richland and go 3 lights to York. Left on York, and go 1.2 miles. On the left.

THE ELITE EPICUREAN, *Exits 64A and 73A, Columbia*

See page 52 for a description of this downtown Columbia institution serving fine Greek and American food.

DIRECTIONS **Eastbound:** Exit 64A puts you on I-26 East. Almost immediately, I-26 traffic must bear right, but you should go straight (Route 76 toward Columbia). This will put you on I-126 and in 4 fast miles you'll be downtown on Elmwood Ave. (don't exit for Huger). Turn right at the third light (Main St.). The restaurant is on the left, at the third light (Laurel).

Westbound: Exit 73A puts you on Route 277 South, a very fast freeway that in 5½ miles becomes Bull St. From that point, it's 1 mile to Laurel (1 block after Richland). Turn right on Laurel and go ¼ mile to the third light (Main). Restaurant is on left.

HERB's GRILL, *Exit 65, Columbia*

See page 51 for a description of this locally loved purveyor of fried chicken.

DIRECTIONS From Exit 65 (Broad River Rd.), head north for 1 mile to the fifth light (St. Andrews Rd.). It's on the corner, on left.

RAY LEVER'S BAR-B-QUE HUT, *Exit 71, Columbia*

Choose between all-you-can-eat and all-you'd-likely-want-to-eat at this genuine pit barbecue that's about 6½ miles from I-20. It's a good chance to sample mustard-based barbecue sauce, an opportunity you won't have outside the Columbia area. See description on page 159.

DIRECTIONS From Exit 71, bear right if eastbound, turn left if westbound, onto Route 21 North. Go 5 miles (fast-moving, no lights) and turn left onto Folk Rd. (large sign for Ray Lever's makes the turn hard to miss). Restaurant is about 1½ miles down Folk, on left.

THUNDERBIRD MOTOR INN, *Exit 141A, Florence*

From I-20 you're just minutes away from this much-loved buffet-style restaurant. See page 291 for description.

DIRECTIONS From Exit 141A, enter I-95 North for 4 miles to Exit 164. At the bottom of the ramp, bear right, and then turn left at the light. You'll see the Thunderbird on your left.

CARRIE NATION'S, *End of Interstate, Florence*

If you've been frequenting the trendy "eating and drinking emporiums" of the Northeast, the Victorianesque appointments of this restaurant will not be unfamiliar: tin ceiling, plenty of brass, ersatz Tiffany lamps, a clutter of old advertising mirrors, and water served in mason jars. We call it the bricks, plants, and oak café, BPO for short. BPO's invariably feature a QRS menu: quiche, Reuben sandwiches, and spinach salad. Carrie Nation's is true to type.

Although common up north, BPO cafés are rare in the Southeast. This one carried the true mark of a South Carolina restau-

rant—she-crab soup, a Charleston original that has spread through the region. Whether or not this heady broth will catch on like fried potato skins and Buffalo chicken wings we do not know, but we wish it well. While Carrie's version isn't quite up to the she-crab standard of Henry's (page 56), it could come close if the kitchen would use just a tad more sherry and a shake less salt.

The steak and cheese sandwich ($3.95) was quite a tasty, well-filled sandwich. Other possibilities, in addition to the quiche, Reubens, and full-meal salads, are spruced-up hamburgers ($3.75), roast beef au jus ($3.95), chili ($1.60), and a few real entrées like shrimp kabob ($8.95) and steak tips ($6.95). Also requisite in this kind of restaurant are alcoholic coffees and overrich desserts. We went for a seductive concoction of cherries, walnuts, and rum in a cream filling with chocolate crust. It's called "Slice of Heaven Pie" and it really was—almost.

The happy crowd of young professionals seemed to enjoy this place greatly, and one couple even told us that Florence had risen inestimably in their eyes since Carrie Nation's opened. One thing no one was able to tell us was why the restaurant was named after the temperance leader whose free-swinging hatchet had demolished many a saloon around the turn of the century. Quite clearly it was not on account of shared sentiment.

HOURS   Mon.–Sat. 11:30 am–midnight. Closed Sun.

SPECS   Florence Mall; (803) 667-1970; major cards; full license.

DIRECTIONS   Stay on I-20, continuing straight past the interchange with I-95. About 2 miles later, go straight through the light and immediately turn left into Florence Mall. Drive past Penney's. Restaurant is in the middle of the mall.

North Carolina
South Carolina

North Carolina

EXPRESSIONS RESTAURANT,
Exit 18B, Hendersonville

The area around Hendersonville and Tryon, North Carolina, is now competing with Florida's West Coast and central Arizona for honors as America's fastest-growing retirement community. It is not surprising, given the influx of urban and suburban natives, that a whole crop of urbane restaurants has sprouted to nourish them. Expressions is one of the best. Bow-tied waiters, plush seats, butcher-block tables, and a quiet, tasteful decorating scheme in forest green and sherry indicate at once that here can be found refuge from what is often euphemistically referred to as "country cooking."

Which isn't to say that regional cuisine is sacrificed entirely. It was here in the Smokies, long before we reached the Carolina coast, that we were introduced to she-crab soup, a richly flavored cream broth made from the meat and roe of the female blue crab (although "once in a while a few males sneak in," our waiter admitted). Expressions's chef Tom Young takes liberties with the traditional recipe, freely adding curry, turmeric, and rum. The result was as delicious as it was sacrilegious.

His salad didn't fare as well. Although propitiously sparked with almonds and sprouts, some ingredients suffered from frostbite. Nevertheless, the Bibb lettuce (which had escaped the low temperatures) was most welcome after weeks of nothing but iceberg.

Tryon, NC

Lunches are *au courant* sandwiches (Monte cristos, Reubens, smoked salmon, turkey breast with watercress), salads (avocado and crabmeat, curried chicken, spinach and mushrooms) and light entrées (linguini Provençale, frittata, shirred eggs Forestière), all in the $3–$5 range. We opted for chicken and mushroom crepes. Two of them in a cucumber and dill sauce made a filling, tasty meal, served with a side salad for $4.95.

At night, the menu becomes more ambitious, moving toward entrées like rack of lamb Dijon, moonfish in lime-flavored hollandaise, or roast duckling in a cassis sauce. Prices on these start at $10.

If you're headed south, it may be a long time before you encounter this kind of food again. Perhaps that's why we saw so many doggie bags going out the front door.

HOURS Lunch: Mon.–Fri. 11:30 am–2 pm. Dinner: Mon.–Sat. 6–10 pm; closed Sun.

SPECS 114 N. Main St.; (704) 693-8516; major cards; full license.

DIRECTIONS Exit 18B puts you on Route 64 West. Go about 2 miles to Main St. and turn left. Go through four closely spaced traffic lights, and it's on your left, just before the light at 1st St.

CARO-MI DINING ROOM, *Exits 28 & 36, Tryon*

If you are heading toward South Carolina on I-26 East, you will reach the Caro-Mi Dining Room via Saluda Mountain, a breathtaking descent that should not be attempted by the acrophobic. It's an appropriate introduction to this restaurant's picture-perfect setting, the closest thing we'd seen to our home state of Vermont—right down to the covered bridge. To sit on one of the rocking chairs out on Caro-Mi's front porch and listen to the gurgling Pacolet River brought on a sweet sort of homesickness; of course, the dogwoods and rhododendrons so typical of North Carolina's mountains brought us to our geographical senses.

It's just as lovely inside, a lodgelike atmosphere dominated by the varnished knotty pine walls, hardwood floors, and red-checked tablecloths on wooden tables, all of it illuminated by candle lanterns that cast a warm ruddy glow.

Fortunately, the food does not take a backseat to the decor. "We really don't have any secrets," says Chuck Tomko, whose parents Carl and Nell have run the restaurant for 25 years. "We just have a few items on the menu and make sure that they're all fresh."

It's straight southern cooking here, some of the best we've had. The two specialties are salt-cured country ham and pan-fried Smoky Mountain rainbow trout; fried chicken, jumbo shrimp, and Delmonico steaks round out the menu, although chicken livers and roast turkey are occasionally available. No matter what your choice, you'll be presented with a seemingly endless parade of homemade side dishes beginning with biscuits and preserves (the latter served in recycled baby-food jars) and moving on to grits with red-eye gravy, macaroni salad, cole slaw, and spiced apples. Then, with the entrée, come green beans flavored by a ham hock, freshly cut french fries, and "tea" (meaning iced tea, shockingly sweet). It's all served family style and the entrée price, ranging from $6 to $9.50, includes everything but dessert.

HOURS Wed. & Thurs. 5–9 pm; Fri. & Sat. 5–9:30 pm; closed Sun.–Tues. There can be a 30–60 minute wait between 6:30 and 8 pm on Sat. nights in summer. Closed for four weeks in Jan. or Feb–call to check.

SPECS 1433 Highway 176 (between Tryon and Saluda); (704) 859-5200; no cards; no liquor (brown bagging permitted).

DIRECTIONS **Eastbound:** From Exit 28 bear right, go 1.1 miles to stop sign at T, turn left toward Tryon. Drive 4.6 spectacular, winding miles down Saluda Mountain. Restaurant is on right. After eating, don't backtrack; reverse directions below to return to I-26; signs will help you find it.

Westbound: From Exit 36, turn left onto Route 108 West. In about 2½ miles, bear right (signs to Hendersonville and Asheville). Go 0.6 mile, turn right onto Route 176, and drive 1.9 miles to restaurant on left. After eating, don't backtrack; reverse directions above to return to I-26. (Ask for directions at restaurant if unsure.)

ELETTRA'S, *Exit 36, Tryon*

We never met her, but we feel as if we know Elettra well. Her personality pervades every corner of the restaurant the way whiskey flavors Irish coffee. There's no separating the two.

Like Cher or Liberace, Elettra is a one-name person. She's an artist, and her electric, mosaiclike oil paintings hang in strategic places throughout the restaurant. She's a designer, and she planned every construction detail. She was a longtime resident of Sicily, and touches of Mediterranean charm are sprinkled throughout the restaurant. Most of all, she's a cook, and every item on the eclectic menu wears her signature.

But before you even address yourself to the menu, you are greeted with a complimentary glass of wine. Then comes a basket of fresh herb rolls and an hors d'oeuvres cart bearing such lovelies as marinated mushrooms, stuffed cherry tomatoes, and chicken salad in cream puffs ($1.50 for six). For soups, choose between black bean, split pea with ham, or a very herby and delicious cream of spinach. The entrée menu, which changes entirely from day to day but not at all from lunch to dinner, ranges in price from about $3.75 to $6.50. We were quite happy at the low end with "risotto Elettra," ground beef and tomato with rice, amply but not overpoweringly seasoned with herbs too numerous to divine. Spaghetti Palmadero, scallops Mornay, and asparagus Benedict were some of the choices we had to pass up.

At the end of the meal, just in case Elettra hasn't made enough of an impression, she has her staff hand out home-baked sour-cream cookies, gratis. It was a sweet surprise.

HOURS Lunch: Mon.–Sat. 11:30 am–2:30 pm. Dinner: Thurs.–Sat. 5:30–8:30 pm. Sundays hours may soon be instituted; call to check. Closed Dec. 25 and 26.

SPECS 121 S. Trade St.; (704) 859-5121; no cards; beer and wine.

DIRECTIONS From Exit 36, head west on Route 108 toward Tryon. In 3½ miles go straight through the light at junction of Route 176, and through the next three lights as well. You'll be on Trade St., and the restaurant will be on the left. It's 4 miles from the Interstate.

NOAH'S GALLEY, *Exit 36, Tryon*

Noah's Galley is open only at the lunch hour, but Kay Mason can be found kneading the bread dough at 6 every morning. At about 9, customers start coming in to the health-foods shop that she runs in tandem with the lunchroom to buy her seven-grain, whole wheat, and pineapple loaves. You can do that too, of course, and you'll probably find something to your liking to spread on a slice or two (cashew butter perhaps, or how about some imported Gruyère?). If you wait until Noah's Galley opens at 11, Kay and her daughter, Debbie, will take care of fixing the sandwich for you.

You won't talk them into putting ham or roast beef in it, but perhaps you'd like to try their version of a Reuben. It consists of vegetarian corned beef (a soy product), sauerkraut, shredded carrots, and melted Swiss on rye bread. Our minds being at least as open as our gullets, we gave it a try. The verdict was—not bad at all, especially the sauerkraut, carrots, cheese, and bread! ($1.95)

Other sandwiches include "chicken little" (a sprouty egg salad), "olive branch" (avocado and black olives, with the appropriate fixings), and "tofunafish." The bread is indeed delicious, as are the homemade soups Kay and Debbie serve in the cute little area they've put together at the back of the shop. Salads are also available, as is a lovely-looking Mexican sandwich made with fresh-baked chapati. Wash it all down with fresh-squeezed orange or carrot juice or some of the silkiest, most seductive fresh fruit smoothies we've ever sipped ($1.25).

HOURS   Mon.–Fri. 11 am–3 pm; closed Sat. & Sun.

SPECS   Highway 108; (704) 859-6356; no cards; no liquor.

DIRECTIONS   From Exit 36, head west on Route 108 toward Tryon. In 2 miles it's on your right (sign says "Nature's Storehouse"). (**Note:** This restaurant is in Lynn, a tiny town about midway between Tryon and I-26, on Route 108.)

South Carolina

NEW PROSPECT SEAFOOD, *Exit 5, New Prospect*

One kind of restaurant we'd not encountered before this trip was the "fish camp." We asked around to find out if it was where your kids went in the summertime to learn how to tie flies. No, we were told. "It's a place where you can get the most seafood for the least money." And then the caveat, "They don't worry about the atmosphere, just the food." In upland South Carolina, New Prospect Fish Camp was often mentioned as a good example.

The place lived up to its reputation. For decor, only a few flimsy fishnets on the walls bespoke the restaurant's genre. The food was served in old stainless-steel army trays, the kind with a separate compartment for each course. But the boundaries were blurred by the mounds of food that spilled freely into neighboring sections without regard for where fried oysters were supposed to end and hushpuppies begin.

Take, for instance, the fish platter. We had our choice of flounder, catfish, or perch as a featured item. With it came a strong supporting cast: fried oysters, shrimp, and (that's right, *and*) scallops, as well as hushpuppies, potatoes (french fried or baked) and slaw. Another choice we had to make was whether we wanted our seafood broiled or fried. Betty Burnett who runs New Prospect Seafood with her husband, Tom, explained that the broiler sees most of its action during what she called the "New Year's Resolution Season."

"After the first two or three weeks of January the orders are back to ninety-nine percent fried," she said. We went along with the majority and found our fish delightfully light, not in the least bit greasy, coated by a thin jacket of flour rather than the thick coat of pancake batter that characterizes inferior seafood.

For our seven-course seafood meal we paid $4.75. Had we gone for the deluxe combination plate, with all three kinds of fish and a crab patty as well as the complete shellfish treatment, etc., it would have been a dollar more and probably would have fed three of us nicely. Children's and senior citizens' plates run about half-price.

The Burnetts recently changed the name of the restaurant to New Prospect Seafood, but locals still know it as "the fish camp." It doesn't much matter: in this town, all you have to say is "fish," and someone will point the way.

HOURS   Thurs. 4–9:30 pm; Fri. & Sat. 4–10 pm; Sun. 4–9:30 pm; closed Mon.–Wed.

SPECS   (803) 592-2691; no cards; no liquor.

DIRECTIONS   From Exit 5, turn left if eastbound, right if westbound; you'll be on Highway 11 headed toward New Prospect. Go about 3½ miles to stop sign and cross the intersection. It's just beyond, on the right.

ANNIE OAKS
ANKIE'S DELI DELIGHTS, *Exit 19, Spartanburg*

See pages 217 and 218 for a truly fine restaurant and an excellent German deli.

DIRECTIONS   From Exit 19 go north on I-85 about 2.5 miles to Exit 73A. Then follow directions given.

BEACON DRIVE-IN, *Exit 22, Spartanburg*

We took five pages of notes on the Beacon and could easily use up that much space writing about it. But where would we start? With the helicopter pad that regularly sees South Carolina's senators and governor drop in? With Sunday morning church services that draw as many as 3,000 worshippers to the Beacon's parking lot? How about the billboard we once saw in Palm Springs, California, that said, "You are only 2300 miles from the famous BEACON DRIVE-IN, Spartanburg, S.C."?

Or should we start inside the building that serves 10–12,000 hungry mouths every Friday and Saturday night? Here you can (and will) meet the now-famous J. C. Stroble, the man whose feats as a fast-food magician have elevated him to the top of his field. So extraordinary is his performance that Charles Kuralt and crew spent a full day taping it for "On the Road." Here, briefly, is how it goes:

J.C. is the first person you encounter in the service line at the Beacon. If it isn't busy at the time, you won't be impressed because you'll simply tell him your order, listen as he calls it out to the fleet of cooks, and stand by as he retrieves it for you. But when the lunch crowds, and the bus loads, and the Saturday night movie-goers start to arrive en masse, J.C. launches into action. He'll take 10, 15, 20 complete orders into his head, sort them out like a computer, and call them back to the cooks: "Hey Fred, six chili cheese with, four without, two cheeseburgers, one with slaw, three outsides, two burgers without, one with, hash a plenty, heavy on the red." His voice is deep and tonal, as rhythmic as a Baptist preacher's. "Come on down, come on down *the line*, come on, next. Frank gimme a beef, make that outside, chili cheese, make that two, come on y'all come on down the line. Next, next." And then, before you can figure out what you're expected to do, J.C. has dashed off and returned with six plates in hand. He's taking more orders as he hands you your plate. "C'mon, c'mon down the *line!*"

All of which is fairly extraordinary, made even more so by the fact that J.C. Stroble is blind.

And we could go on, but we'd better not. However, you might be interested to know something about the food. Bear in mind that this is a drive-in and you won't be disappointed. Actually, the popular chili-topped cheeseburger ("chili cheese"), with or without bacon, was rather good in an unsubtle way. So was our large cup of hot chocolate that floated a scoop of vanilla ice cream. The skins-on onion rings (that's right!) were certainly the most interesting, if not the best-tasting, we'd come across in a long while. The menu is huge and the prices quite small. You'll probably spend around $3.00 for your meal.

This is the fourth building that owner John White has called the Beacon during the past 35 years. We asked what had happened to the other three. "We wore 'em out," he said. We understood.

HOURS Mon.–Wed. 6:30 am–11 pm; Thurs.–Sat. 6:30 am–11:30 pm. In summer, open until 11:30 every night. Closed Sun. (but free watermelon after worship).

SPECS 255 Reidville Rd.; (803) 585-9387; no cards; no liquor.

DIRECTIONS From Exit 22, turn left if eastbound; turn right if westbound. You're on Reidville Rd. and it's 3 miles to the Beacon, on your right.

HERB'S GRILL, *Exit 106, Columbia*

Let's get one thing straight: Herb's will never win a beauty contest. And that's putting it mildly. At first glance, it looks like a salt-of-the-earth workingman's bar, the kind of place you pretend doesn't exist when you're giving out-of-town guests a tour of the neighborhood.

But let's get a few other things straight, too. First of all, Herb's is really a family restaurant. It isn't a bar at all, although you can order a draft to go with your fried chicken. Ah yes, the fried chicken—that's the other thing. Herb's has the best in Columbia. Nobody in town even argues about that. Whether it's the best in the world seems to be the only point in dispute.

We won't take sides. Herb's chicken is terrific, and we'll leave it at that. But you must understand that it's terrific in a roll-your-sleeves-up-to-the-elbows sort of way. Herb seems to have perfected the arcane art of preserving juicy, tender meat beneath a crispy, crunchy skin. And you get two large pieces of breast meat for just $3.25, including slaw and french fries. (One large piece is $2.20). The fries are also notable—none of this frozen crinkle-cut nonsense, but large skins-on wedges of real spud.

The menu at Herb's isn't large, and nine out of ten people

come in for the chicken, but you might be interested in fried rabbit ($3.45 for three pieces). There are also a few steaks, burgers, and meaty sandwiches, all quite reasonable. And if you're there on a Friday, you'll get to try the excellent fiery catfish stew.

HOURS   Mon.–Fri. 10 am–11 pm; closed Sat. and Sun. Herb's Game Room, next door, is open on Saturdays, serving catfish stew, hot dogs, sausage dogs, and pizza (no chicken).

SPECS   3039 Broad River Rd.; (808) 772-9866; no cards; beer.

DIRECTIONS   From Exit 106, turn left if eastbound, turn right if westbound. You'll be heading east on St. Andrews Rd. Go about ¾ mile to the second light (Broad River Rd.). It's at the corner, on the right.

THE ELITE EPICUREAN, *Exit 108, Columbia*

If you were a U.S.C. undergraduate and your parents came up for the weekend, this is where you'd take them to dinner (so long as they were paying). Now don't picture anything la-de-dah. There's no French on the menu, and no vested waiters to stop conversation with two-foot pepper grinders. Columbia isn't that kind of a city, and the Elite Epicurean isn't that kind of place.

In some ways, it's more like a New Jersey diner than an urbane restaurant. The waitresses, for instance, are almost motherly and utterly unpretentious. Most of the seating is in booths that are comfortable but hardly plush; the decor is quasi Greek-tacky. And the menu is a pretty even mix of American and Greek cuisine. But there an analogy to diner food ends. What is served at the Elite can hold its own against most any competitor.

Lamb and shrimp dishes are the dinner specialties, but you can find several preparations of squid, and such delights as whole smelts stuffed with asparagus spears. Lamb chops "bandit style" consists of two double-thick chops topped with onion, tomato, and feta cheese; the portion is large enough that you might easily make out like a bandit yourself by splitting one with a companion. "Shrimp Isle of Scorpios" probably takes the most ohs and ahs; it is a casserole of fresh shrimp, tomatoes, onions, garlic, and feta cheese fortified with cognac and ouzo. At $13.50 and $10.95, these two are at the top of the menu. Many other dinners are $3–4 lower, and all include hors d'oeuvres, salad, and potatoes a la Greque.

Lunch at the Elite is a less Olympian affair. Full meals, including salad, vegetables, dessert, and beverage, run under $4; the entrée list changes daily, but it is strictly American. Likewise for breakfast.

HOURS Mon.–Sat. 6 am–11 pm; closed Sun. There is likely to be a wait at dinner time on Fri. and Sat.; reservations are helpful.

SPECS 1736 Main St.; (803) 765-2325; American Express only; full license.

DIRECTIONS Eastbound: As you approach Columbia, I-26 through-traffic must bear right. You should not; instead, continue straight and you'll be on Route 76, which soon becomes I-126 and in 4 fast miles puts you downtown on Elmwood Ave. (don't exit for Huger). ■Once on Elmwood, turn right at the third light (Main St.). **The Elite Epicurean** is on the left, at the third light (Laurel).

Westbound (actually northbound): Exit 108 puts you on I-126 which shoots you downtown and in 3 fast miles puts you on Elmwood Ave. (don't exit for Huger). Then, as above from ■.

MAURICE'S PIGGY PARK, *Exit 113, West Columbia*

Maurice's Piggy Park is a celebration of everything held sacred by that vast population that used to be called America's great silent majority: an American flag (not just any old flag, but the largest in the state) flies overhead; a fundamentalist chapel on the premises dishes out free Bibles, free refreshments, and free counseling; the great American automobile culture is duly respected with old-fashioned car-hop service; and the clean-scrubbed youngsters who serve you represent what teenage America used to be before it was corrupted by the 60s. Most important, the main act—Piggy Park's *raison d'être* and *joie de vivre*—is that all-American food, barbecue.

You may have tasted "Q" elsewhere, but unless the barbecue trail has led you through central South Carolina, you're in for a new experience. In the area around Columbia, barbecue sauce is a chipper mustard-based blend; when the meat comes off the hickory-fueled grill, it's doused with the bright-yellow liquid and comes to your table looking like something on a color TV screen that's out of kilter. Still, it's got flavor to spare, and if you can see past the peculiar hue, you'll find plenty for your taste buds to concentrate on.

Sample Maurice's mustardy results in a small dose with his "Little Joe" sandwich for $1.85, or go whole hog with the "Q-combo plate"—heaps of pit-cooked pork and beef along with fried chicken, ribs, pork hash, rice, hushpuppies, slaw, and rolls, all for $4.95. There are dozens of possibilities in between, and quite a few things that stray from the realm of pit-cooked "Q": foot-long chili hot dogs, dill pickles, and beefalo burgers.

We liked Maurice's mustard-based barbecue even if it didn't turn out to be our favorite variation on the pit-cooked pig. For anyone wishing to expand his porcine horizons, it's a must. Maurice's hushpuppies are also memorable—huge, rough-textured, irregularly shaped, and deeply flavorful. His onion rings were also winners, big fluffy things with a lovely light breading.

HOURS　Mon.–Sat. 10 am–10:30 pm; closed Sun.

SPECS　1600 Charleston Highway; (803) 796-0220; no cards; no liquor (are you kidding?).

DIRECTIONS　From Exit 113, turn left if eastbound (southbound, actually); turn right if westbound (northbound, actually). In 1¼ mile you'll reach the junction with Route 321. You're looking right at it.

BERRY'S-ON-THE-HILL
DUKE'S BARBEQUE, *Exit 149, Orangeburg*

Finding a memorable restaurant in this part of South Carolina is like looking for a snowflake in a cotton boll. By all accounts Berry's is the best around, and it was certainly the best we came up with. But—the truth must be spoken—our entire meal there, from vegetable soup through pork and onions, rice and gravy, pineapple fritters, and salad was just barely respectable. Only the sweet potatoes, which had a bit of character, and the cake in wine sauce, which showed some real imagination, were exceptions to the less-than-happy rule.

On the other hand, all that cost only $5.50, and the restaurant is certainly pleasant enough—sort of country-simple, with bare wood floors, blue tablecloths, handsome curtains. Hamburgers are $1.85, and all the usual lunch stuff is on the menu.

Berry's has been around Orangeburg for a long time. We can't give it a very enthusiastic review, but we think we can promise you won't find anything better between Columbia and Charleston. The only viable alternative we could come up with was Duke's, and that's one of those Thursday-to-Saturday barbecue pits. We came through on Wednesday, so except to tell you that it's got more character on the outside than within, we have to leave you on your own.

HOURS **Berry's:** Daily 10 am–10 pm.
       Duke's: Thurs.–Sat. 10 am–9 pm.

SPECS **Berry's:** 450 John C. Calhoun St.; (803) 536-5275; major cards; full license.
       Duke's: 1298 Whitman St.; (803) 534-2916; no cards; no liquor.

DIRECTIONS From Exit 149 go north on SC 33 toward Orangeburg for 4.3 miles to the light at US 21. Turn left and go 0.2 mile to light at US 301. For **Berry's** turn right and go 0.2 mile, on the left. For **Duke's** turn left and go about 0.8 mile and turn left just past the RR tracks. Bear right for one block and you're there, on the right.

THE CONTINENTAL CORNER, *Exit 199, Summerville*

Once upon a time Tom Mavrikes and Ernest Yatreles were seminarians in the Greek Orthodox Church. They changed their minds about that, and then frustrations with the red tape of their secular jobs led them to launch a Greek deli together. Only this one's not orthodox. Besides gyros, souvlaki, spanakopita, and loukaniko (Greek sausage with orange peels), there's an English mixed grill ($9.95), pastrami sandwiches ($2.60), and a New York cheesecake that is revered by the congregation of a Charleston synagogue.

We tried a ($2.75) gyro made from chicken, tomatoes, and onions in a sour cream and yogurt sauce, stuffed into a thick, soft, Greek (not Syrian) pita specially brought in from Chicago. It was terrific, its excellence stemming mainly from Tom's light, sensitive touch with the spices. Tom's good on the spiced tea, too, and he also produced an acceptable Greek salad ($1.75). Dinners are mostly in $4.95–$6.95 range, running from a simple feta omelette or Greek-style liver to Greek chicken and pork.

The Continental Corner is a new, clean, and entirely cheerful place, decorated with a Mediterranean touch—walls of rough white plaster, a brick floor, and wooden booths. It bears no resemblance at all to anything that would even so much as suggest the highway, and we're sure you'll leave with your belly pleasantly full and your spirit refreshed.

HOURS Winter: Mon.–Thurs. 11 am–8 pm; Fri. & Sat. 11 am–9 pm. Summer: one hour later, daily. Closed Sun.

SPECS 123 W. Richardson; (803) 871-1160; V/MC; full license.

DIRECTIONS From Exit 199 go 1.8 miles (five lights) to Richardson in the center of Summerville. Turn right and go one block. On the right, parking in rear.

HENRY'S, *Meeting Street Exit, Charleston*

"If there were such a thing as Charleston cuisine, Henry's would be it." That's how restaurant reviewer Frank Jarrell described this funky, venerable Charleston institution. Henry's is the kind of gutsy, frowzy, downtown seafood house where the waiters wear formal coats and go to no pains to make you feel at home. Not rude, as at Durgin Park in Boston, or spiffy as at Joe's in Miami Beach. Just sort of indifferent, as befits a place that's been around for 55 years and no longer has anything to prove.

You enter into a lime-green dining room furnished with just a few empty tables and can't help but wonder if anybody's home. Then off to the left you see another dining room, equally green, but this one populated with pleasant-looking people and decorated with white tablecloths, hexagonal tile floor, wainscoting, and a tin ceiling that looks as if it really belongs. All in all, an appealing combination of funk and formality.

Then, off to the right, there's the bar—red walls encumbered to the ceiling with nautical pictures, comfortable booths, and a wooden bar that is so unpretentiously plain it's hard to believe it's really old. Here sit the young professionals pondering the choice of such delectables as she-crab soup ($1.75/cup; $2.75/bowl), bacon-wrapped shad roe ($6.90), crabmeat and oyster casserole ($7.75), or maybe fried Carolina shrimp a la Gomez ($6.90).

Now we love old places like this. For interest and local color the restaurant business can offer no better. But in all honesty we must tell you that the color is better than the cuisine. It's not bad, mind you. And the she-crab soup, which is Charleston's gift to American cuisine, had a good, mild, creamy flavor and a subtle crab taste, nothing at all like Maryland crab soup, and well worth your checking it out. The corn bread was terrific, and the hushpuppies quite good. But the fried soft-shell crabs were a disappointment, the vegetables mediocre, and the cheese dip unworthy of mention.

One solution to this problem is to order fried oysters wrapped in bacon, which we later learned is what Henry's does best. Another is to have just soup and corn bread here. Then walk into the adjacent historical district and munch a bit of this and a bit of that as you wander. You're probably tired of sitting anyway, and if Charleston's cuisine doesn't rival that of New Orleans, its old section beats the Vieux Carré hands down—cobblestone streets, stuccoed houses with ironwork, businessmen on bicycles, and no strip joints. A great way to break up the tedium of the drive.

HOURS Mon.–Sat. 12 noon–10:30 pm. Closed Sun.

SPECS   48–54 Market St.; (803) 723-4363; major cards; full bar.

DIRECTIONS   The Meeting St./Downtown exit from I-26 puts you on Meeting St. in the right direction. Go nine lights (1.2 miles) to Market St. Then left onto Market and go two blocks. Turn left again and you'll see it on the right in the tan building. Parking lot is in front of you, to the left.

POOGAN'S PORCH, *Meeting Street Exit, Charleston*

Now if you want some really good food in Charleston, try Poogan's Porch. It costs more than Henry's at dinner time, but it too is in the historic district and here you can feast on award-winning Cajun shrimp or Poogan's own scallops Savannah. Or how about stuffed quail, another version of bacon-wrapped oysters, or cobia Calcutta? (Cobia, we learned, is a fish, and for this house specialty they wrap it in ham, marinate it in soy sauce and sesame oil, and finally sauté it lightly in Dijon mustard, honey, and lime.) And as everywhere in this part of the world there's she-crab soup. No two versions are alike. At Poogan's it's wine-flavored and rich, an interesting blend of sensuous, creamy flavors. Full dinners run $10.00–$13.00. The soup is $2.25/cup.

Poogan's specializes in raising Carolina low-country cooking to culinary height. At lunch you can be as down-home as okra gumbo ($1.50/cup; $2.95/bowl) or a humble hamburger ($3.50). But you can also get an oysters-and-parsley omelette ($4.75) or smaller versions of the dinner fare ($4.25–$5.95). Four interesting salads run $3.75–$5.50.

Lest the decor be thought unequal to the cuisine, be assured that this restaurant inhabits a small renovated house in the historical district. The ceilings are high, the walls are a handsome shade of deep blue, and the tables are formally set in white. Quiet music will relax you. The feel is dignified, intimate, pleasant, but not so fancy as to make you feel out of place after half a day at 65 miles an hour.

HOURS   Lunch: Mon.–Sat. 11:30 am–2:30 pm. Dinner: Sun.–Thurs. 5 pm–10 pm; Fri. & Sat. 5:30 pm–11 pm.

SPECS   72 Queen St.; (803) 577-2337; V/MC/AE; full license.

DIRECTIONS   The Meeting St./Downtown Exit from I-26 puts you on Meeting St. in the right direction. Go 1.4 miles to Queen St. and turn right. One half-block up, on the right.

I-40

Tennessee
North Carolina

Tennessee

CROSS-EYED CRICKET
APPLE CAKE TEA ROOM
BUDDY'S BARBECUE

For the 20 miles of road between Lenoir City and Knoxville, I-40 and I-75 run together. See pages 143–47 for descriptions of three likely restaurants. The Cross-Eyed Cricket is a sheer delight. To reach it from I-40 take Exit 364 and go west on TN 95 just a short bit until you see a sign for the restaurant. Turn left and follow the road and the signs for 2 lovely miles. For the other restaurants, just follow directions given.

HAROLD'S KOSHER STYLE DELI, *Exit 388A, Knoxville*

According to Harold Shersky, there aren't more than 300 Jewish families in all of Knoxville. That may explain why, at his deli, you can get hushpuppies with your corned beef on rye. Other than that, however, his little restaurant is the real thing, run by himself and his wife, Adeline, as a labor of love for 35 years. Blintzes with sour cream ($2.25); hot pastrami ($2.35); chopped liver ($2.85); herring, tongue, and borscht—they're all there, along with a few unethnic interlopers like beefburgers ($1.20), chili ($1.55), and hoagies ($2.25). We can't attest to all of it, but we can assure you that the corned beef, at least, is nearly as good as anything you could find in Manhattan.

Adeline does all the desserts herself: a rich, smooth, luscious cheesecake; a carrot cake; coffee cake; and her *pièce de résistance,* pineapple nut pie ($1.25). Harold, a balding man in apron and necktie, insisted we try it. Stuffed though we were, we're glad he did.

The deli looks just as an urban deli should. The place is functionally furnished, and an enameled display case full of tempting meats and fattening desserts is stationed right by the door. In fact, the only important difference we could discover between southern-style Jewish deli and its northern original was the southern hospitality that somehow makes even a kosher pickle seem gracious.

HOURS Mon.–Sat. 5:30 am–5 pm. Closed Sun., July 4, Rosh Hashana, and Yom Kippur.

SPECS 131 South Gay St.; (615) 523-5315; MC/V; beer only.

DIRECTIONS Take Exit 388A (Business Loop) and then immediately exit again for Summit Hill Drive. Turn right at Summit Hill and go two lights to Gay. Turn right onto Gay, one block, on the left.

THE REGAS, *Exit 388A, Knoxville*

The Regas is one of Knoxville's oldest and most famous restaurants. Like many such places, however, it's poshly overdecorated in flocked red wallpaper, red carpeting, and deeply upholstered vinyl chairs. It mistakes plush for class, and in some cases the error continues beyond the decor into the food—a "gourmet cheese sampler," for example, that offers Muenster and what tasted like Velveeta with pimento.

Let it be said clearly that the Regas is essentially a steak house, and that the steak (in béarnaise sauce with onion rings) was really very good. The vegetable soup was OK, as was the salad, and two good croissants came with our dinner. But the string beans were an abomination, pure and simple. So what can we say when dinners run from $9.50 to $13.50? Our guess is that if you stay away from anything green and anything written in French, you'll do quite well.

Lunch, we suspect, is much safer. Half a pineapple stuffed with chicken salad ($5.95) sounds like welcome variety in highway eating, as does an avocado stuffed with shrimp salad (also $5.95) or tuna with almonds ($4.75). An 8-ounce hamburger at $3.95 ought to be a safe bet, but there are only three other sandwiches to choose from. A small prime rib goes for $6.50 at lunch, and it's probably quite good. After that the menu is nearly all steaks and seafood again in the $11.25–$14.50 range.

HOURS Mon.–Thurs. 11 am–3 pm & 5 pm–10:30 pm; Fri. 11 am–3 pm & 5 pm–11:30 pm; Sat. 5 pm–11:30 pm. Closed Sun.

SPECS 318 North Gay St.; (615) 637-9805; all major cards; full bar.

DIRECTIONS Take Exit 388A (Business Loop) and then exit immediately again for Summit Hill Drive. Turn right onto Summit Hill and go two lights to Gay. Turn right onto Gay, two blocks, on the right.

THE MILLSTONE INN, *Exit 435, Newport*

In the '20s and '30s the Millstone was the center of life in Newport—the place where visiting dignitaries stayed, where balls were held, and where in short the town got as close to splendor as it could. Then came the dismal fate that overtook so many old hotels. For 10 years the Millstone was an abandoned shell.

But a unique stone building with fireplaces and oak woodwork was too good to waste. When the World's Fair came to Knoxville, Ron and Mary Jo Bullard decided it was time for the Millstone to be reborn. So they fixed it, cleaned it, and scrubbed it. Now the fireplace in the lobby is aglow again on winter nights, welcoming the highway-weary soul.

And there's lunch to be had here. The desserts and breads are all homemade; simple and fancy sandwiches run from just $.75 to $2.75; and the full lunchtime buffet is $3.25—modest prices indeed for a meal at handsomely set tables beneath a 14-foot tin ceiling. The walls are stone and the floor is bare wood, all of which gives the dining room something of the feel of a comfortable old hunting lodge.

Now the truth of the matter is that the Bullards are new to the innkeeping business, and they've got a difficult task before them. Were the Millstone in New England, it would be an instant success. But Newport, Tennessee, is another matter. The situation is fluid as they look for a formula that will attract tourists from the highway and at the same time bring a local business. How it will all turn out is unclear, as is the future of the dinners that are now served only on weekends. It might be best to give them a call before you go too far out of your way. Rooms are $18.50–$25.00, furnished, unfortunately, with standard motel fittings.

HOURS   Lunch: Every day, 11 am–2 pm. Dinner: Thurs.–Sat. 5 pm–9 pm.

SPECS   402 East Broadway; (615) 623-3592; V/MC/AE; no liquor.

DIRECTIONS   From Exit 435 go north on TN 32 1.4 miles and turn right at the second light. Go four quick lights and then one block more. On the right.

North Carolina

OLDE BELL RESTAURANT, *Exit 31, Canton*

To reach the town of Canton you must drive 2½ miles around the mammoth Champion Paper and Pulp Mill. It's the largest such mill in the world, and from its forest of smokestacks comes the cleanest, whitest, most highly purified smoke we've ever seen. It's almost beautiful, and it's certainly impressive.

At least half the town of Canton must be numbered among the mill's 2,300 employees, and we guess a good many of them must eat at the Olde Bell, a clean and simple working-class restaurant without pretensions that just happens to serve some quite decent southern cooking. The building that houses it is a story unto itself—made partly of metal, partly of stone; and partly a cabin of neatly dovetailed, ancient-looking pine logs. Inside is a scattering of tables, a small lunch counter, and a varnished stone hearth now inhabited only by an electro-glo fire.

The homemade meat and vegetable soup won't win any awards, but it was good and it was filling. So was everything else we tried, most of which was fried, except for the apple cobbler that flirted with excellence. Sandwiches from $1.50 to $2.25; one meat and three vegetables for $2.95.

HOURS   Mon.–Sat. 5 am–8 pm; Sun. 8 am–2 pm.

SPECS   111 Park St.; (704) 648-6381; no cards; no liquor.

DIRECTIONS   From Exit 31 (Canton, NC 215) follow NC 215 south for 2.2 miles as it jogs around the mill to the second light. Turn left and go one block. On your left, at the corner.

THE MOUNTAIN GREENERY, *Exit 65, Black Mountain*

The welcome sign proclaims Black Mountain as the home of Susan Pruffitt, Miss North Carolina of 1978. On arrival we thought of it instead as the home of Black Mountain College, a now defunct experimental college whose faculty once boasted the likes of Joseph Albers and Merce Cunningham. We will remember it, however, for the Mountain Greenery, one of the least likely and best-tasting restaurants we've come across in our culinary wanderings.

The place looks as if it must once have been a florist shop. At any rate, you enter through a greenhouse, pass through a tiny lobby, and find yourself in a quiet, dark, and surprisingly dignified little room. There are but eight tables, handsomely set, and everything seems to be in the best of taste until you hear the country music playing quietly in the background and notice, without quite believing it, the TV set whose silent, printed weather forecasts dominate the room from off in one corner.

Undaunted, we ordered the Reuben pie ($3.95) and sat back to see what would happen. It was delicious, a blend of chopped corned beef, cabbage, mushrooms, bacon, and onion baked in a light pie shell and topped with a tangy cheese sauce. Suddenly the TV didn't matter, and we wanted to try every one of the usual and not-so-usual lunch offerings: applewood-smoked pork sandwich, for example ($3.25), or maybe the house version of nachos ($2.25).

Dinners run from $7.95 for a vegetable quiche to $14.50 for steak Diane. For $9.95 you could try chicken breast topped with prosciutto, Monterey Jack, and mushroom sauce. Italian dishes like shrimp scampi and spaghetti carbonara were especially well represented. Key lime pie for dessert, made to the specifications of the Greenery's Floridian owner.

HOURS   Mon.–Thurs. 11:30 am–2:30 pm & 5 pm–9 pm; Fri. 11:30 am–2:30 pm & 5 pm–10 pm; Sat. 5 pm–10 pm. Closed Sun.

SPECS   401 East State St.; (704) 669-2495; V/MC; beer and wine.

DIRECTIONS   Take Exit 65 for Black Mountain. You'll have no choices to make, and the restaurant will appear on the right in 0.3 mile.

CLINE'S BARBECUE, *Exit 105, Morganton*

Vernon Cline is a very friendly man, and so is everyone who works for him in his new, clean, plain, and plasticky barbecue place. Such atmosphere as there is comes from personal warmth and a mixture of hickory smoke and country music that fills the air.

Vernon's version of North Carolina barbecue is deeply smoked and comes in a pungent vinegar/Worcestershire/mustard sauce—$1.65 for a pretty good sandwich; $3.50 for the complete dinner with hushpuppies, baked beans, cole slaw, pickles, and french fries. There's fish, beef, and chicken, too; but pork, sliced, snipped, minced, and sauced, is what the place is all about.

It was from Vernon that we learned that Morganton is the home of Senator Sam Ervin, chairman of the Senate Watergate Committee that brought Richard Nixon to his knees. Sam still lives here, strolling the streets and taking an occasional meal at the Sterling Snack Bar (and pool hall) in town. That sounded interesting, so we left Cline's, which nestles safely between the fast-food joints out by the highway, and headed for town in search of adventure.

HOURS   Tues.–Sat. 11 am–9 pm. Closed Sun. & Mon.

SPECS   (704) 437-6282; no cards; no liquor.

DIRECTIONS   From Exit 105 (NC 18) go half-mile north. On the right.

STERLING SNACK BAR, *Exit 105, Morganton*

The Sterling Snack Bar is so absolutely local that as we sat at the counter working on "the best breakfast in town" a fellow in a flannel shirt and trucker's hat asked us how the high school football game came out. We muttered something noncommittal over our grits and commented on the excellent flavor of the smoked ham. We all agreed that there really is nothing like a true fresh egg!

At the rear were half a dozen pool tables, separated from the counter area by three frowzy plywood booths. Pictures of Franklin D. Roosevelt and Herbert Hoover hung on walls. There was a beer cooler and eight old theater seats on a platform a few inches above the floor. On them sit the men who aren't eating, looking as if they haven't moved since the pictures were tacked up, talking, talking, talking. We never saw Senator Sam Ervin, whose office is right next door, but we did learn how his North Carolina hometown cultivates in its citizens the gift of gab. Football was the chief subject, but politics came a close second.

If you haven't the courage to enter so funky and down-home a place, you can place your order from the sidewalk. There's a little window that opens onto the end of the counter, and through it pass all the sandwiches and coffee needed to get Morgantown's secretaries through the day. (Perhaps women come in at other times, but the indoor clientele was exclusively male when we were there.)

Needless to say, a meal at Sterling's is not going to send you to the poorhouse. Seven dinners run from $1.50 to $2.75; burgers are $1.00, and other sandwiches start at $.85. If the rest is as good as the breakfast, you'll get a whole lot more than your money's worth.

HOURS Mon.–Sat. 4 am–midnight; closed Sun.

SPECS Sterling and Meeting Sts.; no cards; beer only.

DIRECTIONS From Exit 105 go north on NC 18 for 2.3 miles to the fifth light (Meeting St.). Park. The **Sterling** is one block to your left, then a half-block to the right.

THE STONE HOUSE, *Exit 105, Morganton*

If Cline's sounds too plain and the Sterling too rugged, if you'd care for a touch of class and some of the amenities, then the Stone House is the obvious choice. This gnomelike, stone edifice sits on the edge of the town square offering "classical French" cuisine at dinner in an intimate atmosphere where starched linen and soft carpets set the tone. Entrées go from $9.75 for trout amandine to $13.75 for veal with crabmeat and Swiss cheese. Cornish game hen, chicken florentine, and a few good steaks come in between.

The spirit of the Stone House is nevertheless casual, especially at lunchtime when the menu advertises a "hot diggity dog" ($2.50) and a "quiche me, you fool" (4.25). Deli sandwiches, a good selection of salads, plus soups, burgers, and sinful-sounding desserts complete the choices.

Unfortunately we got to town too late on Saturday night to give the Stone House a try, so we'll have to leave this one to your spirit of adventure.

HOURS   Mon.–Fri. 11 am–2 pm & 6 pm–10 pm; Sat. 6 pm–10 pm. Closed Sun.

SPECS   108 East Meeting St.; (704) 433-7403; V/MC; wine and brown bags.

DIRECTIONS   From Exit 105 go north on NC 18 for 2.3 miles to the fifth light (Meeting St.). Park. Restaurant is half-block to your left.

COUNTRY ADVENTURES BARBECUE BARN,
US 321/64/70 Exit, Hickory

Out here the word "country" is not a geographical term. It is an ethnic and moral term, denoting the simple American virtues of down-home, straightforward talking, feeling, and living. In music this ethos is called "country" music, and in matters of food it is called "barbecue."

Of course we had to seek it out and try to give it to you in its most authentic form. The question arises therefore as to whether a huge, new, commercial operation in a "barn" that has never seen so much as a dog or a cat, much less a cow or a horse, can be called true "country." Eighty long, pine-slab tables and metal folding chairs fill the cavernous space, the service is cafeteria style, and there's another "barn" attached to the first that houses an entire country-western nightclub, complete with glitzy lighting and a stage that often reverberates to the stomping of the Country Cloggers.

Obviously this isn't your "little ol' country place," but the more we thought about it the more it seemed that precisely because it didn't care about authenticity, this might be the "realest" of them all. As Dolly Parton put it, there's something "a little bit phony" about the whole country cult anyway; and of all the folk movements America has given rise to, this one seems least hostile to commercialization. Perhaps it even thrives on it.

Speculation aside, the Country Adventures Barbecue Barn gives you hickory-smoked pork, beef, ribs, and chicken, plus baked beans, potato skins, cole slaw, hush-puppies, tea or coffee. It's all you can eat for $7.50, and while sitting around on a steam table doesn't help the food, we rate it good to very good, especially the ribs.

It's fun and it's an experience.

HOURS Thurs.–Sat. 6 pm–10 pm.

SPECS (704) 324–1488; MC/V; no liquor.

DIRECTIONS From the exit for US 321/64/70 go north on US 321 for 2.6 miles to a light at 9th Ave. Turn left on 9th Ave. and go 0.3 mile up the hill to 9th Ave. Drive. Turn right (following a sign for the airport) and go about 100 yards to a small sign on the right that will point you to another right turn. The barn is 300 yards up this dirt road.

LANDMARK PLACE
SUB-EXPRESS,
Exit for I-77, Statesville

See pages 165 and 167 for a description of as fine and handsome a restaurant as is to be found in this part of the world, and also for a perfectly good sandwich shop.

DIRECTIONS From I-40 turn south onto I-77 and go about a mile to the East Broad St. exit. Then follow directions on pages 166 and 167.

CENTER VIEW INN
SNOOK'S OLD FASHIONED BARBECUE,
Farmington Rd. Exit, Mocksville

We were in hot pursuit of back-country barbecue stands, and we'd heard that Deano's was the pride of Mocksville. So naturally we were disappointed to learn that the Center View Inn has taken over Deano's old stand (only half a mile from the exit) and that the principal offering has changed to pizza. Deano's "Q" is still sold here, but it's made elsewhere and shipped in. That didn't seem down-home enough for us; they were out of barbecue when we stopped in; and the owners themselves told us that the best barbecue in the county was Snook's, four miles down the road.

Now you may be perfectly content with Deano's and a half-minute drive, but off we went. It took about 6 minutes to reach the crudely painted sign depicting a farmer, ax waving wildly above his head, in hot pursuit of a wily porker. More authentic than Snook's you cannot get. The place consists of three white shacks in the middle of nowhere—one for taking your order, one for eating-in at the long Formica counters that run just under the windows, and one for smoking the meat. Unfortunately, authenticity and the best of flavors don't necessarily come together. We found the chipped pork only mildly flavored—not at all the vinegary wonder we were so sure we had come upon—and we're recommending Snook's to you more for the color than the cuisine.

> **HOURS**   **Center View:** Mon.–Thurs. 10 am–10 pm; Fri. & Sat. 10 am–midnight; Sun. 11 am–9 pm.
> **Snook's:** Daily, 11 am–7 pm.

DIRECTIONS   From the exit go south on Farmington Rd. 0.2 mile to a stop sign. For the **Center View** turn right and drive 0.3 mile, on the right. For **Snook's,** turn left at stop sign and go 4.7 miles, on the right.

SALEM TAVERN, *Exit for NC 52/8S, Winston-Salem*

Once Winston and Salem were separate towns. Winston grew prosperous on the tobacco trade, and absorbed its backwater neighbor. No one thought much about it until one day it was realized that Salem was a perfect 19th-century village hiding under a 20th-century veneer. Salem was founded by Moravians, religious refugees from Germany, who built their towns in the new world with a fine eye for beauty and craftsmanship. Now the half-timbered houses and fine old brick buildings have been painstakingly restored, and for the trouble of a two-minute drive you can not only forget the noise and hurry of the highway, you can forget the entire 20th century.

The Salem Tavern will help you do this. It was built in 1816 to the severe religious requirements of the plain people—small, low rooms, bare wooden floors, undecorated walls and windows. It serves as restaurant to the village, and plain as it is, it is a very pleasant relief indeed from the glitzy gaudiness of anything you're likely to find out by the road. When we passed through, the menu featured German items like ragout of pork, spaetzles, and white rice flecked with grains of its wild relative —well-enough prepared, but nothing to get very excited about. All this was due to change, however, with the imminent arrival of the new owners. Since no one even knew what would be on the menu, there's little we can do but tell you that good food or not, you're likely to enjoy an hour spent in these environs.

HOURS Mon.–Sat. 11:30–2:00 pm & 6 pm–8:30 pm. Closed Sun. Hours may change, however.

SPECS 736 South Main St.; (919) 748-8585; major cards; full license.

DIRECTIONS Take exit for NC 52 & 8S (Old Salem) and follow the signs for about 1 mile to the village. Then go one block past the reception center to Main and turn right. It's two blocks down, on the right.

SNOW'S GOOD FOOD, *Exit for NC 66, Kernersville*

It's not easy to find small-town luncheonettes and soda fountains that haven't been run out of business by highway strip development, but we found one in Kernersville, and it's got the added bonus of possibly being the skinniest lunch room in the business. The counter runs almost the entire length of the shop, leaving just room to squeeze by it if you're determined to sit at one of the ever-so-plain-plastic tables at the rear.

Snow's hamburgers were made locally famous by Elizabeth Sparks, who writes on food matters for the Winston-Salem newspaper. In exchange for the compliment, Snow's named one of its creations the Liz-burger, and we tried this concoction of chili, lettuce, cheese, tomato, fried onions, mustard, and mayo on a thick, juicy ground-beef patty. It was pretty fair for that kind of thing, but what impressed us most about Snow's was that they keep refilling the sweet iced tea before you ask for it. The place is as indigenous to the town as a restaurant can be, and it's absolutely friendly. For these virtues we recommend it, and for the prices—$.70 for a hot dog, $1.20 for a regular burger, and $.30 more for Liz's favorite.

HOURS   Mon.–Sat. 7:30 am–8:30 pm. Closed Sun.

SPECS   109 North Main St.; (919) 996-2811; no cards; no liquor.

DIRECTIONS   From the exit go north on NC 66 and continue straight ahead when 66 turns off to the left. It's 0.7 mile to Main St. from the exit. Left on Main, 2½ blocks to restaurant, on the right.

CRAZY ELLIOT'S (also known as HUCK'S),
Jamestown Road Exit, Greensboro

We met Elliot Pearlman standing in line at Bakatsias back in Durham. He's the kind of man who makes you feel within two minutes that you've known him all your life, and if you stay with him two minutes longer you literally will know every detail of his life. Maybe that's why he was so successful at selling women's clothing, and maybe that has something to do with why he then went and built himself a career as "North Carolina's leading character actor." But that is certainly why he bought Huck's Restaurant and determined to turn it into the entertainment and dining center of Greensboro.

Whether he'll succeed or not, we don't know. He'd just bought it when we met, and he was making plans for his innovations. But we do know that he'll have a great time trying out his aggressive familiarity on the customers, guiding them to their seats, seeing to their needs, making whatever grand gesture needs to be made, and generally having a good time. You may enjoy it too, especially if you miss New York. The prices probably won't be bad at this shopping center-nightclub, and the food just may be good. Elliot said he was going to import real New York deli, but we make no promises.

HOURS Currently Mon.–Wed. 11 am–11 pm; Thurs. & Fri. 11 am–1 am; Sat. 4 pm–1 am. Closed Sun.

SPECS 5605 W. Friendly Ave.; (919) 852-0796; V/MC/AE; full bar.

DIRECTIONS Exit is marked Guilford/Jamestown Rd./Guilford College. Go north from exit for 2.2 miles on Guilford College Rd. to light at Friendly Ave. Turn right and go one block to the small Quaker Village shopping center. Park and go inside.

TRAVELER'S ADVISORY

From Greensboro, N.C., to Durham, N.C., I-40 and I-85 run together. See I-85 for entries on this stretch of road.

CLAIRE'S, *Chapel Hill Street Exit, Durham*

We are decidedly partial to fine old houses that get converted to classy, understated restaurants. Such is the basic look of Claire's, but despite its awninged and becolumned exterior, despite its lace curtains, small, carpeted dining rooms, and chrome-framed museum prints, Claire's doesn't quite reach the pitch of elegance to which it seems to have aspired. Perhaps it's the crayons and drawing-paper place mats? But whatever it is, the total effect is likable and relaxed, which may well suit you better than real spiff after three hours in the car.

Absolutely everything at Claire's is fresh, and absolutely everything is from scratch, including the homemade pasta. The menu is an eclectic collection of international dishes with a *nouvelle* American accent. Lunches are on the order of shrimp and pasta seasoned with lemon and Dijon mustard or an omelette of sun-dried tomatoes, zucchini, mushrooms, potatoes, and Parmesan cheese ($4.15). Dinners are very modestly priced for this type of cooking—veal canneloni at $7.25 and Indonesian trout for $7.75. At lunch there are hamburgers, Reubens, and an Irish stew that we found worthy, but less than wonderful.

The menu is quite varied, so that whatever your mood (unless it be for steak and potatoes) you're sure to find something to your taste.

HOURS   Mon.–Thurs. 11:30 am–2:30 pm and 5 pm–10 pm; Fri. & Sat. 11:30 am–2:30 pm and 5 pm–10:30 pm; Sun. 11:30 am–10 pm.

SPECS   2701 Chapel Hill Rd; (919) 493-5721; V/MC; full bar.

DIRECTIONS   Take the exit for Chapel Hill St. near the center of Durham and turn onto Chapel Hill heading away from downtown. Go 0.3 mile to second light and bear left onto Kent. Go 0.4 on Kent and at the light turn right onto Moorehead. Go one block and then left onto Chapel Hill Rd., which you follow for 0.6 mile. On the left, just before the bridge over US 15/501. Sounds hard, but you'll be following the flow of the traffic all the way.

ANOTHER THYME, *Duke Street Exit, Durham*

This most appealing restaurant and its prototype, Some Thyme, are described on pages 232–35. Although both can be reached from I-40, Another Thyme is just a minute away. If you are on I-40, use the directions given here *before* entering I-85 in Durham.

DIRECTIONS   From the Duke St. exit, head north for about ½ mile to the second light (W. Main). Left on Main and pull into the parking lot on the right. **Another Thyme** is across from the parking lot, on Gregson Street (parallel to Duke, one-way in the other direction).

THE ANGUS BARN, *Exit 285, Morrisville*

Steak-and-potato lovers, this is your kind of country, and the Angus Barn is your kind of restaurant. Delicious, thick, juicy steaks and ribs are what the place is about, though they *will* sell you a broiled flounder or lobster tail if you insist. Be prepared to pay. The ground beef "steak" bottoms out the menu at a mere $9.95; chateaubriand is tops at $18.95.

The restaurant, of course, looks like a barn—big, beamy, and bricky. It's commercial and a little phony, but not offensively so, and it smells wonderful, always filled with the aroma of roasting ribs. A local favorite, to be sure, and while it's not what we'd call an interesting restaurant, it's excellent in its class.

HOURS   Mon.–Sat. 5 pm–11 pm; Sun. 5 pm–10 pm. Closed Christmas, New Year's, Thanksgiving.

SPECS   Highway 70 and Airport Rd.; (919) 787-3504; all cards; full bar.

DIRECTIONS   From Exit 285 go north following signs for airport. Continue past the airport to US 70 (3.5 miles, total). Turn right and go 0.1 mile. On the right.

IRREGARDLESS CAFÉ, *Exits 289 & 292, Raleigh*

This restaurant is Arthur Gordon's revenge on all the English teachers and other fuddy-duddies who once plagued his life by correcting his grammar. As an undergraduate at U.N.C., his papers were regularly returned with red circles around his favorite nonword, "irregardless." But in 1974, the young graduate had his way. He opened his own restaurant. Grammarians shuddered, but there it was in big bold letters, THE IRREGARDLESS CAFÉ, and the sign was too high for them to reach with their red pencils.

Arthur's solecistic creation burst upon the Raleigh scene as a 1960s-style vegetarian restaurant. It filled a niche and met with immediate success. Since then, the natural-foodsy flavors have graduated to the '80s and the success has not abated. Arthur's brand of vegetarianism now allows for fish and poultry: he serves wine-poached salmon and champagne chicken alongside spinach brioches and vegetable curries. But, like European cooks, he still shops for fresh ingredients each morning at Raleigh's City Market, and he still throws his heart into everything that leaves the kitchen. We arrived for Sunday brunch, a meal we won't soon forget.

The waitress greeted us with glasses of fresh-squeezed orange juice, and she immediately took our orders for coffee and tea (herb or black). Only then did we address the menu: omelettes stuffed with broccoli-cauliflower-brie or fresh crab in béchamel sauce, mushroom-artichoke frittatas, cheese blintzes, fruit waffles, and more. For bread, another difficult decision to make: whole-wheat roll, raisin-bran muffins, sour-cream coffee cake, or date-nut raisin bread.

The frittata was outstanding, and the cheese blintzes served with an enormous fruit salad rivaled Grandma Pearl Schwartz's. All orders arrived with home fries—not ordinary home fries, mind you, but home fries made from both white and russet-skinned new potatoes and a hint of nutmeg. The date-nut raisin bread, which looked like a slice of bread pie, was unsurpassed by anything of its ilk that we have ever had.

That was Sunday brunch. We didn't get to try a weekday lunch or dinner, but we've heard they are almost as memorable. Expect salads, sandwiches (especially salad sandwiches), bean-burgers, and the day's special entrées.

As for prices, here is a department in which the Irregardless has had difficulty moving forward with the times. At lunch or dinner, light meals run under $3; dinner specials are rarely higher than $6. Complete brunch is $5.50, and you won't have to eat for the rest of the day.

At any time of the week, you'll hear live acoustic music—folksingers, string quartets, ragtime piano, harp. Even the children will be entertained, as the Irregardless keeps a library of juvenile books on hand. From what we could tell, everyone in town loves this place, even (perhaps grudgingly) the staunchest grammarians.

HOURS Lunch: Mon.–Fri. 11:30 am–2:15 pm. Dinner: Mon.–Thurs. 5:30–9:30 pm, Fri. & Sat. 5:30–10 pm. Brunch: Sun. 10 am–2 pm. Closed week of Christmas and week of July 4.

SPECS 901 W. Morgan St.; (919) 833-9920; V/MC; full license.

DIRECTIONS **Eastbound:** Exit 289 puts you on an interstate spur to downtown Raleigh. In about 2 miles exit for US 1 South/Sanford/Pittsboro, also an expressway. Go about ½ mile to the Hillsborough St./Meredith College exit. ■ Bear left onto Hillsborough St. and go about 2½ miles (fast-moving) into town. Just past the light at Ashe, bear right onto Morgan. As soon as you do so, the **Irregardless Café** parking lot is on your left; restaurant is across the street, a few doors further down.

Westbound: Exit 292 puts you on US 1 North, an expressway. Go about 2 miles to Hillsborough St. exit. Then, as above from ■.

T. K. TRIPP'S, *Raleigh*

OK, it *is* a chain, but it's a small, local chain. OK, its decor is the usual clichéd Victoriana, but here the clichés are delivered with verve. The truth of the matter is that before we knew there were other T. K. Tripp'ses we had already downed a very tasty, full-flavored bowl of vegetable beef soup ($1.95) and enjoyed a very good hamburger on a real kaiser roll ($3.55). So why not tell you about it? We could have found something more authentic, but for this kind of food, it wouldn't have been any better.

Since Tripp's is your basic BPO café (bricks, plants, and oak), it comes with the mandatory QRS menu (quiche, Reuben, and spinach salad, around $4.00 each). Potato skins, too, of course, but somehow the carrot cake got replaced by "old world" apple pie.

Dinner consists of your basic steak and seafood standbys pepped up with an occasional outsider like chicken cordon bleu. It runs from $6.95 to $9.95, and you'll get your money's worth. Tripp's doesn't take any risks, but what it does, it seems to do very well.

HOURS Mon.–Fri. 11 am–11 pm; Sat. 5 pm–11 pm; Sun. 11 am–10 pm.

SPECS 3516 Wade Ave.; (919) 821-3990; V/MC/AE; full bar.

DIRECTIONS **Eastbound:** Exit 289 puts you on an interstate spur toward downtown Raleigh. In about 2 miles, just past the junction with US 1, the spur becomes Wade Ave. Go straight onto Wade and turn left at the first light. There will be a small shopping center on your right. In there, at the far end.

Westbound: Exit 292 puts you on US 1 North, an expressway. Go about 2.5 miles to the Wade Ave exit. Take Wade Ave. east toward downtown Raleigh. Turn left at the first light. There will be a small shopping center on your right. In there, at the far end.

DON MURRAY'S BARBECUE RESTAURANT, *Raleigh*

It's nice to know that someone was serving all-you-can-eat buffets long before Morrison's and Ballantine's. It's even nicer to know that they are still doing it at competitive prices, and that you can taste the difference.

A local institution for as long as anyone in Raleigh can remember, Don Murray's is a top choice for anyone with a voracious appetite and a slim wallet. If you've got a station wagon full of kids, it's a godsend.

The barbecue itself is nothing to write books about. It's perfectly acceptable, mind you, but the meat that comes to the steam table has never seen the embers of hickory or any other wood. That's OK so long as you're not seeking the pinnacle of pit-cooked "Q." Look at what Don Murray gives you along with barbecue on his daily dinner buffet. There's fried chicken and what around here is called chicken pastry (we would have called it chicken pot pie). For vegetables you'll find yams and marsh-mallows, corn, black-eyed peas, macaroni and cheese, cole slaw, applesauce, fried onion rings, spinach (overcooked, but what can you expect on a steam table?), and green beans (likewise). And, in case that's not enough, Murray's has recently added fresh trout. For $4.35 you get to partake of this to your heart's content. Forsaking the all-encompassing buffet, you might opt for a trout dinner: unlimited fish plus french fries, slaw, and hushpuppies for $3.50.

If all you can eat is more than you'd care to, there are all kinds of dinner specials with finite quantities, most of them around $3.

With low prices and prodigious portions, you might expect that Don Murray's would be little more than a cement-block bunker, but actually it's quite nice in a family restaurant sort of way, with calico curtains, wagon-wheel light fixtures, and vaguely Colonial pictures on the walls. Come here for quite re-spectable, eminently affordable food and the satisfaction of knowing that even if family-run, family-style restaurants are en-dangered, they're not extinct.

HOURS   Mon.–Sat. 11 am–9 pm; Sun. 11 am–8 pm.

SPECS   2751 North Blvd. (US 1); (919) 872-6270; no cards; no liquor.

DIRECTIONS   **Eastbound:** I-40 East ends at Raleigh, but eastbound travelers will continue on the Cliff Benson Beltline, which is US 64 at this point. Just east of Raleigh, US 64 leaves the Beltline and heads east to Rocky Mount and I-95, but for **Don Murray's** do not take this exit. ■ Stay on the Beltline for 2 more miles and take the exit for US 1 North/Louisburg/Richmond. Go ¼ mile to second light, turn left and look left. You'll see it.

Westbound: I-40 West begins at Raleigh, so it's not strictly possible to be westbound on I-40 toward Raleigh. However, US 64, a 4-lane express-way, runs from eastern North Carolina to Raleigh, where it becomes I-40. To get to **Don Murray's** from US 64 West, you should leave 64 at sign for Durham/West 70/North 401/North 50. This will put you on the Cliff Benson Beltline. Then, as above from ■. (**Note:** After eating, back-track 2 miles on the Beltline, and you will be on I-40 West.)

Virginia

THE WATERSIDE, *Downtown Exit, Norfolk*

First there was Boston's Quincy Market. Then the Harbor-place in Baltimore. Now no city worth its smog can be without its very own "eating mall"—a conglomeration of snackeries and serious restaurants under one rather sizable roof. Norfolk's is called the Waterside.

Perhaps you detect an undertone of sarcasm. It's not that we don't like Quincy or Harborplace or Waterside (or New York's Seaport or Washington's Pavillion, etc.). It's just that we find it difficult to wax enthusiastic over a clever thing that's become a fad.

Just the same, any interstate traveler would be well advised to stop at Waterside. For a pleasant diversion from the drive, a little exercise to limber up stiff joints, and a veritable United Nations of eateries from which to snack or feast, it compares with the best of this genre. Here are just a few of the possibilities:

Pierce's Pitt Bar-B-Q of Williamsburg (page 83) has opened a second branch, and here it is. It's got the same hickory-smoked Boston butt, the same sauce, the same everything (except prices, which are slightly higher). **Phillips Waterside** has three separate locations in the Waterside; each is distinguished by the method of seafood preparation—fried, steamed, and raw. At **Pasta & Company** you'll find all kinds of irresistible salads that you can ogle through the glass display cases before deciding. Highish prices.

Cheese steak is the featured item at **Philadelphia Steak & Sub Co.;** fried vegetables are the **Veggie Patch**'s stock in trade.

Hasskin's French Fries and **Cee Cee's Hamburger Classics** purvey the obvious; **Potatoes Unlimited** seems to have endless variations on the spud.

If you want to eat ethnic, you might try sio-pao, pancit, lumpia, or empanadas at **Filipiana;** the dishes are all explained on the display menu. **Szechuan Garden** is fast-food Chinese, and **Takis Gyros** has many Greek specialties including spanakopita, beef kabob, and souvlaki as well as its namesake, gyros.

All of these eateries are located on the perimeter of the Waterside's first floor. In the middle you'll find butcher-block tables and chairs. When we're at one of these restaurant marketplaces we like to eat a little, walk a little, eat a little, walk a little. But if your digestive system prefers to stay put, you might like to steer yourself toward one of Waterside's "sit-down" restaurants, among them **Il Porto** (Italian), the **Tandoor Restaurant** (Indian), and **Reggie's British Pub.**

HOURS   Something will be open between 11 am & 9 pm every day; some of the places are open later yet.

SPECS   333 Waterside Dr.

DIRECTIONS   From I-64, 10 miles east of Hampton Roads Bridge Tunnel, take I-264 (sign says I-264/Downtown Norfolk/Portsmouth), which shoots you downtown. Stay on it to the very end (about 5 miles), following signs for Waterside Drive. Almost immediately you'll see the **Waterside** complex on your left, at Atlantic St. Turn right onto Atlantic for paid parking (50 cents/hour).

OLD POINT STEAK AND SPAGHETTI HOUSE,
Exit 5, Hampton

The name is deceiving—this restaurant is neither Italian nor an AAA-style steak emporium with foil-wrapped baked potatoes and chick-peas on the salad bar. It's primarily a Greek restaurant, and although you'll find Delmonicos and other beefy things featured prominently on the menu, you'll also find dolmadakia, pastichio, and souvlaki. And the decor is certainly not what steakhouses bring to mind. Located in a downtown shopping district, it's compact, homey, a little heavy on the plastic, but unpretentious and quite pleasantly 15 to 20 years behind the times.

The spaghetti sauce is Greek, a lighter shade of red than its Italian counterpart. Its spices are more aromatic and its flavors more complex than the usual pasta topping. In response to an inquiry about the seasonings, owner Peter Kilopoulos would reveal their number (17), but not their names. Along with the sauce comes the usual run of mushroom, meat ball, and pepperoni acompaniments, priced between $2.65 and $3.85.

Another standout was the Greek salad. At $1.65 it was really quite sizable, and suitably appointed with black olives, feta, and peperoncini. Although the ratio of iceberg lettuce to endive and red cabbage was too high for our taste, its dressing, like the spaghetti sauce, was wonderful. We suggested to Mr. Kilopoulos that he market it by the bottle, and he told us that two patent lawyers had tried to talk him into just that. No thanks, he said. He preferred to keep serving the family recipe to restaurant guests and let it go at that.

HOURS Sun.–Fri. 11 am–10 pm; Sat. 4–10 pm.

SPECS 33 E. Mellen St.; (804) 722-8880; major cards; beer and wine.

DIRECTIONS From Exit 5, turn right if westbound, left if eastbound. Go about ½ mile to light at Mallory St. Turn right, go one block, and turn left on Mellen St. (Route 143). In 1 block you'll see it on your left. Free parking around back (turn left at corner).

PIERCE'S PITT BAR-B-Q, *Exits 55 & 56, Williamsburg*

Reserve a spot for Pierce's in the Barbecue Hall of Fame. It deserves honors on three accounts. First, the barbecue itself, among the very best we've tasted. Second, Pierce's worthy function as an alternative to ye olde touriste trappe, of which there is no shortage in this towne. And third, its history, a heartening sidebar on what can happen (as opposed to what usually happens) to local restaurants when an interstate highway arrives in town.

Pierce's is on old Highway 168, the main route across southern Virginia before Interstate 64 came along. Within a year of that event, virtually every small business on 168 closed up tight. Despite a loyal following of interstate truckers and Virginians who came regularly from Richmond and Norfolk, the prognosis for Pierce's was poor. The local exit ramps hadn't been completed and there was no way to reach Pierce's without a considerable detour.

But the love of fine barbecue runs deep, and those who loved Pierce's weren't willing to let an 8-foot fence conquer the romance. So they parked their cars and trucks beside the Interstate and hopped the fence, much to the consternation of state police. The resulting squabbles between the law and the lovers of barbecue resulted in nationwide publicity for Pierce's, spreading its fame, increasing its clientele, and exacerbating the problem. In the end, the state built two exit ramps that made Pierce's a very convenient Interstate stopoff, and everyone was happy, even the state police, who are among the restaurant's best customers.

So what it is about Pierce's Pitt Bar-B-Q, besides the misspelling in the name, that is unique? For one thing, the meat is all Boston butt, slaughtered to order the day before it's smoked on hickory embers in the barbecue pit out back. Julius "Doc" Pierce and his son, "J.C.," prefer butt for its lower fat and bone content, and its slightly deeper, darker flavor. But most of the flavor comes from the sauce, top secret of course, which we found utterly delightful. It is tomato-based, with vinegar and peppers, a concoction that tingled, but didn't burn, its way to our hearts.

Prices at Pierce's are typically low—$3.95 is about the most you can spend, and $1.85 for a jumbo sandwich might be all it takes. As for decor, it's all on the outside. The buildings are

vibrant orange with yellow trim, an antidote, perhaps, for highway drowsiness. You should be aware there's no place to sit
down, except for a few shaded picnic tables and, of course, your
car seat. Stock up on napkins—the sauce likes to travel.

HOURS Winter: 10 am–8 pm, 7 days a week. Summer: 10 am–9
pm, 7 days a week. Closed Dec. 23–Jan. 2.

SPECS 447 Rochambeau Dr.; (804) 565-2955; no cards; no liquor.

DIRECTIONS **Eastbound:** From Exit 55, turn right and take the
first left onto Route F137 (Rochambeau Dr.). Go 1.3 miles; it's on right.
Return to Interstate by reversing westbound directions (below); do not
backtrack.

Westbound: From Exit 56, turn left, cross over the highway, and take
the very first right (Route F137/Rochambeau Dr.), a service road that
runs parallel to the Interstate. Go 3.2 miles; it's on left. Return to Interstate by reversing eastbound directions (above); do not backtrack.

O'BRIENSTEINS, *Exit 37A, Richmond*

Richard Ripp is a clever man. He wanted to put a restaurant
in Richmond's biggest shopping mall, but he also wanted to
avoid the stigma usually attached to mall food. Enter two
"friends," Mr. O'Brien, publican extraordinaire, and Mr. Stein,
deli proprietor and bagel maker.

It seems that Messrs. O'Brien and Stein were at one time
quarreling neighbors. Tensions rose to the point that a hole was
punched in the wall separating their two shops. The hole was
enlarged, and pretty soon the wall was virtually gone. Customers
streamed in. They liked the Jewish deli/Irish pub combination,
and with business skyrocketing, O'Brien and Stein suddenly
found that they liked each other after all. So, combining their
respective talents, the two became partners, moved out to the
mall, and opened an Irish-Jewish restaurant-pub.

Such is history as O'Brienstein's patrons hear it from their
waiters and waitresses (if they ask). Although a mural celebrates
the moment of interethnic understanding, the story is pure fic-
tion.

It works. If Richard Ripp, the real proprietor, intended to make customers forget they're in a mall, he has succeeded. If he intended to attract attention to a novel culinary marriage, he has achieved that too. People talk about O'Brienstein's, and they enjoy eating there. We have to admit we did too.

The first thing that reaches the table, even before a glass of water, is a basket of freshly baked bagels (not the best, but not bad at all). The Jewish side of the menu promises deli sandwiches like pastrami on rye, burgers on bialy, ham and cheese blintzes (no one said Stein was kosher), and a variant of eggs Benedict using cream cheese and lox, with an onion bagel instead of an English muffin. O'Brien contributes a very respectable Irish beef stew, stuffed baked potatoes, corned beef and cabbage with buttered potatoes, and Irish coffee.

Straying from the theme, O'Brienstein's has diversified its menu, allowing in stragglers from all over the globe: fettuccini carbonara, chicken and vegetable stir fry, ratatouille, quiche, and —here's an odd hybrid—nacho bagels. There are a number of vegetarian selections such as vegetable strudel and avocado sandwiches, and one of the swankiest-looking salad bars we've ever seen, sparkling with fresh fruit and gorgeous vegetables. With a bagel and soup, it can be visited (and revisited) for $4.95. Most menu items run $4.25 to $5.95, with the salad bar optional for an extra $2.75.

The restaurant itself is a modish, lively, delightfully confusing maze on many levels, loosely centered around three atria with hydroponic gardens. Exposed ductwork and support pillars have been artfully incorporated in the scheme, and a nifty series of pulleys and belts run several interconnected ceiling fans. An uncountable number of waiters and waitresses scurry about in their blue and green getups.

If you like restaurant theater (not to be confused with dinner theater, in which all the acting is on stage), you'll love this place. The food may be secondary to the theatrics, but it's not too terribly far behind.

HOURS Mon.–Thurs. 11:30 am–10 pm; Fri. & Sat. 11:30 am–11 pm; Sun. noon–6 pm.

SPECS Regency Square Mall, corner Parham and Quoccasin; (804) 740-2707; V/MC; full license.

DIRECTIONS Exit 37A puts you on Parham Rd. South. In about 1¾ miles, you'll be at the corner of Quoccasin Road, looking at Regency Square Mall. To get to O'Brienstein's, turn right on Quoccasin, get in the left lane, and bear left into mall. Turn left at stop sign, and park in front of Miller & Rhoades. Restaurant is just inside the mall entrance.

TONY'S CHUCKWAGON, *Exit 23, Charlottesville*

Tony's Chuckwagon is a great restaurant. We had to think twice before raving without qualification about so simple (and inexpensive) a place, but reconsideration brought us to the same conclusion: Tony's is just great!

Example: the hamburgers are freshly ground right here every morning; they're served, if you request it, on an outsized biscuit (also made here, of course). Delicious.

Example: the chicken salad is absolutely tops, even better than the apparent sum of its parts—chopped fresh chicken, boiled eggs, sliced tomatoes, Spanish onions, and cucumbers. Either there's some herb or spice nobody mentioned, or Tony simply has the Midas touch.

Example: the cole slaw is superb, having achieved just the right tension between sweetness and tartness.

And so on. There's one more item we must mention, the cobbler. Please understand that, having spent the previous six weeks in southern restaurants, we were up to our eyeballs in cobbler, doubtful that the dish could hold any further interest even if it were made with mangoes and kiwi fruit. But Tony's apple cobbler sang out to our taste buds and stood out from the crowd like Luciano Pavarotti in a junior high school choir.

It hasn't always been this way. Each of Tony's kitchen successes is the product of hard work. Not just the work of opening up every morning at 6:30 and sticking around until many hours after the lunch crowd has left, but the hard, constant work of experimenting with recipes, day after day after day, until he was absolutely sure that everything was as good as he could get it.

With such outstanding food and prices that peak at $3.25 (most items are $2.50 or less), you may be preparing for us to say that Tony's is a hopeless dump, that to enjoy the tastes you'll have to close your eyes, or worse. But we're delighted to report that it's a charming place. Not in the least bit fancy, of course, but a sweetly if plainly decorated room with big windows, nice oak window frames and doors, a few watercolors on white walls, and cloths on the tables.

It seems that all Tony's effort has paid off, and the word is out. Arrive at the lunch hour and you'll join company with a diverse collection of doctors, judges, merchants, professors, students, secretaries, and self-described eccentrics, including one who parks his 1952 Rolls Bentley out front.

HOURS Mon.–Thurs. 6:30 am–4 pm; Fri. & Sat. 6:30 am–8 pm; closed Sun. (A new Tony's Chuckwagon, location given below, serves dinner as well as breakfast and lunch: Mon.–Thurs. 5:30 am–9 pm; Fri. & Sat. 5:30 am–10 pm; closed Sun.)

SPECS 114 4th St. N.E.; (804) 296-6509; no cards; beer. (The other Tony's is at 1540 East High St.; (804) 977-9714.)

DIRECTIONS From Exit 23, head north toward Charlottesville. In about 2½ miles, turn right on Preston Ave., which soon becomes Market St. In about ¼ mile, turn right on Fourth St. It's half a block down, on right.

(Other location: From Exit 25, turn left if eastbound, right if westbound onto Route 250 West. In about 2 miles, at the corner of High St.—Route 20 South—look left. It's in back of the former gas station.)

LITTLEJOHN'S NEW YORK DELICATESSEN,
Exit 23, Charlottesville

Across Main Street from the University of Virginia's impeccable campus (designed by Charlottesville's favorite son, Thomas Jefferson) is a row of inexpensive eateries of the sort that lie at the outskirts of any large university. A standout with the students, partly because of its unflagging hours, is Littlejohn's Deli.

We liked it here. Contrary to expectations, it wasn't visually or acoustically loud; while not exactly subdued either, the tones of natural hardwood, a pressed tin ceiling, and a few obligatory plants made for a pleasant, not overstimulating, environment.

Above the cafeteria-style counter is a blackboard on which are chalked, in rainbow colors, a hundred different sandwiches, most in the $2–$3 range. (Note the impromptu illustrations that accompany the sandwich names.) Other blackboards call your attention to drinks (Dr. Brown's is a favorite), desserts (cheesecake and apple strudel among others), soups, chili, and various snacks.

Sandwich spreads are made fresh daily, and the turkey salad we tasted was quite good. Meats are roasted on the premises, and our roast beef sandwich was thick and properly rare. Among students, the sandwiches of choice appear to be the Italian sausage sub and Littlejohn's Special—corned beef, pastrami, cheddar, tomato, herb mayo, and spicy mustard.

HOURS   Open 24 hours a day, 7 days a week, except for the week of Christmas when it's closed.

SPECS   1437 W. Main St.; (804) 977-0588; no cards; beer and wine.

DIRECTIONS   From Exit 23, head north toward Charlottesville. In about 2 miles, turn left on W. Main St. and it's exactly 0.9 miles down, on your right.

ROWE'S FAMILY RESTAURANT,
I-81 Interchange, Staunton

If you're looking for a place with low prices, an attractive family atmosphere, and genuine southern cooking, you won't have to stray far from I-64 to reach Rowe's. A description is on page 189.

DIRECTIONS   **Westbound:** At the I-81 interchange, enter I-81 North. Almost immediately, take Exit 57. Turn left and you'll see it on your right.

Eastbound: I-64 and I-81 run concurrently for about 40 miles, as you know because you have been driving them. At the point where I-64 splits off to the east, do not take it. Stay on I-81 until Exit 57 (almost immediately after the split). From Exit 57, turn left and you'll see **Rowe's** on your right.

THE PAMPERED PALATE, *I-81 Interchange, Staunton*

If you're in the mood for a cheery little gourmet shop that also serves light meals, check out the Pampered Palate. See page 190.

DIRECTIONS **Westbound:** At the I-81 interchange, enter I-81 North. Almost immediately, take Exit 57. Follow the directions given on page 191.

Eastbound: I-64 and I-81 run concurrently for about 40 miles, as you know because you have been driving them. At the point where I-64 splits off to the east, do not take it. Stay on I-81 until Exit 57 (almost immediately after the split). Follow the directions given on page 191.

THE PALM PARLOR, *Exit 13, Lexington*

On page 187, we describe this up-to-date café that serves fine soups, sandwiches, and pasta dishes.

DIRECTIONS From Exit 13, follow signs toward Lexington. In about 1 mile, bear right onto Business 11. Go with the flow for another mile and you'll soon be on Jefferson St. The second light in the business district is Nelson; the **Palm Parlor** is on the right, at the corner of Jefferson and Nelson.

Florida

STATE FARMERS' MARKET RESTAURANT,
Exit 23, Ft. Myers

As you've probably surmised, this restaurant is adjacent to the State Farmers' Market, where produce from all over South Florida is weighed, inspected, and shipped off to retailers all over everywhere else. If what's served in the restaurant next door isn't fresh, it sure isn't going to be any fresher in Peoria.

Many of the market's workers take their meals here; they're joined by truckers, local families dressed in their informal best, and anyone else who knows a very good deal when it's put on the table in front of him. This is a busy, lively, happy place where banter between the tables is commonplace, and the waitresses sit with the customers to take a breather.

All meals start with wonderful bread. You will be asked your preference, corn bread or dinner rolls. Say both. After a sizable basket is plunked down in front of you, you'll have to choose your main course—chicken fried steak, meat loaf, spare ribs, prime rib, ham steak, mullet, veal, grouper, chicken livers, or chicken gizzards.

We'd heard raves about the chicken parts, and we were feeling adventuresome, so we went for the livers (evidently we weren't adventuresome enough for gizzards). Breaded and fried, they came out looking like dark brown cauliflower pieces, not at all what we had expected to see. Nor was the taste anything we had predicted. It was simply marvelous. There were 10 of these surprising livers on the plate—about twice what one hungry person who has already pigged out on corn bread could possibly consume.

Vegetables like turnip greens, black-eyed peas, and okra and tomatoes come on the side, and the price for a full meal is an incredible $3.30.

If that's too much, have a sandwich or a salad. Big breakfasts too.

HOURS   6:30 am–8 pm, 7 days a week.

SPECS   2736 Edison Ave.; (813) 334-1687; no cards; no liquor.

DIRECTIONS   From Exit 23, head west toward Ft. Myers for about 3¼ miles to the light at Palm Ave. Turn left, go ½ mile to stop sign at Edison Ave. Turn right on Edison and it's on the left.

JOE'S HOME COOKING,
Exit 29, Punta Gorda

In *Eating in America*, a history of the United States through its stomach, authors Waverly Root and Richard de Rochemont lament that after World War II Americans traded oranges for orange-juice concentrate. "Even in Florida," they write, ". . . with orange trees all around you, you will find it difficult to get fresh orange juice unless you squeeze the fruit yourself."

Little has changed since Root and de Rochemont wrote in 1976. We'd already been down the east coast of Florida and were heading up the west before we ran into a restaurant that prided itself on its juice—juice that is freshly squeezed from oranges and grapefruits the owner grows in his backyard. Boxes of them sit unceremoniously at the end of the serving counter, and every so often one of the kitchen helpers gathers an armload and carries them back to be converted to delicious, reassuring fresh-squeezed juice (50 cents per large glass). It's filtered before it comes to your table, but your taste buds will immediately tell you that it's the real thing.

Joe's is a budget bet, though unextraordinary except for juice. The surroundings are nondescript, save a few imitation Tiffanies that add little in the way of atmosphere; what there is in that department comes more from the clientele than the decor. It's a popular place with the locals, and on a Saturday at peak breakfast hour we found it hopping. Unfortunately, our omelette (sausage and cheese, $2.60), while passable, didn't earn marks nearly as high as the O.J. Hamburger baskets are favorites at lunch and dinner ($2.15, with fries and slaw), along with inexpensive sandwiches and dinner platters in the $3.50–$4.50 range.

Come for the local color, the low prices, and the juice.

HOURS   Mon.–Fri. 5:30 am–3:30 pm; Sat. 5:30 am–2:30 pm; closed Sun.

SPECS   226 Tamiami Trail; (813) 639-1214; no cards; no liquor.

DIRECTIONS   From Exit 29, turn left onto US 17 South toward Punta Gorda. In about 2 miles you reach the junction with US 41. **Joe's** is 1 block to your left, but the road is one way (the wrong way) so you must go around the block.

JAMES PLACE, *Exit 35, Venice*

Although it sounds like a property on the Monopoly board, James Place is actually a modest restaurant, the culinary domain of James Corcoran, a Londoner who's broken with his native tradition by learning the secrets of simple but wonderful cooking. How nice for us to find a working person's eatery for which we must make no apologies. Pleasant in every respect, but not in the least bit pretentious, with large windows on Venice's palm-lined business street, James Place invites you to come in, sit down, read the paper, and enjoy one of James's now-famous omelettes.

It seems he had been open no more than two weeks when his omelettes were the subject of a Washington, D.C., television show. Apparently, a TV chef from the capital had breakfasted at this restaurant and gone home to talk about it on the air.

They *are* good, made with three eggs, stuffed with three fillings, and then served with toast, home fries, and a fresh fruit garnish. For this you pay $2.75, reasonable by any standards.

Of course it's not all omelettes. There are fresh muffins every day, and English muffin sandwiches ($1.25), as well as the usual morning standbys. And at lunch, homemade soups (65/95 cents) and quiche come to the fore, the latter served with fresh fruit for $2.95. Or get big, juicy hamburgers (or baconburgers, mushroomburgers, etc.), any of several full-meal salads, or an up-to-date sandwich. Very few items have crept above $3.00.

It was breakfast and lunch only when we passed through, but there are plans for a dinner menu. It would be worth a call to check.

HOURS   Mon.–Fri. 7 am–4 pm; Sat. 7 am–3 pm; closed Sun.

SPECS   117 W. Venice Ave.; (813) 485-6742; no cards; no liquor.

DIRECTIONS   See **Helena Café,** below.

HELENA CAFÉ, *Exit 35, Venice*

The New Helena Shop is a women's specialty department store selling ladies' apparel, custom furniture, designer wallpaper, and dance exercise outfits. The Helena Café originated to serve the shoppers, and although its reputation has spread, there's little arguing the fact that this pert, pretty, skylit café is designed to appeal to women.

One of the lunchtime favorites among shoppers are the finger sandwiches—spiced cream cheese, ham salad, chopped walnuts in cream cheese, for instance. An assortment comes with a bowl of soup for $3.65. Instead, you might choose an unusual pecan-sparked chicken salad accompanied by a mini-Danish and an absolutely spectacular fruit garnish ($4.65). Other possibilities include seafood quiche, salad Niçoise, and broiled hamburgers.

Dinners at Helena, most in the $6–$9 range, are eclectic—veal picante, steak Diane, chicken kabob, shrimp curry—with a nod to American light cuisine, especially quiche and meal-sized salads.

If you're anything like us, at least one of the pastries or cakes that present themselves to you on the dessert cart will end up on your table. They are all from St. Armand's Bakery, Sarasota's finest, and since the interstate passes too far from downtown Sarasota for the purposes of this book, this is a good chance for a taste of that town.

HOURS Lunch: Mon.–Sat. 11:30 am–2:30 pm; dinner: Tues.–Sat. 5–9 pm; closed Sun. (no dinner Mon.).

SPECS 141 W. Venice Ave., 2nd floor; (813) 488-5324; major cards; wine.

DIRECTIONS From Exit 35, head west toward Venice. In about ½ mile, turn right at the flashing light onto Venice Ave. In 3 miles, cross US 41, go over the bridge and straight through the light at Tamiami Trail. **James** is on the left in the middle of the next block. For **Helena,** continue to next light (Nokomis Ave. S.). It's on the corner, on left. Entrance is from Nokomis Ave.; restaurant is on second floor. Ten minutes.

THE CRAB TRAP, *Exit 43, Palmetto*

Owner Lee Cline is a Maryland native who built the reputation of his Florida restaurant around his home state's greatest contribution to the culinary world—the blue crab. A wood carving above the dining room entrance and crab-trap light fixtures pay homage to that species. But Lee doesn't serve Maryland crab very often anymore, and never in the authentic Baltimore fashion. He's found a better, far more indigenous cuisine for his restaurant. This is, in many ways, the most "Florida" of Florida restaurants.

It was here, for instance, that we first tasted alligator. Now that may sound illegal, alligators being an endangered species and all, but in fact it's not. Restaurants need a license to buy alligator meat, and they must purchase the meat only from licensed "gator agents" who are authorized to shoot nuisance gators—those who show up at golf courses, swimming pools, etc. (Environmental note: this behavior on the part of the reptiles is usually a result of people feeding them table scraps, a practice that should be discouraged.) At any rate, the gator's tail meat comes as nuggets, breaded and sautéed. The flesh is white, firm but not chewy, fine-grained, and sweet-tasting. It's a bit like chicken but has much more personality.

And then there's turtle. Served in the same way, it is darker and slightly rubbery, still delicate, yet with an exotic undertaste reminiscent of faraway places. (A local freshwater species is served here, not sea turtles which are protected by law.) And at the Crab Trap we also ordered black-tip shark, a very firm-fleshed fish that was the least distinctive of the three, and less satisfying than the other two newcomers to our diet.

We were too full to go whole hog, but at the Crab Trap you can order Florida wild pig. Or choose among frogs' legs, stone crabs, Okeechobee catfish, and Caribbean lobster. You want something really different? Lee is considering armadillo.

What's nicest is that you don't have to make much of a commitment to sample these delicacies. Lee wants his customers to tease their palates with new foods, and to encourage that he makes all of them available as appetizers ($3–$4) as well as dinner entrées ($7–$11). That's what we did, and our estimation is that these two appetizers and a side order of excellent "house fries" (skins-on wedges of potato that have been boiled and then fried) would quite adequately squelch one lively appetite.

If your taste for the exotic can't abide anything more bizarre than tuna salad, you won't go hungry at this rustically appointed yet very comfortable nautical-style restaurant. You can get that too, along with sandwiches, steaks, and traditional seafood dishes.

HOURS Sun.–Thurs. 11:30 am–9:30 pm; Fri. & Sat. 11:30 am–10 pm. Closed Thanksgiving and Christmas.

SPECS Route 19, Terra Ceia Bridge; (813) 722-6255; major cards; beer and wine.

DIRECTIONS From Exit 43, bear right onto Route 301 South. In 3½ miles, bear right onto US 19 North. About 2 miles further, bear left with US 19 toward Saint Petersburg as US 41 splits off toward Tampa. One mile further up US 19, the restaurant is on your left. This is further from the Interstate than most, but where else are you going to get turtle? Traffic moves well. If continuing to Saint Petersburg, do not backtrack to I-75; go straight to Sunshine Bridge Skyway.

Note 1: When an exit for Rubonia is completed (2 miles south of the existing Moccasin Wallow Rd. exit), this will be the best way for southbound travelers on I-75 to reach the **Crab Trap.** We cannot give you exact directions; call the restaurant.

Note 2: Travelers who are coming south from Saint Petersburg on I-275 will find the restaurant on the right, two miles south of Sunshine Skyway toll plaza. Do not try to come via I-75.

Entering I-275

TRAVELER'S ADVISORY

Unfortunately, I-75 is not a *fait accompli* in Central Florida, and travelers on that highway must detour through sections of I-4 and I-275. See page 19 for a description of restaurants accessible from I-4; those off I-275 follow. It is important to note that I-75 through traffic will pass the exits for Mel's Hot Dogs and Brett Brett's Sandwich Shop, but the Lincoln Restaurant requires a 2-mile detour, as explained in the **DIRECTIONS** section below.

LINCOLN RESTAURANT, *Exit 23A (I-275), West Tampa*

It's a simple matter to get from I-75 or I-275 to this wonderful Cuban restaurant. Read a full description on pages 17–18.

DIRECTIONS Southbound: Normally you would be routed from I-275 to I-4 East before picking up I-75 South. For the **Lincoln,** *don't* take

I-4; instead, stay on I-275 South to Exit 23A, a 2-mile detour. ■ From Exit 23A, bear right onto Dale Mabry Highway North (Route 92 East) and go about ¾ mile to the light at Columbus. Turn right. In ½ mile it's on the left, at the corner of Lincoln Ave.

Northbound: Northbound I-75 travelers are routed through I-4 West; at the junction of I-275, they normally head north. However, to reach the **Lincoln,** it is necessary to take I-275 *South* for 2 miles to Exit 23A. Then, as above from ■.

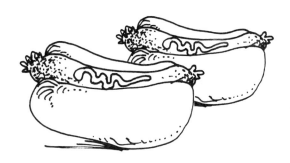

MEL'S HOT DOGS, *Exit 33 (I-275), Tampa*

Can you believe it? A hot dog joint with red-checked tablecloths, ice-cream-parlor chairs, picture windows, the day's newspapers for the reading, and framed reviews on the walls? The reviews are what really got us—there must be fifteen of them, all raves, and some from as far away as Philadelphia! Clearly, this is no ordinary hot dog joint.

Mel Lohn is no ordinary hot dog vendor. Lohn was a sax player in a Chicago rock band when he first came to Tampa and fell in love with the place. It's the same old story—he moved to town but couldn't find a decent hot dog anywhere, so decided to correct the situation. That was in 1973; the rest is Tampa history.

Although he'd never sold a hot dog before in his life, he had eaten more than a few. Mel claims he's dined at most of the three thousand hot doggeries in Chicago and suspects he's probably downed more franks than anyone else in the world. His favorite breakfast? A hot dog and coffee. If he's in a hurry, he'll skip the coffee.

The dogs he serves in Tampa are Chicago-style, meaning they are kosher all-beef hot dogs, hand-stuffed into natural casings (that's what gives them the "pop"). They're served on poppy-seed buns with bright yellow mustard (none of that Dijon stuff) and all the trimmings—onions, kraut, relish, and pickle. Although Mel's dogs can get fancier, we suggest you not confuse your palate; rather, sample the basic version first ($.99; $1.59 with french fries and cole slaw). We think you'll agree that a better hot dog cannot be found. Then, having experienced the naked work, you can dress it up a little—with chili, baked beans, cole slaw; Swiss, American, or cheddar cheese; or lettuce and tomato ($.25 per). Or wander into exotic territory with a bratwust, kielbasa, or Italian sausage.

If it just happens that you hate hot dogs but have been dragged along by carmates who see things quite differently, fear not. You can take refuge in a roast beef sandwich, fried chicken breast, or even a hamburger. But we doubt many will.

Mel is full of hot dog trivia and even a few hot dog proverbs. He believes his profound interest in the subject is entirely becoming so noble a food. As he puts it, "The dog is the noblest of all animals and the hot dog is noblest of all dogs because it, and it alone, feeds the hand that bites it."

HOURS   Mon.–Sat. 10 am–10 pm; Sun. 11 am–8 pm; closed only Christmas and New Year's Day.

SPECS   4136 E. Busch Blvd.; (813) 985-8000; no cards; no liquor.

DIRECTIONS   From Exit 33 of I-275, turn left onto Busch Blvd. In about 2½ miles you'll reach the main entrance to Busch Gardens at 40th St. Keep going straight on Busch Blvd. and in 0.2 miles it's on your left. After eating, return to I-75 North via I-275 North; take I-275 South to signs for I-75 South.

BRETT BRETT'S SANDWICH SHOP,
Exit 34 (I-275), Tampa

Brett Brett's goes down in our Book of Bests. For it was here that we had our most delicious slice of on-the-road cheesecake, a cheesecake that can hold its head up high to the best of New York or L.A. or anyplace else you want to name. But we're getting ahead of ourselves. You're not going to—at least we didn't —start out with cheesecake.

We began with a roast beef sandwich. Not any old roast beef sandwich, mind you, but one that was about 2 inches thick, properly rare, topped with crispy sparks of bacon and a super garlic mayonnaise. And on the side, a most enjoyable potato salad. Costing $3.95, this sandwich/salad combo is the most expensive item on a list that starts at $2.25. A few other choices are turkey with curry mayonnaise, Genoa salami, and herbed garlic cream cheese with bacon. Or you can get a full-meal spinach salad, chili, or empanadas (spicy meat-filled pastries). Half-sandwiches are available at half the price plus 50 cents.

OK, now can we talk about the desserts? First we should say that there are cookies, rum and carrot cakes, a variety of pies (including one called "no-name"), banana bread and cranberry bread, and more—all of them originals prepared from absolute scratch. Then (finally!), the cheesecake.

People (like us) who hate to make decisions will, in a perverse way, find the list of cheesecakes distressing. How do you choose between mocha, oreo, cappuchino, chocolate chip, mint, praline, orange, coconut, pineapple, Grand Marnier, and what's unassumingly called "original"? When you learn that these aren't just differently flavored or alternatively topped versions of the same thing, but *entirely different recipes*, it becomes even more difficult. Somehow, we settled upon pineapple. Rapturously smooth and thick with pineapple it was, but not murderously rich and not in the least bit heavy or dry. We've already told you how we felt about it; to carry the description further would be to risk purple prose.

HOURS Mon.–Fri. 10 am–6 pm; Sat. 10 am–4 pm; closed Sun.

SPECS Plaza del University, 1120 N. 30th St.; (813) 971-5621; no cards; beer & wine.

DIRECTIONS From Exit 34 of I-275, head east on Fowler Ave. (turn right if northbound, left if southbound). In about 1¾ miles, turn right at the light at N. 30th St. In one block pull into Plaza del University, a small shopping center on your right. It's toward the far end of the plaza.

NOTE FOR SOUTHBOUND TRAVELERS

Those who are southbound on I-75 (and are therefore following this book backwards) should see **TRAVELER'S ADVISORY,** page 96.

BARNES' FAMILY RESTAURANT, *Exit 63, Bushnell*

Given the number of billboards that tell the I-75 traveler where (not) to eat, we were pleased to find a place that neither wants nor needs roadside advertisting, because its local clientele already knows all about it.

Although this restaurant's food is not what anyone would call gourmet, it's perfectly respectable home cooking, featuring such items as braised short ribs, chef's salads, standard sandwiches, fried oysters, "fresh-caught catfish" (which turned out to be "fresh frozen"), and, the big seller, meat loaf. We asked Blondell Barnes, who oversees the kitchen, why meat loaf should outsell catfish here in the Okeechobee region, and she said, "Why, because we make it from outright 'scratch,' " which we assume you can't do with catfish. The prices for dinner items (with three vegetables, bread, and coffee) run $5–$6; sandwiches are $1–$2.

We might be able to express genuine enthusiasm for the food served here if the setting was a bit more appetizing. "Funky," we fear, is too mild a term. Of course, there's no denying that the Barnes' Family Restaurant provides a window on rural Florida life—rare in a state that's practically become a suburb of the North—and no one can complain about lack of local color. Just the same, we don't imagine anyone would complain if Mrs. Barnes set loose a troop of fund-raising boy scouts with scrub brushes, scrapers, and paint cans.

Still, that meat loaf *was* good.

HOURS Mon.–Sat. 6 am–8:30 pm; Sun. 6 am–8 pm.

SPECS Highway 301 South; (904) 793-4891; no cards; no liquor.

DIRECTIONS From Exit 63, head east. In about 2 miles turn right at the stop sign onto Main St. Go ¾ mile to the restaurant on right. Don't be confused by the Barn, a large package store/bar along the way.

LE PARIS, *Exit 69, Ocala*

When we visited, Le Paris was owned by a French family whose various members did everything from boiling the veal bones for consommé to baking the croissants and pastries daily. The light lunch we had there was delicious—a chicken salad sandwich on a large and excellent croissant, with a fine leaf-lettuce salad on the side (only $3.00). And the decor had a simple kind of relaxed charm. But as we paid our check, we learned that a change of ownership was imminent. And so we shall cut this entry short, not wanting to entice you with a description that may fail to materialize. On the other hand, the new owners, we were told, are also French, experienced in the restaurant business, and determined to preserve Le Paris' estimable cuisine.

We wish them well.

HOURS As we found it, **Le Paris** was open for lunch, Mon.–Fri., 11 am–2 pm; dinner, Mon.–Sat., 5–10 pm; closed Sun.

SPECS 1618 S.W. Pine Ave.; (904) 622-1506; major cards; beer and wine.

DIRECTIONS See **Miss Pearl's Soul Café,** below.

MISS PEARL'S SOUL CAFÉ, *Exit 69, Ocala*

Before we ever met Miss Pearl we had heard a lot about her. That she served the best black-eyed peas in the state of Florida, for instance, and the best meat loaf "this side of heaven." That she was the type who would scold you for not finishing your butter beans. That after eating at her place you wouldn't have to eat again until tomorrow (and this at 10 am!). Most of all we had heard it would be an experience.

The experience begins just inside the door. The modest but cheerfully decorated room is silent, save for Miss Pearl and her daughter Betty, rattling off the day's menu for each customer, their voices often crossing in antiphonal harmony: "Beef stew, fried chicken, barbecued ribs, smothered pork chops in *brown* gravy [emphasis theirs]; biscuits *or* corn bread; rice, Northern beans, butter beans, *candied* yams, collard greens, turnip greens . . ." It doesn't matter what they say—everyone wants meat loaf. "Meat loaf is on *Friday*," Miss Pearl says emphatically. Beef stew is the winningest second choice.

Once the plates have been piled high, the business of eating begins, and a serious business it is. No one talks, no one looks up, no one moves anything but his jaws. In walks a dignified gentleman who removes his suit jacket as he intones to the crowd, "How is everyone today?"

"Just fine," come the muttered replies. Nobody misses a chew.

The arrangement is thus: For $3 you get one entrée, rice, two vegetables (out of a dozen or more), and corn bread or biscuits. There's no menu, just what the cooks announce as you approach the L-shaped counter that rims the exposed kitchen.

Not exactly experts on soul food, we will nevertheless attempt to critique Miss Pearl's results. The pork chops were tender as butter, their sauce rich and dark with molasses. The okra and tomatoes, which we had come across repeatedly in the South, seemed the apotheosis of so prosaic a dish. The beef stew was delicious, and the black-eyed peas just full of flavor.

Perhaps the following will stand as a more credible testimony: On her way through Ocala recently, Brenda Boozer, the opera singer, pulled up in a mile-long limo, ate lunch with her entourage, and left with $8 worth of collard greens.

Things livened up a little before we left, by the way, as families began to replace the crowd of workingmen on lunch break. All kinds of fun broke out when a toddler wandered into the kitchen area. "He's just going to do some cooking," said the aforementioned gentleman, now seated at the counter. "Oh, oh, oh," exclaimed Miss Pearl. "He's coming back here to cook and in no time at all he'll be sittin' under a whole case full of sugar!"

HOURS   Mon.–Sat. 11:30 am–5 pm; closed Sun.

SPECS   223 W. Broadway; no phone; no cards; no liquor.

DIRECTIONS   From Exit 69, turn right if northbound, left if southbound, onto Route 40 toward Ocala. In about 2¼ miles, go straight through the light at S.W. 16th Ave. One-quarter mile later, Route 40 bears slightly to the left and up over a bridge. At this point you should not go over the bridge but bear right for Broadway (there's a sign for Broadway, but it was rotated 90° so as to be unnoticeable). You'll immediately come to a light at South Pine Ave. For **Miss Pearl's** go straight across Pine; in one block you'll see it on the left at the corner of S.W. 3rd Ave. For **Le Paris,** turn right onto South Pine and go one mile; it's on the right, with parking at the motel immediately following.

DIXIE CREAM RESTAURANT,
Route 227 Exit, Gainesville

Youthful, happy, friendly, and woody describe the Dixie Cream, with the undisputed best breakfasts (darn good lunches, too) in Gainesville. "We don't do anything that anyone else shouldn't do, but they don't," says proud, immodest co-owner Jim Larson.

What Jim and his staff do is prepare everything, absolutely everything except the Heineken and the Coca-Cola, from scratch, using the best possible ingredients: imported Swiss and blue cheese, their own blend of orange blossom and wildflower honey, eggs fresh from the henhouse. They serve generous portions in an informal and delightful atmosphere of butcher-block tables and spindle-backed chairs with handmade Appalachian quilts hanging on the ceiling. There's also a hand-crafted brass cash register built in 1903. Jim finds its weight helpful during hurricane season.

The food here leans toward the whole-grain and natural-foods end of the spectrum, but there's plenty for everyone. You can have a tofu and sprout salad ($3.75) or an "Egg-A-Muffin"— grilled ham and sliced tomato covered with two poached eggs and a Swiss cheese topping ($3.75). An interesting version of the latter is "Eggs Popeye"; we'll quote its description from the menu: "two eggs panfried inside portholes of oatbread, covered with sautéed spinach and onions, and topped with sour cream" ($3.75). And so on.

We had huevos rancheros, as good a rendition of that dish as you're likely to find east of Albuquerque ($1.50) and an order of corn cakes, two plate-sized behemoths that will fill your fiber quota for a week ($1.50). The corn cakes (which also come as plain or whole-wheat pancakes) can be had with banana, apple, blueberry, pecan, or chocolate chip fillings.

At lunchtime there are burgers, full-meal salads, stir-fried tofu, a variety of imaginative sandwiches ($2.75–$3.00), and some very tempting baked goods. The breakfast menu is available at all times.

HOURS   Mon.–Sat. 7 am–2 pm; Sun. 8 am–2 pm.

SPECS   2226 N.W. 6th St. (cor. N.W. 23rd Ave.); (904) 372-5642; no cards; beer & wine.

DIRECTIONS   Use Route 222 Exit (no number). Head east for 7 miles to the light at N.W. 6th St. Turn right and go 1 quick mile to light at N.W. 23rd Ave. It's on the southeast corner of that intersection.

Note: If you are southbound there is another way that is quicker and more direct, but it has you leaving the Interstate well before Gainesville. Use exit marked Route 441 South/Alachua. Turn left onto Route 441 South and go 13 miles (it's a traffic-free four-lane highway), and then bear left onto Route 20 as 441 goes straight. Route 20 is N.W. 6th St., and in 2 miles you'll find the restaurant on your right at the corner of N.W. 23rd Ave. Consult a map to see why this does not take you far out of your way.

AW SHUCKS, *Route 26 Exit, Gainesville*

Since it opened in April 1983, Aw Shucks has had Gainesville's piscivores puffing out their gills with civic pride. The city's inland location had previously discouraged the development of a top-notch seafood restaurant, but Aw Shucks has put an end to that.

Not only does owner Don Holbrook make sure his seafood is as fresh as possible, he also sees to it that it's cooked just right, which means no more than just enough. To aid him in this end, he's hired Cathy Bastion, a graduate of the Culinary Institute of America, to oversee his kitchen. Cathy prepares three homemade chowders, two shellfish and several fish entrées, a daily quiche, fresh vegetable dishes and desserts, and she also makes up to 15 different "gourmet" sauces—classical French sauces like béarnaise and Dijon, as well as more recent immigrants like Jamaican and Indian infusions. From her list, which changes each day, you can choose one to accompany your dinner.

We found a daily lunch special of fresh smoked mullet with stuffed potato and a tossed salad to be well worth its $3.95 price tag. There are also five or six tempting sandwiches and salads, as well as stir-fried vegetables with tofu and brown rice, all in the $3–4 range. At dinner time the entrée prices go up to $9–$11, but light lunch items are still available.

Aw Shucks is in a single oblong room with a lengthwise wall divider separating the prominent bar on one side from the serving area. Although basically rustic in feel, there are touches of gentility, and the redwood tables are cloaked with white tablecloths come 6 pm. At that hour, the midafternoon rock music changes to jazz and the volume is lowered, or so we were told.

HOURS Mon.–Wed. 11:30 am–1 am; Thurs. & Fri. 11:30 am–2 am; Sat. 4 pm–2 am; Sun. 4 pm–10 pm.

SPECS 4212 N.W. 16th Blvd.; (904) 372-0332; MC/V; full license.

DIRECTIONS From Gainesville exit for Route 26 turn right. Go 1 mile to light at N.W. 8th Ave. and turn left. In ¾ mile turn left at light for N.W. 43rd St. It's 1 mile to the light at 16th Blvd. **Aw Shucks** is in the Market Place, the shopping center facing you and slightly to your right.

THE ORIGINAL PIZZA PALACE, *Gainesville*

In case you've ever wondered what a pizza parlor looked like before the days of Formica and fluorescents, this is your chance to find out. This white clapboard building has been serving University of Florida students and faculty since 1953, and a Gainesville friend of ours says it's hardly changed at all since he came to town in the early '60s. The old hardwood floor wears the patina of age, as do the well-worn chairs and beige plaster walls. Overhead are ceiling fans that clearly predate the days when such items could be bought at K-Mart. Only in a place like this could a four-foot-diameter Coke sign from the '50s stand proudly and naturally behind the bar, appearing perfectly at ease in the '80s.

And the food is good. Real good. We never tried the pizza, but only because we'd heard so much about the pasta. So, pasta it was. We had the choice of white or green, spaghetti or fettuccine, all four possibilities freshly made right here. Sauces include meatballs, marinara, mushrooms and scallions, white clam, fettuccine Alfredo, and what's called "sautéed seasonal vegetables." That last one sounded rather forgettable, but it was precisely what our informant had extolled. His advice was good: the dish was outstanding—five or six fresh vegetables sautéed *al dente*, and held lightly together with a marvelous cream sauce on perfectly cooked pasta. Each bite asked for two more. The marinara was also a winner, pungent with the flavors of onion, garlic, and anchovy. Each of these pasta dishes, we found, made a full meal; they come with garlic bread and salad for around $4.00.

There are also pasta salads, an Italian chef's salad, a colossal antipasto, and dinners of the lasagna, manicotti, eggplant parmigiana sort ($6–$7). Next time, we'd like to try the cheesy, New York Style pizza, but the memory of those "sautéed seasonal vegetables" may not allow it.

HOURS Sun.–Thurs. 5–11 pm; Fri. & Sat. 5 pm–midnight.

SPECS 608 N.W. 13th St. (corner of N.W. 6th Ave.); (904) 372-1546; no cards; beer and wine.

DIRECTIONS **Northbound:** Use Gainesville exit for Route 24, turn right and go about 3¼ miles before bearing left onto S.W. 13th St. From here it's about ¾ mile to University Ave. Cross University (S.W. 13th will become N.W. 13th, but don't worry about it) and in ¼ mile the restaurant will be on your left (corner of N.W. 6th Ave.).

Southbound: Use Gainesville exit for Route 26, turn right and go about 5 miles to the light at N.W. 13th St. Turn left, go ¼ mile to corner of N.W. 6th Ave. It's on left.

ROBERT'S DOCK, *Route 90 Exit, Lake City*

Lake City is a good many miles from either Florida coast, and although it's in the heart of Suwannee River country, Robert's Dock, despite its name, is not "way down upon" that or any other river. It isn't far from the unpronounceable Ichetucknee Springs, a major draw for inner-tubers and scuba divers, and many of them retreat to this restaurant after a day on or below the water. But its most loyal clientele, as you will see if you arrive at the lunch hour, are the business people of Lake City, who don't mind driving a good three miles out of town to enjoy the quality home cooking of Robert and Emmie Chasteen. Unfortunately, you'll have to drive a little further than that (see **Note** under **DIRECTIONS,** below), but if you're interested in good food and a good deal, it's worth it.

Lunch is basic American fare like chicken and dumplings, fried chicken, and baked pork chops (with *brown* rice, to our surprise). For $3.25 it comes with two vegetables and a sizable basket of muffins—white, corn, and bran raisin, all obviously homemade and fresh out of the oven. Unfortunately, ours were a little burned on the bottom but the bran-raisin muffins survived that fate enough to bring their deep, dark taste to the fore. Our chicken and dumplings came in a minicrock, crowded onto a large plate with other dishes bearing a broccoli casserole and fried sweet-potato patties. Not bad, really, and a remarkable quantity of food for $3.25.

At dinner time, seafood is added to the traditional southern dishes of the lunch menu. The Chasteens' seafood casserole is their trademark. With shrimp, scallops, oysters, fish fillet, and deviled crabs, it does sound enticing, although the creators do not hide the fact that its base is canned cream of mushroom soup. At dinner, this is $9.95; other seafood specialties run the plank from $3.25 (fish 'n' chips) to $18.00 (Alaskan king crab). You'll still be able to get a hamburger or fish sandwich for under $1.50.

Desserts are homemade, and the pleasant taste of Emmie's chocolate peanut-butter pie lingered all the way to Jacksonville.

HOURS Mon.–Thurs. 11:30 am–9 pm; Fri. 11:30 am–10 pm; Sat. 4–10 pm; Sun. 11:30 am–8:30 pm.

SPECS US 90 East; (904) 752-7504; MC/V; beer & wine.

DIRECTIONS From exit marked Route 90/Live Oak/Lake City, head east toward Lake City. Go straight through town, never veering off Route 90. The restaurant is 7 miles from I-75, and you'll find it directly across from the airport, on the left.

Note: If, after eating, you are headed for I-10, do not backtrack to I-75. Instead, take Route 90 West to the junction with Route 441. Turn right and take 441 North directly to I-10.

MAE'S COUNTRY KITCHEN, *FL 136 Exit, White Springs*

It wasn't food but the lure of a boatride on the primeval waters of the Suwannee River that brought us to White Springs and the Stephen Foster State Folk Culture Center. Just as we expected, the live oaks were hung with Spanish moss and reached out over the black waters so as to make us feel near to the source of things. We left with a deepened appreciation of Thales, the first philosopher, who said that all was water.

Metaphysics notwithstanding, we got hungry, insisted to the park attendants that this town *must* have a restaurant, and finally came across tumbledown Mae's Country Kitchen where we tasted the best fried chicken of our southern journeys.

Mae's has been here since 1912, and we do not mean it entirely as a compliment if we say that it seems little has changed since that date. The place is, in short, a dump—a peeling brick box with the word "luncheon" in one window and in the other some plants that desperately needed a bit of Thales's water. We'll say no more on this score, except to add that the restaurant's character is in keeping with the rest of this tiny town and that to expect more would be a mistake.

At lunchtime $3.75 will buy you a buffet piled high with the day's offerings—liver, chicken, and six vegetables when we were there. The vegetables were only fair, and we passed on the liver. But the chicken's delicious, spicy coating was stupendous. It made the whole trip worthwhile and put the Colonel to utter shame. We tried to learn its secret, but Julia Mae Wilson, who has been the cook here for eight years, would say only that she believes in spices. If you can put up with the place's faults, she'll make a believer out of you too.

It pays, by the way, to visit memorial parks. We learned many things in White Springs while watching dioramas of Camptown Races and Ol' Black Joe. Not only did Foster never see the Suwannee River, he originally titled the song "Way Down Upon the Pee Dee River" and changed it after glancing through an atlas in search of something more sonorous. Worse, Foster never set foot south of Philadelphia.

Such is the birth of myths. Mae's Country Kitchen, however, is the real thing.

HOURS Mon.–Sat. 6 am–2 pm (maybe later in summer).

SPECS Highway 41; (904) 397-2866; no cards; no liquor.

DIRECTIONS Go east on FL 136 for 3.3 miles to a stop sign. Turn right and the restaurant will be immediately on the left. The memorial is about a mile from this point.

Georgia

C. H. MITCHELL, THE BARBECUE KING,
Exit 4, Valdosta

We had heard that this joint's name was no idle boast, so we plopped ourselves down at a plastic table, ignored the dingy paneling, and ordered without a second thought. Now barbecue comes in many styles, and we are prepared to award C.H. top honors in the more-tomatoey-than-spicy-or-vinegary category. It was really very good, and the $1.30 sandwich came piled as high with meat as a corned beef sandwich at an expensive Jewish deli. All the same, we have to reserve the best-in-the-show awards for Pierce's (page 83), the Lexington (page 225), and the Fresh Air Barbeque (page 120).

No matter. Mitchell's Brunswick stew was outa sight, absolutely the best version of this specialty that we found anywhere. Its flavor was rich and deep, the corn was still crunchy, and though strongly spiced, it was not so hot as to obliterate a delightfully complex concatenation of flavors. If you're a fan of Brunswick stew, don't miss it.

Barbecue, of course, is what this place is all about, but they do offer other items at eccentric prices—$2.08 for breakfast, fries for $.53, $.94 for a burger. Scoops of ice cream run $.26 each, and cookies cost two cents.

The counterwomen couldn't have cared less, so don't come looking for southern hospitality. Settle for great Brunswick stew.

HOURS　Daily, 8 am–1 am.

SPECS　515 S. Ashley Street; (912) 244-2684; no cards; no liquor.

DIRECTIONS　From Exit 4 go east on Hill St. for about 2½ miles to Paterson. Turn right on Paterson and in 2 blocks you'll be led to a bridge. Go over the bridge and just on the other side of it make the sharpest possible U-turn to the left. **Mitchell's** will be on the right in a small brick building.

MAGGIE FOSTER'S RESTAURANT, *Exit 5, Valdosta*

We can't prove it, but we'd bet our last gallon of gas at 3 am Sunday morning that Maggie Foster's is the best restaurant there is in this corner of Georgia. Maggie's could compete well in *any* city, but in Valdosta the only competition is a movie-set, suburban Chinese-food palace and a German place decorated like, if you can imagine it, a brothel for little old ladies.

But Maggie's is classy—white tablecloths at dinner; chilled fork salad service; small, tastefully decorated dining rooms; and here and there an archway or twisted, stuccoed column. The staff is young and just learning the ropes, but they are doing it well, and making every effort to please.

The menu is seafood and includes oysters Bienville ($9.20), shrimp scampi ($9.20), and scallops baked in a butter sauce with scallions and mushrooms and topped with Parmesan ($9.85). The cream of broccoli soup with scallops was a true delight—light, smooth, subtle, and with just enough spice to make things interesting. The preparation of the new potatoes in cheese sauce was just about perfect, and while the main dish was not so excellent, it certainly was quite good.

Such fancy dinner-time cooking does not prevent the lunch menu from being quite down to earth. Any of ten good deli sandwiches come with homemade potato salad and a kosher pickle for just $2.20–$2.75. There are subs for around $3.50, and nine-inch from-scratch pizzas for $3.85.

Maggie's is obviously a blend of some plain and simple American favorites with the "hautest" cuisine Valdosta will tolerate. But plain or fancy, it's all done with sophistication and obvious pride in the craft of cooking, the efforts of two brothers who learned their trade in Daytona and Jacksonville and brought it to Valdosta.

We must tell you, though, that Valdosta water is all but undrinkable. At a minimum you should squeeze some lemon into it before letting it get anywhere near your lips. That black mark aside, we can just about guarantee that this restaurant will provide you with a most welcome break from the road. Just drink Coke or wine.

HOURS   Mon. 11:30 am–2 pm; Tues.–Sat. 11:30 am–2 pm & 6 pm–10 pm; closed Sun.

SPECS   103 W. Brookwood Drive; (912) 247-0100; V/MC; beer and wine.

DIRECTIONS   From Exit 5 turn left if northbound, right if southbound; go 0.4 mile to Gornto Road (just before a shopping mall). Left onto Gornto and go 0.3 mile to Baytree. Right onto Baytree and go 1.9 miles to light at Oak. Right on Oak, 1 block to Brookwood. Left on Brookwood. One block to **Maggie's,** on the corner, on the right.

111

LANKFORD MANOR, *Exit 19, Tifton*

We consider it our sacred duty to enter forbidding, run-down restaurants in search of the perfect "find." From a distance Lankford Manor had all the earmarks—a long-established restaurant in a handsome but weathered old house. But as we got closer it seemed there was just *too* much peeling paint, the grounds were just *too* neglected, and there were just *too* many dry and barren flowerpots placed higgledy-piggledy in the windows of the glassed-in porch. Our courage faltered. We hesitated, debated, and returned to the car. We debated again. Finally duty overruled prudence, and in we went.

Billy Lankford had been watching our antics. "I know it looks bad," he said, "but it tastes good." This after we had negotiated our way through half a porch of Coke machines, cane chairs, and seashells into the dingy green dining room that was barricaded behind a wall of venetian blinds. Billy was long, tall, and graying, wearing a red cardigan sweater and necktie that made him look out of place in his own establishment. He carried himself like a gentleman and spoke in a slow, gentle Georgia accent. What's more, he spoke the truth, except that the food was better than just good. It was delicious, the best true, down-home southern cooking we came across in ten thousand miles of exploration.

We knew we were onto something the moment we tasted the wonderful vegetable soup, enlivened by subtle seasonings and big chunks of fresh tomato. Then the nutty flavor of the fried okra sent us into near ecstasy. The best was yet to come, however. We were soon feasting on a concoction of ground beef and fresh string beans, carrots, and tomatoes, baked under a cornbread crust and spiked with hints of mustard and cinnamon. It went by the humble name of "hamburger pie," and while that name may not sound very interesting, we promise it was as good as any moussaka you've tried. That this meal—with salad, beverage, rolls, and two vegetables—cost only $3.50 was a miracle. Dessert was only $.25 more—a light and tasty lemon chess pie, slightly on the tart side.

The same $3.50 could have bought us any of ten other dinners, or we could have had the house specialty, fried Georgia quail on toast, for just $7.00.

Billy Lankford is a friendly man. Almost before we sat down he wanted to know all about where we were from and what we thought about this and that. Here conversation has been elevated to high art, graced by a southern languor that makes the simplest gesture seem gracious. It turns out that Lankford Manor was a Depression-era boardinghouse that was opened in 1932 by Billy's father after his bank failed. Billy has an engineering degree from Georgia Tech, but, as he put it, "I couldn't take the rat race." "We're just hangin' in here," he said. "The place doesn't make any money. Keep it open just because I'm afraid to be unemployed. Make my living from the stock market." To prove it he went back into the house to find a piece of cardboard richly shingled in little yellowed corporate earnings reports clipped from the *New York Times.*

So we talked about the market, about a Mr. Bailey who had lost his cane last week, about the women who now do the cooking, about the recipes and the weather. Time passed in a dreamy haze, and nothing, absolutely nothing, moved.

HOURS   Daily 6 am–9 am, 11 am–2 pm, & 5 pm–8 pm.

SPECS   401 Love Ave.; (912) 382-9172; no cards, personal checks; no liquor.

DIRECTIONS   From Exit 19 go east 1.3 miles to center of Tifton and turn left onto Love St. (US 41). Two blocks, on the right, on the corner.

PERLIS TRUCK STOP, *Exit 31, Cordele*

This no-nonsense truck stop is clean, bright plasticky, and almost as classy as a Howard Johnson's. Civilians are segregated from truckers by forbidding signs, and ordinary folks don't get phones in their booths. But the food is definitely above average for this kind of place—properly cooked pole beans flecked with ham, tender and flavorful short ribs, good gravy for the mashed potatoes. Coffee and corn bread were poor, and the salad dull, but that's a good average for a 24-hour truck stop a stone's throw from the road. More expensive than you'd expect, however—$4.45 for meat and three vegetables; $5.99 for the all-you-can-eat version of the same.

They've got a TV room, showers, diesel repair, a copier, a motel, a gas station, and a general store that sells cowboy boots and everything else you'd need to haul a rig from Savannah to Santa Fe.

HOURS   24 hours daily.

DIRECTIONS   Right at Exit 31.

THE COLONIAL INN, *Exit 36, Vienna*

Though locally respected, we judged this would-be posh, would-be colonial restaurant only a little better than most motel dining rooms. On the other hand, there's nothing offensive about it either. Lunches for about $3.50; lunchtime sandwiches $1.65–$3.95; salad bar for $2.75. Dinners run $5.00–$10.00, and the menu is your standard steak and seafood affair.

Nice people.

HOURS   Daily 6:30 am–9:30 pm.

SPECS   (912) 268-2211; major cards; no liquor.

DIRECTIONS   Just west of Exit 36. Millions of signs; can't miss it.

NEW PERRY HOTEL, *Exit 43, Perry*

We like hotel dining rooms, and if the hotel itself is still alive, so much the better. Thus the Perry, which for 58 years has lodged motel-disdaining, Florida-bound Midwesterners, had little chance of displeasing us.

Now we want to make it clear right off that although the food here occasionally rises above average, it doesn't stay there very long. Those in search of a culinary souvenir should really go elsewhere. But perhaps you, too, are tired of motels. Or maybe you could just enjoy the homespun formality of an old southern dining room. There are gestures at elegance here, like white tablecloths and fresh flowers (and, let it be said, such amenities offer great relief from the tedium of the road). But the net result is almost more kitschy than formal. There's no mistaking the straightforward friendliness of the waitresses for anything but just-folks hospitality.

The menu is pure American stuff. About $4.00 for lunch and $6.75–$9.25 for dinner; $2.00 for a hamburger; $3.25 for a two-egg breakfast with meat (try the salt pork, if you want something different). Rooms are $17.00–$24.00 for a tiny green affair with a curvilinear bed, venetian blinds, and a skeleton-key door lock. There's a modern motel out back ($32.00–$34.00), and in the spring, 1,000 tulips bloom.

HOURS   Daily 7 am–9:30 am, 11:30 am–2:30 pm, & 5:30 pm–9 pm.

SPECS   800 Main Street; (912) 987-1000; major cards; no liquor.

DIRECTIONS   From Exit 43 go 1.1 miles east on US 341 to the town square in Perry. Can't be missed.

LEN BERG'S RESTAURANT, *I-16 Exit, Macon*

Len Berg's is one of those crusty, ancient downtown institutions that any city worth its salt must have. Such places serve good food at reasonable prices and make no concessions to suburban values. Len Berg's goes even further—very good food and unreasonably low prices in a decor that even the most dedicated aficionado of funk would find hard to love.

Imagine, if you will, low ceilings and seven teeny, tiny rooms populated by the plainest of plastic tables. Add a counter reminiscent of a northeastern diner, and paint everything, booths included, that shade of green appreciated only by institutional maintenance men. Adorn all this with a few pictures of Civil War battles and golfing trophies, and you've got Len Berg's

When you're 76 years old, you don't have to be beautiful, especially if you can cook, and when they bother to cook the rice in chicken broth for a $2.95 dinner, you know you're on to something good. Len's prices encouraged our extravagance, and we blew all of $5.25 for a bacon-wrapped filet mignon. It wasn't the most tender cut of meat we ever tasted, but it had a fantastic flavor for the price. The German fried potatoes were very good, and the rolls were excellent. We are deeply grateful to the waitress for insisting we try the cream-topped macaroon pie. For all of $.75 you can try this delightful blend of macaroons, pecans, dates, soda crackers, and egg whites, satisfaction all but guaranteed.

Though it has a reputation throughout Georgia, Len Berg's is still a local eatery and shows no signs of aiming for the big time. We watched a wonderfully friendly waitress read the menu to a regular customer with poor eyesight, which drove home the fact that for many Maconites this restaurant is a second home.

Downtown Macon, by the way, is a very pretty place—preserved and done up, but not made to look like a shopping mall. After your meal, consider a walk down Cherry Street, just two blocks from Len Berg's.

HOURS Mon.–Sat. 11:15 am–2:30 pm & 5 pm–10 pm. Closed Sun.

SPECS Post Office Alley; (912) 742-9255; no cards; beer.

DIRECTIONS Do not take the I-475 bypass around Macon. Stay on I-75 toward downtown Macon. Then, near downtown, follow signs for I-16 East (toward Savannah). Take Exit 4 off I-16, which is still in downtown Macon. The sign may say 5th St., but 5th St. has been renamed Martin Luther King Blvd. At the end of the exit ramp turn right onto MLK Blvd. and go 2 blocks to light at Walnut. Turn right onto Walnut and in 1½ blocks you'll see a small sign for the restaurant on your left. Turn left into the alley, and you're there. It's much easier than it may sound.

BEALL'S 1860, *Exit 52, Macon*

If you feel you've just got to have more class than Len Berg's can offer, perhaps you'd enjoy a meal in this just barely antebellum mansion, so grandiose you could easily mistake it for a Greek temple, or at least a government building. Dine under 20-foot ceilings and elaborate moldings, but be prepared to tolerate steak-and-ale appointments. It seems that this restaurant is in the process of evolving from a plain beginning to something more elegant. In the meantime, prime rib ($8.95–$12.95) is still the specialty, and the menu is still basically that of a good steak and seafood place. Sandwiches and lunch entrées are from $3.15–$4.95, dinners from $6.50–$14.95 for a rack of lamb.

At a minimum you'll get to see the other fine old houses that line College Street.

HOURS Mon.–Sat. 11:30 am–5 pm (lunch menu) & 5 pm–10:30 pm (dinner menu); closed Sun.

SPECS 315 College St.; (912) 745-4768; major cards; full license.

DIRECTIONS **Southbound:** Do not take the I-475 bypass. Stay on I-75 to Macon. From Exit 52 turn right onto Forsythe Street ■ and go two lights to College Ave. Left on College and just past the second light the restaurant will appear on the left. Can't miss it.

Northbound: Do not take the I-475 bypass. Stay on I-75 to Exit 52. Go straight at the light at the end of the exit ramp and turn left at the next street (Forsythe). Then as above from ■.

THE LEFT BANQUE, *Exit 62, Forsythe*

The slogan for this odd and multifaceted establishment is "the necessities for an elite way of life." Such necessities include "gourmet shopping," "gourmet luncheons," and "gourmet travel." Yes, it's a gift shop, travel agency, and restaurant all in one, the gift shop spilling over into ten or so rooms, each named for its particular type of merchandise (Christmas room, children's room, etc.)—a sort of, you should pardon the expression, "gourmet" department store, with the brass knickknacks kept in the vault of the renovated "banque."

Forsythe is a very plain town, and we wondered how such pretensions sat with the local folks. No matter. If you want a Greek or spinach salad, a quiche of any kind (much less one made from mozzarella and lappi cheeses), or perhaps some ricotta blintzes, the Left Banque is the only place to get it in this part of the world. Travelers weary of catfish and barbecue may well find this sufficient reason to pay a visit. We can tell you that the quiche we tried was quite good, its flavor helped along by the chunks of country ham. Good hearty muffins, too, flecked with bits of fresh fruit. Maybe there's something to be said for this business of elitism.

Whether you pick one of these or perhaps the elite version of Georgia fried chicken breast (described on the menu as "strips of chicken breast deep fried with sweet and sour chicken"), you will get to eat it in a truly unique restaurant decor—odd, contrived, inconsistent, and yet somehow pleasant. One bare wall is adorned only with local art; opposite it a room-length mural duplicates about half a block of Main Street. A third wall is festooned with balloons, and four street lamps stick up among the red-checked tablecloths like pine trees from a picnic ground.

Or perhaps you'd prefer the more sedate library room where there are white tablecloths, bookshelves, and far fewer gimmicks. The owner's husband was once a priest, and if you look closely you'll see that the books are all weighty tomes of theology in German.

It's a hodgepodge of well-meaning gestures in the direction of class, and we have to confess that we kind of liked it, especially when the owner admitted that she had just tumbled progressively deeper into the restaurant business. The Left Banque began as a very modest tearoom meant only to serve the lightest of meals to people shopping for fancy candlesticks. (And well we understand the need for something besides fried chicken!) What's more, the prices aren't all that elitist. Most salads are around $3.00; full luncheons are $4.95 or less, and sandwiches run from $2.00 for the humble grilled cheese to $4.25 for the Parisian Reuben, about which we could find nothing particularly French, unless Parisians make their Reubens from corned rib eye instead of brisket.

HOURS Tues.–Sat. 11:30 am–2 pm. May soon be open for dinner Fri.–Sun. ($14.00–$20.00 range). Now closed Sun., Mon., & major holidays.

SPECS 11 W. Johnson St.; (912) 994-5505; major cards; wine.

DIRECTIONS From Exit 62 go half-mile west to the center of Forsythe. **The Left Banque** is on the town square.

FALLS VIEW RESTAURANT, *Exit 65, High Falls*

We sorely missed the chance to experience what many have claimed to be the best catfish in Georgia. But the old black man who serves as guard gave us a guided tour of the place, and we did get to talk to owner John Wilson on the phone. So while we must remain silent on the quality of cooking, we can at least tell what we *did* learn.

The Falls View is in a pleasant-looking board-and-batten building, stained green to match the pine trees that surround it. And, yes, there once was a waterfall right across the road. But the creek's been dammed, and all that's left of the falls is a concrete spillway that, while not ugly, won't make you feel especially at one with nature.

The restaurant is truly one man's dream. John Wilson not only built the place with his own hands, he even sawed up the pine trees to make the lumber! We suspect that once upon a time it was all more funky and down-home-looking than it is now, what with its cathedral ceilings, carpeting, and high-backed oak chairs around wood-grained Formica tables. But that's what tends to happen with success. Like the falls itself, there's nothing offensive or unpleasant about the restaurant as it is now, but nothing really charming either.

None of which will bother you if the catfish is as good as they say. It's $6.50 for the all-you-can-eat special, including cole slaw, hushpuppies, french fries, onions, pickles, and tomatoes. If you're not that hungry, $5.25 will buy the meal with no reorders, and $4.25 will buy the catfish to go (eat it in the state park across the road). Fresh shrimp and oysters ($6.00/dozen), broiled flounder ($6.50), steaks ($6.95 for an 8-oz. rib eye), and burgers ($2.00) pretty much complete the menu. Kids' servings at about $3.00.

HOURS   Mon.–Thurs. 4:30 pm–9 pm; Fri. & Sat. 4:30 pm–10 pm; closed Sun., 3 days at Christmas and Thanksgiving.

SPECS   (912) 994-6050; no cards; no liquor.

DIRECTIONS   1.4 miles east of Exit 65 on High Falls Road. On the right.

FRESH AIR BARBEQUE, *Exits 66 and 67, Jackson*

If you are willing to drive 10 miles out of the way, Jackson, Georgia, offers the chance to taste what well may be the best barbecue in the South. Actually we judge it a draw between the Fresh Air Barbeque, the Lexington (see page 225), and Pierce's (see page 83), a tie that could not be resolved because the styles of barbecue are so different there is no standard that would apply to all three. The Fresh Air's entry is a hearty, tomato-based, *very* pungent version, with the deepest, richest, fullest smoky flavor we encountered anywhere.

   Toots Castor's family has been producing this treat for over 50 years now. The secret, we were told, is long, slow smoking—24 hours minimum over the hickory logs before the meat gets anywhere near your table.

   If mere taste is not enough to tempt you 10 miles off the Interstate, then let us hasten to add that the Fresh Air is everything an authentic country barbecue joint should be—a long, tin-roofed, log-cabiny sort of shack, pierced by a huge brick chimney from which alluring aromas never cease to pour. There's another shack off to one side where cord upon cord of oak and hickory lie drying, and picnic tables line the front porch for dining *al fresco rustic*. If it's too cold for that, go inside and enjoy the knotty pine walls darkened by a half-century's worth of hickory smoke, and meet whoever sits next to you at the long wooden tables.

   Service is all but instantaneous, and you're sure not to go broke—$1.25 for the sandwich, $1.10 for Brunswick stew (less of a wonder, we thought). Except for soft drinks, slaw, and barbecue to go ($4.95/lb.), that exhausts the menu.

   There's something to be said for doing one thing and doing it superbly well.

   HOURS Mon.–Thurs. 8 am–7:30 pm; Fri. & Sat. 8 am–9:30 pm; Sun. 8:00 am–8:30 pm. Closes half-hour later in summer.

   SPECS Highway 23; (404) 775-3182; no cards; no liquor.

   DIRECTIONS Northbound: From Exit 66 turn right and go 8.4 miles east on GA 36 to the center of Jackson. Turn right at the town square and go 2.8 miles on US 235. On the right.

   Southbound: From Exit 67 go 8.1 miles east on GA 116 to the town square in Jackson. Continue straight ahead and out of town on US 235. On the right in 2.8 miles.

COUNTRY KETTLE, *Exit 70, McDonough*

   Since we can't try everything on the menu, we usually adopt a benchmark meal that becomes the standard for testing roadside eateries—something that is common, popular, and challenging to the cook. We were not deep into the South when Brunswick stew and a barbecue sandwich became our yardsticks, the former because it can be as complex and interesting as the cook's imagination can soar, the latter because it is both a cult item and Dixie's unique contribution to edible Americana.

When we applied this test to the Country Kettle, it passed with flying colors, which surprised us. We are decidedly prejudiced and don't expect much from large, spanking new, commercial operations made to look like barns. Especially if they call themselves family restaurants, and have gift shops and sell that triangular peg game on every table. No matter if they're clean and inoffensive; such places often try to sell you a copy of their mechanical salt and pepper shaker, and that usually is enough to rule them out.

Perhaps it is because the Country Kettle was not very long ago a more down-to-earth barbecue stand, or perhaps it's just because they try hard and do a good job. In any case, the Brunswick stew ($1.75/bowl) was really very good—full-flavored, spicy, and filling—and it got better with every spoonful. While the barbecue sandwich ($1.75) was not the equal of the stew, it had that true smoky flavor and was entirely acceptable.

Meat and two-vegetable dinners, $3.59; $1.00 less for children; all you can eat catfish, $6.95. For $4.95 you'll get a plate of beef or pork barbecue with the Brunswick stew, as well as bread and cole slaw or country fries.

HOURS   Daily, 6 am–9 pm.

SPECS   Highway 81; (404) 957-2411; V/MC/AE; no liquor.

DIRECTIONS   Immediately west of Exit 70.

ABOUT ATLANTA

Traveling down I-75, you have two ways to deal with Atlanta —you can either obey the highway signs and go around the western edge of the city on the I-285 bypass, or you can stay on I-75 and drive right through the heart of the new South. Either way there's good food and lots of local color. We doubt there's much of a time difference, except at rush hour.

If you opt for the bypass you must then choose between **Aunt Fannie's Cabin,** where the menu is recited by a black boy who wears the chalkboard around his neck as an oxen wears its yoke, and the **Beautiful Restaurant,** a soul-food cafeteria run by a black, apparently Muslim, fraternal organization on the edge of a very prosperous black suburb. The food in either is very good southern cooking, though we imagine the owners would disagree on more than just the recipe for sweet-potato pie.

If you go through Atlanta, you'll find two much-loved Atlanta institutions right by the road in the heart of downtown—the **Varsity,** which holds the undisputed title as the world's largest drive-in, and **Mary Mac's Tearoom,** where southern hospitality and cooking go hand in hand. Or you can go to **Melvin's** (home of the world's best breakfast). The place seems well on its way to becoming another Atlanta institution.

If you're willing to detour a bit up I-85, you can add to these choices **Joe Dale's Cajun House** and **Katz's Kosher-Style Deli,** either of which is sure to please. See map for details.

THE BEAUTIFUL RESTAURANT, *Exit 5, Atlanta*

Some of the best and least expensive southern cooking we found was at the Beautiful Restaurant, a soul-food cafeteria run by what is apparently a Muslim religious/fraternal organization. We spent $3.95 for a dinner of short ribs in tomato sauce and can give it nothing less than a rave review. In this kind of barbecue mere heat does not stand in for flavor, and we were so delighted with it that we had to order another full dinner just to see if such quality could be consistently produced.

It was. The chicken baked in a light butter sauce was only a shade less wonderful than the ribs; the corn bread was superb; and the rutabagas, despite their straightforward treatment, were an exaltation of this pedestrian food to the level of high art.

This quality continued right through the black-eyed peas and renowned banana pudding ($.90 extra), failing us only at the cherry cheesecake (which was simply the wrong kind of thing to order in a restaurant like this).

At $3.65 for the chicken and only a few cents more for the ribs, oxtails, or Salisbury steak, you'd think the Beautiful would have to be an utter dump to break even. Not so. Maybe it's subsidized, but the fact is that though it is simple, there is nothing about the place that is stark or tasteless. The Beautiful sits at the edge of a prosperous and lovely black suburb. The tone in the restaurant is quiet and dignified, and the clientele is pretty classy. In fact, we doubt you'll find a more dignified cafeteria anywhere on earth.

The bright orange headdresses of the serving staff piqued our curiosity. We tried desperately to learn the meaning of it all, and though everyone was entirely friendly, they were also very publicity-shy. We got referred to one phone number after another and ended up departing Atlanta without the story. But who needs it when you're talking about one of the world's greatest restaurant bargains?

HOURS   24 hours, daily.

SPECS   2260 Cascade Rd. S.W.; (404) 752-5931; no cards; no liquor.

DIRECTIONS   Northbound turn right and southbound left onto GA 154 (Cascade Rd.). Go through 2.4 quick miles of handsome homes. On the right.

AUNT FANNIE'S CABIN, *Cobb Parkway Exit, Atlanta*

If Aunt Fannie's is the most politically sensitive restaurant we've ever written about, it is because it's so easy to confuse her cabin with Uncle Tom's. "Liberals choke on this place," said Atlanta restaurant reviewer Harold Schumacher, "but it's great for tourists." "It's not racist," said manager George Poole, "it's just a tradition, and if we didn't do it we wouldn't be in business."

Fact: After you take your seat in this pleasantly rustic, barny sort of restaurant, a young black boy approaches wearing a chalkboard menu around his neck. This board does not hang by a chain. Rather it is a sideways oval with a large hole near the upper edge through which the boy's head fits. It looks like the yoke of some beast of burden. The boy then recites the menu to you in a breathless, preadolescent singsong, and you are left with a not very vague feeling of acute discomfort. We noticed that at every single table this performance was followed by silence, and when an unrelated word was finally spoken, the entire table leaped at the subject with unusual zeal. We deeply suspect business would not suffer if this particular tradition were eliminated.

Fact: The owners and management seemed to be all white, the waiters and waitresses all black. Every now and then several of the waitresses mount a small stage and sing the likes of "Comin' Over Jordan" or "Dixie." They sing very well, they sing with gusto, and they seem to enjoy it.

Fact: Aunt Fannie's has a reputation for being touristy, and certainly it is from tourism that the bulk of its business comes. All the same, there is little that is Disneyesque. Part of the building really was a cabin on the Campbell plantation 130 years ago. The more recent additions are well conceived, and the result does not feel inauthentic. There really was an Aunt Fannie. She was born on the plantation in the 1850s and really did work here until her death in 1949. It is said that she told stories of Sherman's march through Georgia and that many of the current recipes are hers.

If that is true, she must have been a very good cook. The food at Aunt Fannie's Cabin is very good—fried chicken that was moist, tender, and flavorful; macaroni and cheese that is as good as we suppose that dish can get. Light biscuits and baked squash that was more than tasty—it was actually interesting. The apple cobbler was too sweet for our taste, but that too seems to be part of the tradition.

Fact: Lunches are $5.00; dinners are $10.95–$13.95. Besides the chicken, you can choose Smithfield ham, rainbow trout, or N.Y. strip. Soup, salad, biscuits, three vegetables, dessert, and beverage are included in the dinner, and lunch gives you almost as much.

HOURS Mon.–Fri. 11:30 am–2:30 pm & 6 pm–10 pm; Sat. 6 pm–10:30 pm; Sun. 1 pm–10 pm, dinner menu only.

SPECS 2155 Campbell Rd.; (404) 436-5218; major cards; full license.

DIRECTIONS Go north on Cobb Parkway (US 41) about 0.2 mile to light at New Spring Rd. Turn left onto New Spring, and go 4 lights (0.8 mile) to Campbell Rd. Left on Campbell, quarter-mile, on the right.

THE VARSITY, *Exits 96 and 100, Atlanta*

The world's largest and second most colorful drive-in sits smack in the middle of downtown Atlanta, right at an I-75 exit. Frank Gordy's Varsity is the kind of place that sells 15,000 hamburgers a day along with several miles of hot dogs and a ton of onions. You can eat it in your car, but the real Varsity experience is to be had indoors.

It begins when you approach the block-long counter and try to figure out which line to stand in. There are special lines for drinks, dogs, onion rings—and God help you if you pick the wrong one or haven't made your decision when you reach the counter. Speed is the Varsity's soul. The counterman shouts out your order in an incomprehensible code, the food arrives, and your change is made, all but instantaneously. So swift is the operation that cash registers and even computers could not keep the pace. Until not long ago the money was simply stuffed in a jar or tossed down a hole. If the turnover falls below six orders a minute, the counterman's pride is hurt and he's likely to get irritable.

After you survive the counter experience, you carry your prize to one of the many large, bright, bare rooms and grab a plastic chair. Then unwrap the food and gaze at the color TV while munching away. As the Varsity's eight-page color brochure says, dining here is on the "informal" side.

The food? It's fresh, it's fast, and it's cheap—burgers for $.65; hot dogs with chili for $.75; buttermilk is $.45, and nothing costs more than $1.10. But you'd best come for the color, not the cuisine. If the onion rings hadn't been so greasy, they would have actually been quite good, but nothing, unfortunately, could lift the hot dogs above mediocrity. The Varsity is good-humored about all this. Taped to the wall was an article from a health-food magazine arguing that cholesterol is good for you.

We fear Atlantans will be offended at our awarding the Varsity only second place in the color category. But the Beacon in Spartanburg, South Carolina, is a very similar sort of operation, and there the counterman exhibits such unbelievable skill he was featured in Charles Kuralt's "On the Road" (see page 50). And the Beacon holds prayer meetings in the parking lot. Not even Los Angeles can match that.

HOURS   Sun.–Thurs. 7 am–12:30 am; Fri. & Sat. 7 am–2:30 am.

SPECS   61 North Ave.; (404) 881-1706; no cards; beer only.

DIRECTIONS   Northbound: Take Exit 96 and turn immediately right onto Piedmont. Go five blocks to North, then left four blocks. On the right.

Southbound: Take exit 100 (North Ave.) and turn left at the end of the ramp. One block, on the left.

MARY MAC'S TEAROOM, *Exits 96 and 100, Atlanta*

Perhaps you like the idea of fast service in a revered downtown Atlanta institution, but you're looking for a mite more class than the Varsity can offer. Then by all means try Mary Mac's and add to the list of allurements good plain southern cooking and some of the friendliest people on earth.

According to Margaret Lupo, the current owner of Mary Mac's, the tearoom tradition began after the Civil War when southern women began casting about for a way to augment their diminished fortunes. Cooking was what they knew, so their parlors became tearooms. Eventually the tearooms left home, but their domestic origin still shows in their small size and generally dainty offerings.

Such was Mary Mac's once, but success has enlarged both the menu and the building. And while the friendliness of home still abounds, the tone is not exactly genteel. "Mary Mac's is the place for good food—for fast service—for value given," says the menu, "not for a leisurely luncheon, a business meeting, or for customers who are not in a hurry."

For these virtues Atlantans love it. There's always a fast-moving line at Mary Mac's, and the buzz of lively conversation over smoked sausage or baked chicken never stops. "Food tastes better when the waitress smothers you with attention," we were told. The staff never forgets the amenities, not even when snatching away your empty plate just as the last crumb is lifted to the mouth. It's fast, all right, but somehow all that smothering keeps you from feeling rushed.

Lunch and dinner at Mary Mac's are pretty much the same. Choose your meat from the likes of shrimp creole, catfish, smothered steak, or grilled liver. Combine this with vegetables like rice and gravy, pickled squash, fried okra, spinach soufflé, or turnip greens. With bread, beverage, and four vegetables, dinner will come to around $5.00—a dollar less if you can settle for only two vegetables. Lunch is a little cheaper still, and the food is always respectable. Occasionally it gets better than that, as did the broccoli soufflé, but you should arrive with appropriate expectations.

You should also try Mary Mac's pot likker, an earthy-tasting soup distilled from turnip greens, and you may want to check into the various presidential puddings. Carter custard is a big favorite, made with peanut butter, cream cheese, and confectioner's sugar, and topped with peanut crumbs. There was a Reagan rum-raisin pudding, but it didn't sell.

HOURS Mon.–Fri. 11 am–4 pm & 5 pm–8 pm. Closed Sat. & Sun.

SPECS 224 Ponce De Leon Ave.; (404) 875-4337; no cards; full license.

DIRECTIONS **Northbound:** From Exit 96 turn right onto Piedmont at the first light and go 6 blocks north to Ponce De Leon. Right onto Ponce De Leon, one block, on the left.

Southbound: From Exit 100 turn left onto North Ave. and go east for 6 blocks to Myrtle St. Turn left and go 1 block, then left again onto Ponce De Leon. Immediately on the right.

MELVIN'S, *Exit 104, Atlanta*

Melvin's is one of those delightful exceptions to the rule of commercial development. Here local control has triumphed over corporate cooking, producing a nearly perfect pit stop—convenient, inexpensive, colorful, and tasty.

Ten years ago Roy Rogers threw in the towel and turned his roast beef emporium over to Melvin Frazier. Melvin promptly desterilized the place, converting it to what good, cheap restaurants used to be—bustling, colorful centers of local life where the waitresses know what the customers want before they're in the door and tease them about their diets.

Just to make sure you don't mistake his place for some plastic palace with pretensions to class, Melvin tore out the kitchen walls to expose a forest of galvanized steel pipes and billowing steam. The counter faces directly into all this and as you eat, you watch about a dozen people scurrying frantically about trying to keep up with the flood of orders. Tempers don't seem to fray, however; and despite the hectic pace, the tone is friendly.

We were told that Melvin's had the best breakfast in town, and the minute we walked in we began to suspect it was true. Whenever you get a lively mix of truck drivers and college students, lawyers, bank tellers, washing-machine repairmen, and professors, you know the food's going to be good. So we plunged into the breakfast special (pork loin with two eggs, biscuits, and grits—$2.95), astonished at the two huge tender cuts of meat and the ocean of red-eye gravy in which it all floated. It was all good —nothing fancy, mind you, but really tasty, straightforward

American cooking that's about as good as this kind of thing can get.

Whether Melvin's lunch and dinner are also the best in town, we were too full to learn. But the restaurant is as cheap as it is good—meat, two vegetables, dessert, and beverage, about $2.95–$4.75. Steaks are a dollar more; half a dozen fried chicken gizzards (the place *is* authentic) are a dollar less.

HOURS Mon.–Fri. 5:30 am–9 pm; Sat. 5:30 am–11 am; closed Sun. and major holidays.

SPECS 1330 Northside Drive; (404) 352-2124; no cards; no liquor.

DIRECTIONS **Southbound:** From Exit 104 turn onto US 41 South and go 0.8 mile to restaurant, on the right.

Northbound: Northbound traffic may have to go to the exit half-mile north of 104 and double back. But they were working on Exit 104 when we came through and it looked as if a northbound exit ramp was being built. If so, take it and follow the directions above.

THE BRICKWORKS, *Exit 112, Marietta*

The menu at the Brickworks is a seven-page tome with two columns of reasonably sized type per page. Thus you get no fewer than nine full-meal salads to choose from (Cobb, crab Louise, pasta seafood, etc.; $4.00–$5.50), ten plain and fancy burgers (about $4.00), eighteen imaginative sandwiches, plus quiches and omelettes. There is also a wide selection of American dinners in the $6.00 to $7.00 range and five tempting variations on the fettuccine theme (around $5.75). Too much to do well, you think? Local judgment has it that it's all good, and so far as we can tell from our sampling, it's true. We tasted a fine smoky bean and bacon soup and a delightful chicken Parmesan sandwich with enough subtlety to seem like far more than just a sandwich.

Take this variety, quality, and value and wrap it up in a tastefully renewed old brick hotel in which plantation owners danced, Sherman slept, and the Daughters of the Confederacy were born.

We think that makes for about as tasty and interesting a highway stop as can be had.

They grind their own hamburger at the Brickworks, and they do their own dressings and desserts. Everything except the fish is fresh; there's a full bar and friendly, unpretentious service.

Admittedly the place is a shade on the trendy side, leaning toward the now-standard look of bricks, plants, and oak. But, its name notwithstanding, the bricks here have yielded to carefully chosen wallpaper, and nothing gets out of hand. It's all light, cheerful, and entirely pleasant.

HOURS   Mon.–Sat. 11 am–midnight; Sun. 11 am–10 pm.

SPECS   1 Depot St.; (404) 426-0544; V/MC/AE/DC; full license.

DIRECTIONS   Take Exit 112 for GA 120 (Marietta Parkway) and go west on 120 for 1.8 miles to a light at Fairgrounds Rd. (movie theater on corner). Right on Fairgrounds for 0.5 mile to first light and turn left onto Roswell. Go 0.8 mile on Roswell and you're at the Marietta town square. **Jimmy's** is on your left just before the square. **Shilling's** and **Guiseppe's** are to the right. **Mitch's** is directly opposite you on the west side of the square, and the **Brickworks** is in the middle of the block behind **Mitch's** (not on the square itself).

JIMMY THE GREEK'S
SHILLING'S ON THE SQUARE
GUISEPPE'S STREETS OF NEW YORK PIZZA
MITCH'S COZY KITCHEN & ICE CREAM PARLOR,
Exit 112, Marietta

Marietta is the kind of town we like. First of all it's only five minutes from the road, and second, it has a square, which, we have learned, is always a good sign for the hungry traveler. Third it's got a respectable bookstore, which is an even better sign, and finally there are no fewer than five restaurants built around the square, thereby rendering Marietta a sort of mealtime shopping center with something to please everyone. Our quick survey suggests that the best of these is the Brickworks, for which see the previous entry. For variety, however, read on.

Oldest and best known of the Marietta culinary quintet is **Jimmy the Greek's.** To the best of our knowledge no one's ever accused Jimmy of reading *Gourmet* magazine in his spare time, but he does serve up shrimp scampi and scallops ($9.00); baby squid fried in lemon butter ($5.95); gyros, souvlaki, a burger with a kosher dill ($2.95 each); and appetizers of kalamata olives and Salonica peppers for $1.25. Also available are Greek standbys like lamb shank ($6.95); a variety of American dinners ($5.00–$10.00); and that great Greco/Georgia synthesis, moussaka with fried potatoes ($5.95). Half the place looks like a Vermont country store, and the rest is woody Victoriana.

Shilling's, on the other hand, is half-tavern, half-restaurant, and entirely woody Victorian with a real tin ceiling. The seafood salad we tried in the pub was nothing to crow about, unfortunately, but they do offer a good selection of fancy sandwiches in the $4.00–$6.00 range; the place is tastefully put together, its hours are long, and the service was very friendly. The restaurant upstairs is a separate operation entirely, featuring mostly steaks and a few continental dishes in the $8.00–$14.00 range.

So far as **Mitch's Cozy Kitchen and Ice Cream Parlor** goes, the name says it all. **Guiseppe's,** on the other hand, is as handsome as a pizzeria can get, what with its brass rails, carpeted seating area, wicker-backed chairs, ceiling fans, tablecloths, and hanging cheeses. And what's more, the pizza was pretty good ($6.95 for a sixteen-incher), and he's got inexpensive versions of fettuccine Alfredo, linguini with clam sauce, and eggplant parmigiana, not to mention a good variety of subs, hoagies, grinders, po'boys, heroes, or whatever they're called in your part of the country.

HOURS   **Jimmy's:** Mon.–Thurs. 11 am–10 pm; Fri. 11 am–11 pm; Sat. 5 pm–11 pm; closed Sun.
Shilling's: Pub—Mon.–Sat. 11:30 am–2 am; Sun. 12:30 pm–10 pm. Restaurant—Mon.–Sat. 6 pm–11 pm
Guiseppe's: Sun.–Thurs. 11 am–midnight; Fri. & Sat. 11 am–1 or 2 am.

DIRECTIONS See directions for the **Brickworks,** page 131.

THE COUNTRY PLACE, *Exit 124, Cartersville*

Southern restaurants called the "Country Place" are about as rare in the South as fleas on a hound dog. Though this one has the usual meat-plus-one-, two-, or three-vegetable menu ($2.15, $2.75, $3.25), it's all nicely decked out in a sandblasted brick wall, some plants, bentwood chairs, and even a brown carpet. Not exactly country, but it doesn't come off as trendy either; you won't find a quiche in the house, and nary a crumb of carrot cake.

The food was entirely acceptable, and the restaurant is a pleasant place to spend an hour. But we have to confess that our real love here was the town of Cartersville itself. To begin with, there's the town square on which the restaurant sits—not exactly beautiful, but endearing. Then there's the wonderful old Victorian train station, so diminutive it looks more like a model than the real thing, and dilapidated enough to satisfy any aficionado of nostalgia-in-the-rough.

The real attractions, however, are off the square on the street right behind the restaurant. There we stumbled upon what may be the most beautiful small-town city hall ever erected in America —a perfectly proportioned Renaissance Revival edifice in yellowed brick, built with meticulous attention to detail and materials. Such a building would make paying your tax assessment almost a pleasure.

Even better was the Confederate war memorial directly across the street. We made a point of reading every such monument we saw, and since virtually every southern town has one, we read a lot of them. Cartersville's was far and away the best, and at the risk of being thought sentimental or chauvinistic, we hereby offer it to you in full:

> Let the stranger who may in future time read this inscription recognize that there were men whom power could not corrupt, death could not terrify, defeat could not dishonor; let these virtues plead for just judgement in the cause for which they perished. Let Georgia remember that the state taught them how to live and how to die, and that from her broken fortunes she has preserved for her children the priceless treasure of her memories, teaching all who may claim the same birthright that truth, virtue and patriotism endure forever.

They just don't write them like that anymore.

HOURS   Mon.–Fri. 6 am–3 pm; Sat. 6 am–noon; closed Sun.

SPECS   300 S. Tennessee St.; (404) 386-8040; no cards; no liquor.

DIRECTIONS   From Exit 124 follow GA 113 west for 2.4 easy miles to the center of town. Just after the RR tracks, turn right. Restaurant is half-block down, on the left.

SHEPHERD RESTAURANT, *Exit 129, Calhoun*

It didn't look promising from the outside—just a nondescript modern building right by the exit that was attached to a small motel. The inside wasn't reassuring either—pleasantly but innocuously plastic, with vertical blinds in the picture windows. But Matthew Robertson is a man who doesn't spend his money on decoration. As our hostess put it, "He's always going to cooking school in Atlanta, and he's always coming up with something new."

Listen to what $4.25 bought us: We were trying out the more exotic variants on southern cooking, and so our three "vegetables" began with stupendously wonderful banana fritters in a bed of powdered sugar (worth a visit for their own sake). Then came fried cheese, which turned out to be inch-thick cylinders of breaded American cheese accompanied by a bowl of hot sauce. Third, there was perfectly cooked broccoli in a very good curry sauce.

Which brings us to the entrée, an enormous trout, fried to a moist and tasty perfection. And as if all that weren't enough, tea and dessert were included in the price. Feeling flush, we blew another $.95 and again struck gold, this time in the form of a lovely vegetable-beef soup just loaded with all sorts of good things.

Such meals at the Shepherd Restaurant can be chosen from about 30 main dishes and 15 "vegetables." They run from $3.25 to $4.95, but after 3:30 pm they're a dollar more and you have to pay extra for beverage and dessert. Sandwiches at all hours, $1.25 to $2.95.

Though the Shepherd is right by the road, there was nothing of the usual grab-a-buck-while-you-can tourist trap about it. The customers seemed mostly local, probably for the simple reason that people hereabouts know a good thing when they taste it.

HOURS Sun.–Thurs. 6 am–10 pm; Fri. & Sat. 6 am–11 pm.

SPECS Highway 53 East; (404) 629-9152; major cards; beer and wine.

DIRECTIONS Just east of Exit 129 in the Shepherd Motel.

GRANDMA'S, *Exit 136, Dalton*

Grandma's is an airy, cheerful B.P.O. (bricks, plants, and oak café), low on brick and high on natural wood. Grandma is a fellow who used to manage the Chattanooga Sheraton and whose father was a German chef in New Jersey. It seems to be a propitious mix, since almost everything we tried at Grandma's was very good, and we have no doubt you won't do better for many miles in any direction.

The menu includes homemade pasta in several Italian dishes ($6.00–$7.00); a variety of tempting salads ($3.50–$4.75); chicken with Dijon sauce ($5.75); and a wide range of Mexican, oriental, and down-home appetizers ($4.00–$6.00); a pleasant change from fried chicken and sweet potatoes. So we were a bit disappointed when the house specialty turned out to be the Grandwich, a $4.95 slice of N.Y. strip with onions and provolone on a soft roll with fries and slaw. All the same we ordered it, and were delighted with the tender, delicious meat and the thoughtful fresh-fruit garnishes. The cole slaw was very nice, and the honey-mustard dressing on our more-than-just-iceberg salad was subtly tasty. Clearly they are trying here to do things well; we could find only mushy french fries to quibble about, and we're confident you'll enjoy the barbecued scallops or spinach fettuccine with pignola nuts that are soon to be added to the menu.

For such delights we can put up with water served in mason jars and salt and pepper in Perrier bottles.

HOURS   Mon.–Sat. 11 am–midnight.

SPECS   143 Brynam's Plaza North; (404) 226-3663; V/MC/AE; full bar.

DIRECTIONS   From Exit 136 go east on Walnut for 1.7 miles to a light at Thornton. Go past the light for 1 block and turn left into the small shopping plaza (Brynam's Plaza North). At the far right end of the plaza.

OAKWOOD CAFÉ (INC.), *Exit 136, Dalton*

Dalton has the widest streets and the largest Christian bookstore of any small town we've found. And it has the Phoebus Apollo Center for the Fine Arts, located behind a purple-painted storefront with heavily curtained windows. Finally there's the Oakwood Café, the only in-town eatery, a cute little '50s-ish affair with paneled walls, green and yellow vinyl booths, and venetian blinds in the windows. It is for these merits alone that we recommend it. We passed through on Sunday, and the café was closed.

HOURS   Mon.–Sat. 6 am–8:30 pm; closed Sun.

DIRECTIONS   From Exit 136 go east on Walnut for 1.7 miles to a light at Thornton. Left onto Thornton for 3 lights (0.5 mile) to Cuyler. Right onto Cuyler, one block, on the right.

Tennessee

THE COUNTRY PLACE, *Exit 1B, Chattanooga*

It's plastic, it's bright, it's a local chain, and it's in a motel. On the other hand, it had the best black-eyed peas we came across (unfortunately a holiday special, usually unavailable), plus light, tasty biscuits. What's more, it was the only half-reasonable restaurant we could find in Chattanooga that was really close to the road, and that is why it's here. Meat and three vegetables around $4.50; sandwiches $1.00–$2.00.

HOURS   Mon.–Thurs. 5:45 am–9 pm; Fri.–Sun. 5:45 am–10 pm.

DIRECTIONS   In the Rodeway Inn immediately west of Exit 1B.

BETHEA'S, *I-24 Exit, Chattanooga*

Bethea's doesn't try hard to be anything at all, and so it succeeds absolutely in being exactly what it is—a homey, folksy, friendly southern restaurant with some very good cooking. For decor there's just a warm hodgepodge of booths and tables surrounded by down-home paneling here and wallpaper there. Add prints of prize bulls and country scenes, a few real oil paintings, and a couple of fireplaces of one kind or another, and you've got the picture—an old Chattanooga institution that doesn't have to make a point, where you'll feel as comfortable in jeans as you would in a three-piece suit.

Bethea's (that's Beth-EA-a's, by the way) does not boast an extensive menu. Besides the ever-present fried chicken, there are snapper ($5.45, broiled or fried), pork chops with dressing ($4.95), trout ($6.95), and broiled ham in fruit sauce ($4.95). Add a few Italian dishes at $5.00, steaks, frogs' legs, omelettes, and a handful of sandwiches ($1.30–$3.95), and that's about it.

We tried the Tennessee fried chicken ($4.60), and yes, indeed, we did end up licking our fingers. The vegetable soup was very good, with little tangs of flavor that proved someone in the kitchen was trying hard to go beyond the ordinary. The rest was good enough, except for the heavy white gravy that is locally much loved, but which we could not abide here or anywhere else.

What Bethea's lacks in variety it makes up for in the friendly efficiency of its service. Our waiter was a charming fellow, just as pleasant and helpful as could be. Bethea's may not be spectacular, but his courtesy makes for a fond memory.

HOURS   Tues.–Sat. 5 pm–10 pm; Sun. 11 am–3 pm. Closed Mon.

SPECS   3850 Brainferd Road; (615) 629-4489; MC/V/AE/DC; beer only.

DIRECTIONS   Take the exit for I-24 toward Chattanooga and go two quick exits to the Belvoir Ave. exit. From the ramp go straight for 2 blocks to the light at Belvoir. Turn right and go half-mile to Brainferd. Turn left and go 0.2 mile. On the left.

CHROME PLATE CAFETERIA, *I-24 Exit, Chattanooga*

We'll well understand if you don't want to drive the 9 miles into downtown Chattanooga for food that's no better than ordinary. If you'd make the drive for a grand old hotel, skip to the next entry and learn about the Read House. But perhaps you'd enjoy the delightfully simple experience of a restaurant that somehow captures the innocence of life in Chattanooga—a cafeteria where no dinner costs more than $3.00, where the southern-style food is acceptable (though no better), and where families go for dinner in their Sunday best (at least on Sunday).

The Chrome Plate Cafeteria is one of the few southern cafeterias that have escaped both urban decay and urban renewal. The second you enter you become aware of a slower pace of living, where pleasant unaffected gestures count for more than trends, good taste, or ideas. Though old, the restaurant is clean, pleasant, and light, looking as if it were born yesterday. And therein lies its charm, indescribably epitomized in the plain blond hardwood chairs with green vinyl seats and the matching green carpet. And in the owner, an old Tennessee gentleman, tall and thin, who watches out over everything with an air of slightly self-conscious dignity.

We loved it, and the muffins were actually quite good.

HOURS Mon.–Sat. 6:30 am–9:15 am, 11 am–2:30 pm, & 5 pm–7:55 pm; Sun. 11 am–6:55 pm.

SPECS Cherry and 7th Streets; no cards; no liquor.

DIRECTIONS See directions for **Read House.**

THE READ HOUSE, *I-24 Exit, Chattanooga*

We like old hotels, the grander, the better. Nothing drives away the tedium of interstate travel quite so thoroughly as lunch in a dining room with 40-foot ceilings, stately columns, starched white tablecloths, and a pretentious Second Empire decor. If the ceiling is decorated with so much gold filigree it would embarrass a generalissimo, so much the better. And if the electric organ plays an all but unrecognizable version of "Summertime," if here and there a metal chair can be spotted peeping out from under a tablecloth right next to its Queen Anne cousins—well, that's just fine too. Camp theater, of course, but good medicine for the travel-weary.

All these delights are offered by the Green Room of the Read House Hotel. And the meat salad was delicious, selected from an overwhelming display of cold dishes that included white asparagus, chocolate mousse, and brie. There were other good choices, too, but we have to tell you that the hot dishes at this $10.00 Sunday brunch were an unmitigated disaster—bland, limp, tasteless, and uninteresting.

Maybe the food here is better when it isn't served buffet style, or maybe you ought to just stick to the cold dishes. More likely you should wait until the menu changes back to straight American fare from its currently continental pretensions, a change due any day now. The best bet may be to pass up the Green Room altogether and pick the Tavern just across the lobby. It offers a deli-bar for $4.75 that features sandwiches, omelettes, pancakes, etc.

However you decide to handle this problem, if you want grandeur in Chattanooga, those are your only options.

HOURS   Green Room: Mon.–Thurs. 11 am–2:30 pm & 6 pm–10 pm; Fri. 11 am–2:30 pm & 6 pm–10:30 pm; Sat. 6 pm–10:30 pm; Sun. brunch 11 am–2:30 pm. Tavern: daily 7 am–10 pm.

SPECS   827 Broad St.; (615) 266-4121; major cards; full license.

DIRECTIONS   Take Exit I-24 toward downtown Chattanooga and go 9 miles to I-124. Go just a bit on I-124 to the exit for Martin Luther King Blvd. Turn right at end of ramp and go 1 block to the **Read House** on the left. For the **Chrome Plate Cafeteria,** go 2 more blocks (2 lights) to a little traffic circle at Cherry St. Make the sharpest possible left here (Cherry St.) and go 2 blocks to 7th. On the corner.

COUCH'S REAL PIT BARBEQUE, *Exit 11, Ooletawah*

We ran out of courage on this one. Traveling south from Athens we'd been striking out at restaurant after unimpressive restaurant, when in despair we turned to the girl behind the counter and pleaded with her to recommend a *real* place nearby, not a plastic-plus-kuntry-ham tourist trap. Southerners love to be helpful. She gave us a knowing wink, thought hard, and came up with Couch's, a place her daddy always stopped at on his old milkman route.

That sounded right, so off we went to the next exit and then a couple of miles into the backwoods, past two trailers that housed rural massage parlors (red lights and all), to Couch's, which turned out to be a dingy green affair plunked down by the road, looking more like an abandoned railroad shack than a restaurant.

As we said, our courage failed us, and we drove on to Chattanooga wondering what we were going to tell you about this stretch of I-75. Later, of course, came dereliction-of-duty pangs and the certainty that at Couch's we'd have found the best and "realest" barbecue ever. We decided to tell you just that, and if you're more daring than we, tell us what we missed.

HOURS Tues.–Sat. 11 am–8 pm.

DIRECTIONS From Exit 11 go east 0.3 mile. Just before the Exxon station turn right and then right again (in effect a U-turn) onto old US 11 (unmarked). Follow it for two miles. It's on the right. The trailers are on the left.

THE RAFTERS, *Exit 49, Athens*

This is steak-and-potatoes country, and though the Rafters is no more or less than a country steak house, it is considered by many to be the best "full-menu" restaurant between Knoxville and Chattanooga. It's the kind of place with real stone walls, bits of barnboard, plastic chairs, a fireplace, exposed rafters, and a brick-patterned linoleum floor—not authentically anything, but sort of hodgepodgey country-posh.

They cut their own prime steaks here, and the fillets are wrapped in bacon before they reach the char-broiler. A small fillet can be had, with shrimp, for just $8.95, which is also the price of an 11 oz. rib eye and the New York strip. Six fried seafood dinners ($6.00–$8.00), ham, chicken, and pork chops (about $6.00), plus the sandwich basics (about $1.50) complete the dinner menu. At lunchtime a meat, two vegetables, and salad bar and soup cost only $3.25. With the dinners comes a football-sized baked potato that almost guarantees you won't have room for the apple pie.

It's worth the five-minute drive to the Rafters just to take a look at Athens, a town that is both pretty and pretty much unchanged since the '30s. We loved the barbershop that seemed more like an ancient photograph than a living business, and in the haberdashery next door we met Miss Teenage America. She'd won the title last year and was helping out the owner while laying plans for a career as a country singer.

HOURS Mon.–Thurs. 10:30 am–9:30 pm; Fri. 10:30 am–10:30 pm; Sat. 3 pm–10:30 pm; Sun. 10:30 am–2 pm.

SPECS   411 South Jackson St.; (615) 745-7671; no cards; beer only.

DIRECTIONS   From Exit 49 follow TN 30 east for 4 miles until you see a sign for the **Rafters**. Turn left, and then immediately left again onto Jackson. Up Jackson 0.1 mile, on the right.

WILSON'S DRIVE-IN, *Exit 60, Sweetwater*

We tend to trust words of restaurant advice when delivered in a French accent, even if they come from behind the counter of a fireworks stand in roadside Tennessee. Sure enough, as promised, Wilson's Drive-In had great ribs, smoked right outside the restaurant in a contraption that looked like a model steam locomotive, cooked to perfection, and then doused with a spicy sauce. A terrific sweet and tangy cole slaw, too, and fine corn bread fingers, the latter baked by Harold Wilson's 75-year-old mother-in-law.

What's more, you'll get to meet Harold. His is not the kind of place where you can be a stranger for long. He likes people; he'll want to know where you're from and how you liked the ribs. In no time at all you'll forget that the decor is mostly bare pressed board and that the picture windows look out onto the asphalt lake that surrounds this humble eatery. All is quite new and clean, however, and when the rib dinner costs only $4.50 (or $4.55 a pound for the meat alone), and when a barbecue sandwich goes for $1.35, you shouldn't ask for more. Barbecued chicken, too ($3.95), all the usual sandwiches, and pies baked by the same lady who did the corn bread. But you might want to pass on the soup. We've a strong suspicion it started life in a can.

HOURS   Every day, 6 am–10 pm.

SPECS   (615) 337-3144; no liquor; no cards.

DIRECTIONS   From Exit 60 go 1 mile east on TN 68 toward Sweetwater. On the left.

THE CROSS EYED CRICKET, *Exit 81, Lenoir City*

It was Sunday when we passed through Lenoir City, so we didn't get to try the famous fried trout and catfish at the Cross Eyed Cricket, but we're prepared to go out on the limb and predict you're going to love it.

First of all, sometimes you *can* tell a book by its cover. No one is going to pick one of the most beautiful spots in the land, lovingly restore an old 1850 grist mill and log cabin, stock the pond with trout, and manicure the grounds so as to produce a superbly beautiful and tranquil retreat from a too busy world, and then go and serve up mediocre food. It just doesn't happen that way, at least not often, and even if it did the Cross Eyed Cricket would be worth the trouble just to rest your soul.

Later we got owner Jim Lockwood on the phone. A few minutes' conversation had us ready to up the ante. Not only does he raise the trout he serves, he actually hatches them himself and supervises every detail of their lives from fry to frying pan. Nor does Jim just take what he can get in the way of fresh catfish. The water the fish live in is the key to its flavor, he says (agreeing, by the way, with the purveyor of the best catfish we *did* taste, see page 281), and so the live fish from Arkansas and Mississippi are sweetened for three days in Jim's pure country water before they meet their fate. How could anything but a superb product come from such attention to detail?

You say you want more proof? Then how about the fact that the old mill is actually in use and is the source of the cornmeal batter? That's right, Jim grinds his own, the yellow cornmeal destined for the fish, and the white meal ending up in the hushpuppies. The complete dinner—fish, hushpuppies, french fries, and cole slaw—is $5.95 ($6.25 if you want both trout *and* catfish). Homemade pies (black bottom, banana cream, French coconut, and apple) complete the meal which you can take in the cabin by the fireplace or on the porch that overlooks the pond. And that's the menu, except for one minimal concession to those suffering from fresh-fish phobia—hamburgers at $1.30.

If you've got a tent with you, you're in luck. The Cross Eyed Cricket is also a campground, and one so lovely that not even an entire fleet of Winnebagos could destroy its beauty. If you've got a fishing pole, your luck is even better. Catch your own, and the same dinner goes for $3.55.

HOURS April–Oct.: Mon.–Sat 5 pm–9 pm (often later); closed Sun. Nov.–March: same hours but closed Sun. & Mon. Closed on major holidays.

SPECS (615) 986-5435; no cards; no liquor.

DIRECTIONS From Exit 81 go 5.1 miles west on TN 95 to a sign for the restaurant just after the road passes under I-40. Turn left, and for two winding, gorgeous miles of Tennessee countryside just follow your nose and the signs.

APPLE CAKE TEA ROOM, *Exit 373, Concord*

For a long time the Mmes. Slagle, Hiner, and Henry wanted to open a tearoom, a place where women could relax while shopping, enjoy pleasant surroundings, friendship, and true home cooking. A place that would be an extension of their own homes and hospitality. But none had any restaurant experience or, for that matter, any business experience at all. So they prayed over

144

it and finally decided that "the Lord will close the doors if He doesn't want it."

He must have wanted it, since there's not been a moment's rest for these lovely ladies since the doors opened. The women like it, and so do the men. Already there's talk of expansion, but it seems fairly well agreed that enlarging might destroy the warm and homey character that made the Apple Cake Tea Room an instant success.

It *is* pleasant—tastefully decked out in antiques, stenciled walls, and brown carpeting, and not overdone (except for maybe the skirt under the washroom sink that matches the wallpaper to a T). Our waitress was as friendly as could be, perhaps because she once managed restaurants for Sambo's and now need never see the inside of a fast-food joint again.

All that we tasted was quite good, beginning with an absolutely wonderful cheese soup that was both rich and subtle, proceeding to some wonderful bran muffins that come with honey butter, and moving on to the coffee and apple crumb cake (a little on the sweet side). The chicken salad croissant ($2.50) was not quite the equal of its accessories, but who's going to complain when you're having a wonderful time?

Such is the fare on the small Apple Cake menu, augmented by a roast beef sandwich ($3.00), a quiche of the day with glazed fruit ($3.25), a pair of salads ($3.00), and a few more tempting

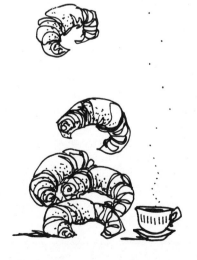

desserts. But make no mistake about it, the Apple Cake is southern home cooking, not a sophisticated quicherie. In proof of this we offer the recipe for one of the house specialties, friendship tea: 18 ozs. of Tang, 1 cup sugar, half-cup presweetened lemonade mix, half-cup instant tea, 13 ozs. apricot Jell-O, plus some anise and cloves. Now that's a recipe we don't expect to see in *Gourmet* magazine, but don't be too quick to thumb your nose. It was surprisingly good—in a southern kind of down-home way.

HOURS   Tues.–Sat. 11 am–2:30 pm.

SPECS   620 Campbell Station Rd.; (615) 966-7848; V/MC; no liquor.

DIRECTIONS   It's just 50 yards east of Exit 373 in a small tasteful shopping center. Sign by the road says "Station West." Go around to the side of the shopping center that's closest to the Interstate and you'll see it.

BUDDY'S BBQ, *Knoxville*

Short on atmosphere and long on taste, Buddy's acquired a national reputation introducing visitors to the delights of southern barbecue during the Knoxville World's Fair. This local chain is set up as a fast-food emporium in a barn of a building that features real wooden tables, color TV, and country/western music live on Friday and Saturday nights.

Now normally we shun anything that so much as reminds us of fast food, but the truth is that any barbecue joint, no matter how truly country, is essentially fast food, where your "Q" is minced in a flash and handed to you over a counter before you can find your wallet. So for barbecue we make an exception to the rule, and for Buddy's we make a double exception since the fare is really quite good. The ribs were great, and the barbecue was soft and tender with a strong, clear, smoky flavor; the sauce was mild but tasty. Even the hushpuppies were good—light, tasty, and spiked with chives. Though they were on the greasy side, we just couldn't stop eating the danged things. The standard barbecue sandwiches come in $1.29 and $1.79 sizes. Thirty cents will buy four hushpuppies. Dinners are around $3.09.

HOURS   Mon.–Sat. 10 am–10 pm; closed Sun.

SPECS   5820 Kingston Pike; no cards; no liquor.

DIRECTIONS   **Northbound:** From Exit 383 go straight at light at end of ramp for 0.5 mile to Kingston Pike. Left onto the pike for 0.2 mile. On the right.

Southbound: From Exit 383 go left at end of ramp 0.3 mile to a light at Northshore Drive. Left onto Northshore and go half-mile to Kingston Pike. Left onto Kingston for 0.2 mile. On the right.

THE REGAS
HAROLD'S KOSHER-STYLE DELI, *Knoxville*

Travelers on I-75 may not want to pass up these Knoxville restaurants, each a fine representative of its own kind of food and atmosphere. But I-75 goes around Knoxville, so that technically these places are on I-40 even though they are fairly easy to reach from I-75. See pages 60–62 for descriptions.

DIRECTIONS   **Northbound:** Do not turn onto the I-75/I-640 beltway around Knoxville. Go straight into downtown Knoxville on I-40 when it splits off from I-75 and then follow directions given on pages 61 and 62.

Southbound: Do not go around Knoxville on the I-75/I-640 beltway. Go straight into downtown on I-275 and then turn onto I-40 East. From there follow directions on pages 61 and 62.

COVE LAKE STATE PARK RESTAURANT,
Exit 134, Caryville

This stretch of I-75 is simply littered with billboards advertising chain restaurants and others that wish they were chains. In an old stone building set in a lovely sylvan park, with expansive views of the backwaters of Norris Lake and the Cumberland Mountains beyond, this restaurant seemed to hold much greater promise than any of its competitors. Alas, we never got to put it to the test because it was closed for the season.

We did ask someone in the ranger's office her opinion, and she seemed to corroborate our hunch. She was especially enthusiastic about the fact that here you could get salads and "vegetable-type meals."

We peeked in the windows to espy an attractive decor of pine paneling, house plants, candle lanterns on the tables, mate's chairs beside them. And through the wall of windows, that wonderful view.

Everything else we know about the restaurant we learned from a sign just inside the front door:

> COVE LAKE RESTAURANT
> HOSTESS ON DUTY
> OPEN 10:30 AM UNTIL 9 PM
> WE HAVE CATFISH

HOURS Tues.–Sun. 10:30 am–9 pm; closed Mon.; open spring, summer, and fall; closed winter.

SPECS Cove Lake State Park, Route 25W; (615) 562-6554.

DIRECTIONS **Northbound:** From Exit 134, bear right onto Route 25W North. In 1 mile, park is on left.

Southbound: From Exit 134, turn left onto Route 25W North. In about 1½ miles, park is on left.

Kentucky

THE HUNGRY PIONEER, *Exit 15, Williamsburg*

A quick glance around the parking lot told us that this was the restaurant for us. Despite its extreme proximity to the Interstate, there was nary an out-of-state car to be found, yet the place was hopping.

The draw was the Hungry Pioneer's $5.45 all-you-can-eat buffet. Take your pick, or take them all: country ham, roast beef, chicken and dumplings, pork barbecue, fried catfish, creamed corn, spinach, green beans, mashed potatoes, yams with marsh-mallows, salad bar, yeasty homemade rolls, soft drinks, and cof-fee. Everything was quite passable, and the catfish was especially good—tender and light, not at all greasy. We began to under-stand why the South is hooked on catfish.

This buffet, which costs $5.45 (children 10 and under, $4.15), runs only on Saturday nights and Sundays. During the rest of the week, a more modest (though ample) variation comes out with two meats and four vegetables plus salad bar. But here's an inside tip for weekday visitors: if (and only if) you request it, they'll bring you a piece of catfish at no extra charge. Do it, but don't tell them who clued you in. The cost for the scaled-down buffet is $3.60 (kids, $2.60). On Friday nights there are catfish fries. Same deal: unlimited portions ($3.45/$2.50).

If this all-you-can-eat talk turns you off because you're more interested in how little you can eat, you can order something off the menu. Sandwiches, burgers, and standard southern entrées start at $2.50, but you won't find quiche or spinach salad.

This is an unadorned roadhouse with Formica booths, panel-ing on the walls, and picture windows that afford a marvelous view of the parking lot. There isn't even an attempt at decoration, but who cares about the decor in a place like this? The atmo-sphere and authenticity come from the people and the food—both of which seem to be plain but good, and very well propor-tioned.

HOURS Winter: every day, 5:30 am–8 pm. Summer: every day, 5:30 am–9 pm.

SPECS Route 25W; (606) 549-1753; major cards; no liquor.

DIRECTIONS From Exit 15, head west. It's the first left you can make, less than ¼ mile from the Interstate, but hidden behind a tree-topped hillock.

D & W CAFETERIA, *Exit 29, Corbin*

Corbin has one great distinction in Kentucky history. It is the home of Colonel Harlan Sanders, who is celebrated in a commemorative plaque that calls him the state's "Most Famous Citizen" and "Goodwill Ambassador to the World."

All right. Let's find out what Corbin residents think of their town's favorite son.

"Excuse me, ma'am, can you tell us who has the best fried chicken in town?" we asked in an impromptu and very unscientific survey taken in downtown Corbin. "I don't know, but it sure isn't him," she replied, casting a disparaging glance in the direction of the Colonel's modern edifice.

"Sir, can you tell us who has fried chicken better than the Colonel's?"

"Most anyone."

Eventually we concluded that either Sanders's product is as undistinguished as we've always thought or that everyone in Corbin resents his success. Maybe they think he stole the recipe from their grandmothers. Either way, the consensus was clear, and eventually we hit a recommendation for the D & W Cafeteria. So there we went.

We'd love to tell you that D & W's fried chicken was the best we've ever had, but that wouldn't be true. It was quite decent, and it certainly compared favorably with that of you-know-who (which, at the time, seemed to be the main point). But it wasn't an undiscovered gem waiting to be unearthed next door to the world's most famous fried-chicken maker.

At any rate, it'll cost you $1.45 for dark meat or $1.85 for white, all in very large pieces. We also spent 45 cents on a potato cake—mashed potatoes made into hamburger-sized patties and fried—and found them to be quite tasty, almost latke-like. You can get chicken croquets, chicken barbecue, pork chops, vegetables, salads, etc., all of it perfectly acceptable though hardly divine. The same can be said of the atmosphere in which it's eaten.

After dinner, we went back to Colonel Sanders's. It had been quite a while since either of us had partaken, and we wanted to see if our memory served us well.

It had.

HOURS Mon.–Sat. 11 am–8 pm; Sun. 11 am–7 pm.

SPECS Trademart Shopping Center; (606) 528-8847; no cards; no liquor.

DIRECTIONS   From Exit 29 turn right if northbound, left if south-bound, onto Route 25E South. Go 2½ miles to Trademart Shopping Center, on right. It's in there, on the right side of the parking lot.

BOONE TAVERN HOTEL, *Exit 76, Berea*

So much has been said in the travel literature about Boone Tavern that we risk redundancy in writing about this wonderful hostelry run by the work-study students of Berea College, who do everything from building the tables and chairs to preparing and serving the food. It's a risk worth taking.

Unlike many such (dare we say most?) well-touted attrac-tions, this one is well worth a stop, although you'll have to time your visit. Most meals are served in seatings—three at lunch, two at dinner (see **HOURS,** below). And since reservations are occasionally critical, advance planning is advised.

If you arrive early, sit in the comfortably appointed lobby and read about this fascinating college that was founded in 1855 for underprivileged mountain youth. To this day Berea College charges no tuition. Instead, all students are required to work 15 hours a week in any of 145 different jobs. Some are employed in traditional Appalachian craft industries—woodcraft, weaving, and broomcraft, for example—and you can shop for the pro-ducts of their labor while waiting for the dining room doors to open.

Once they do, expect to find a gracious, formal dining room staffed by students who are eager to please and equally eager to be engaged in conversation about their college. (Our waiter, as we found to our considerable surprise, was not majoring in dul-cimer making or chair caning, but—of all things—robotics!) The food is traditional southern cuisine, generally well prepared but somewhat spotty, and served with great enthusiasm, if not aplomb.

All prices ($6.50–$8.95 at lunch; $9.95–$14.95 at dinner) are for complete meals, starting with pickled carrots and other coun-try relishes and ending with homemade ice cream or Kentucky lemon pie. The Boone Tavern's signature dish is spoonbread, something of a cross between a soufflé and a custard, rich with eggs and cream, filled out with cornmeal. In our case it was a little too filled out, and we can't rave about it but will report that we've heard it's usually lighter. Entrées are the likes of fried chicken, honey ham, roast leg of lamb, and broiled fresh Chinook salmon (how'd that get in?); with them come special breads, assorted salads, and some unusual vegetable dishes (pineapple beets, for instance).

Were we to be nit-picky about our meal at Boone Tavern, we might say we liked the carrot soup but didn't care for the rolls, that we loved the pie but found the ice cream disappointing, and so on. In the end we'd probably conclude that the food was good, but that the charming atmosphere made it taste better than it really was. Yet the atmosphere is what makes Boone Tavern special—not a pasted-on decor of the sort found in overrated restaurants, but an engaging spirit born of the college's rich history, carried on by today's students and communicated to every guest. And for that, the Boone Tavern gets four stars.

A couple of other things, one good, the other possibly inconvenient, for highway travelers. No tipping is permitted at Boone Tavern, a policy that's strictly enforced. Equally strict is the dinnertime dress code: men who arrive without a jacket will be issued a well-worn "loaner" at the door, but women not attired in dresses, skirts, or pants suits are out of luck.

Should you arrive in the evening, you might well want to spend the night. The comfortable rooms are very low-priced, and infinitely more inviting than any motel.

HOURS Breakfast: served continuously, 7–9 am, every day. Lunch: Mon.–Sat. seatings at 11:30, 12:45, and 1:20; Sun. seatings at noon and 1:20. Dinner: seatings at 6 and 7:30, every day (Sun. included).

Note: Dress code in effect for all evening meals and Sunday lunch.

SPECS Berea College; (606) 986-9341; major credit cards; no liquor despite the name.

DIRECTIONS From Exit 76, head east toward Berea. You'll reach **Boone Tavern** in 1½ miles, on left. No missing it.

PAPALENO'S, *Exit 76, Berea*

You just missed the last seating at the Boone Tavern, or you didn't want to spend that much money, or you can't stand southern cooking, or you don't have a jacket and can't abide the thought of wearing someone else's. Relax. There's another good choice in Berea, just around the corner from the town's landmark hotel.

Nobody will care what you wear to Papaleno's, nor when you arrive (within reason). The prices are quite affordable, and the food's not southern. Here we enjoyed an altogether superior bowl of cheddar cheese soup flavored with bits of green pepper and pimento. And there are a few imaginative sandwiches like olive nut and tuna apple, as well as turkey served on top-notch bread. Other than that, however, Papaleno's is a pizza and sub shop.

One of the best things about it, especially for gourmands on the run, is that pizza can be ordered by the slice (95 cents). Often that is a sign of an inferior product, but Papa Leno's pizza is very, very good—a perfect crust, good sauce, lots of cheese. Whole pizzas, which are made from scratch as you watch, range in size from 10 to 16 inches, and in price from $3 to $6.75 (more for extras, up to $10.85 for a 16-inch "Mountaineer" with 10 different items from anchovies to black olives). And the subs (Italian sausage, stromboli, meat ball, vegetarian, etc.) are served on homemade rolls, priced under $2.50; half-portions are available at such minuscule prices as $1.10 or $1.29.

The setting seems appropriate both to the region and the food —exposed brick walls, handmade wooden booths, and excellent black and white photography of rural scenes. A few touches of red, white, and green remind you that the menu is mostly Italian.

HOURS Mon.–Thurs. 11 am–11 pm; Fri. & Sat. 11 am–midnight; Sun. 3–11 pm.

SPECS 108 Center St.; (606) 986-4497; no cards; no liquor.

DIRECTIONS As for **Boone Tavern** (above). Turn left to pass in front of the Tavern, then take the first right. It's just around the corner, on the right.

THE SARATOGA, *Exit 110, Lexington*

It has been said that Kentucky is a Commonwealth because it has two parts—the common and the wealth. Here is where you can dine with the former. For more opulent surroundings and a window on horsey wealth, head for Griffin Gate (page 157).

Which isn't to say that Lexington's prominence in horse breeding is forgotten at the Saratoga: Pictures of famous thoroughbreds, native sons no doubt, line the walls. Otherwise, this is the kind of authentic neighborhood restaurant found in authentic neighborhoods everywhere.

Its lino floors, old-style Formica-topped tables with metal edgings, ancient (but still comfortable) pea green booths, and cream-colored plaster walls have aged without ceremony over the Saratoga's 40-year history. Someday an oil painting, then an arty postcard, will celebrate its type as a slice of Americana.

The waitresses, most of whom have been here 20 years or

longer, know the menu inside out and expect you to do the same. Don't let that intimidate you—they'll start smiling as soon as you order. And if you like good, plain American cooking, you too will smile when the food arrives.

Certainly it's not extraordinary or extravagant, but it's well prepared, generously proportioned, and easily worth the modest sums charged. The day's lunch special was a large plate of tender short ribs doused in a molassesy sauce, along with a whole boiled potato, tomatoes and okra, corn bread, and a roll. The cost: $3.25. Not bad. (Our dessert, carrot cake, was a surprisingly trendy offering for so unstylish a place.) Other complete lunches might have been pan-fried pork chop, baked flounder, or roast beef; chili, sandwiches, and fried seafood are also available. Dinners are much the same sort of thing, with prices a couple of dollars higher, although sandwiches and burgers continue to be available.

The Saratoga isn't the kind of place you rave about for weeks, but it's liable to become a regular stopoff just the same.

HOURS   8 am–midnight, every day.

SPECS   856 E. High St.; (606) 269-9953; no cards; full license.

DIRECTIONS   From Exit 110, turn left if northbound, right if southbound, onto Route 60 West toward Lexington. Go about 4 miles to the junction with Route 421 (Main St.) and turn left. In ½ mile, turn right onto Ashland Ave. Go 0.4 mile on Ashland to light at E. High St. Left on E. High; it's on the right in 0.1 mile, at corner of Fontaine.

ALFALFA RESTAURANT, *Exit 113, Lexington*

Located across from the main gate to the University of Kentucky, the Alfalfa, as its name suggests, is Lexington's purveyor of things sprouty, whole-wheaty, and vegetarian. But don't immediately cast it into a type, even though its funky decorating scheme of bark slabs and old wooden pallets, its odd assortment of chairs, and its carpet in bad need of replacement might encourage you to do so. The food here is delicious. And judging from the diverse clientele, it seems to be widely recognized as such.

For starters, it should be stated that although the emphasis is on meatless cooking, you'll find crêpes with beef and mushrooms, chicken breast parmigiana, and fresh pan-fried trout. But you'll also find a vegetarian chili made of kidney and garbanzo beans, mushrooms, cabbage, and whatever else the cook thought would go well on that particular day (that variability being "the charm of the Alfalfa," a regular told us). On our particular day it was beyond reproach. A simple but marvelous cream of potato soup featured dill and caraway, and a thick, cheesy spanakopita, while not traditional, was thoroughly enjoyable. Lunch prices hover around $3.

Weekend brunches get somewhat fancier, but only slightly more expensive. Look for matzo brei, huevos rancheros, omelettes, sourdough blueberry pancakes, and "eggs Benedict Arnold" (with avocado instead of ham) at brunch. At the dinner hour, expect to pay between $4.50 and $6.95 for crêpes, stuffed turbot, ratatouille, and pasta dishes. Inquiring about the noodles (which, like everything else, are made from scratch), we were informed that whole wheat is in the bread but not in the pasta. "Don't worry, we don't serve cardboard and call it lasagna," our waitress assured us.

It's that kind of sensible place.

HOURS Lunch: Tues.–Fri. 11 am–2 pm. Dinner: Tues.–Thurs. 5:30–9 pm; Fri. & Sat. 5:30–10 pm. Brunch: Sat. 10 am–1:30 pm; Sun. 10 am–2 pm. Expect a wait for Sunday brunch. Closed Mon. Also closed Thanksgiving, Christmas, July 4.

SPECS 557 S. Limestone; (606) 253-0014; no cards; beer and wine.

DIRECTIONS From Exit 113, turn right onto Route 27 toward Lexington. This is Northern Parkway, which will become Broadway. Go about 3½ miles to Boliver (one block past Cedar). Left on Boliver and right at the T onto Upper. It's about ¼ mile to the restaurant, on the right, between Montmullin and Prall. From the Interstate, the trip can take as much as 15 minutes (less in evenings).

Parking: There's a lot on Prall, just past the restaurant; it's free evenings, and when the university is out of session. At other times, 75 cents/hour.

THE MANSION AT GRIFFIN GATE,
Exit 115, Lexington

You stride beneath 200-year-old oak, ash, and hackberry trees, up the brick steps and between classical columns of the antebellum mansion. Turn the brass doorknobs and lean into the heavy wooden doors. Then sink into the plushly carpeted vestibule. Your attention is drawn upward, past the crystal chandelier and the gilt-framed oil paintings, and you peer up the curving, balustraded staircase. Who will descend those stairs? Will it be Scarlett herself?

Pity be, but all good fantasies must come to an end. Your host is not the belle you may have been hoping for but maitre d' Thomas Brady, a perfectly cordial fellow who will seat you in one of five richly appointed dining rooms in this renovated plantation house.

Examining the menu, somewhat pretentiously bound in leather (if any place can be allowed pretension, this ought to be it), you discover that what you must pay for all this luxury is somewhat less than you might have imagined. Most lunch entrées, for instance, are under $5; you can even have Griffin Gate's notorious steak soup with half a sandwich for $3.75. The decor and a cup of coffee alone might be worth that much.

About that steak soup. It's become the restaurant's trademark, an original item developed by chef Wayne Wells. The reviewer for the *Lexington Herald-Leader* wrote, "Hearty is too weak a word for its overpowering flavors," which we found to be an apt description ($1.25 on its own). House salads, served with entrées, include a variety of leaf lettuces and baby shrimp; vegetables come family-style, and with them you have a choice of rice or cheese grits, an applaudable version of that ordinarily bland southern staple.

Griffin Gate smokes all its meats on the premises; look for smoked turkey sandwiches, and brisket of beef used in a native Kentucky sandwich called Hot Brown—open-faced beef and country ham doused in a rarebit sauce. Other lunchtime choices include sautéed chicken livers; strip steak; half-pound burgers; and some imaginative variations on chicken salad, including one with kiwi fruit and cranberry sauce.

The dinner menu promises a choice of traditional southern and American steak-house fare; most entrées are in the $10–$14 range. The biggest sellers are pan-fried catfish and pork tenderloin glazed with a sweet apple brandy sauce.

Though it's surrounded by the impeccable bluegrass pastures and white painted fences of Kentucky's renowned horse farms, Griffin Gate's closest neighbor is a Marriott hotel that was built to accommodate the horsemen who come from all over the world to buy animals during the November trading season. That's when we want to come back. We're dying to see what a fellow orders after he's sold a horse for a million dollars.

HOURS Lunch: Mon.–Fri. 11:30 am–2 pm. (See also Sunday dinner.) Dinner: Mon.–Thurs. 6–10 pm; Fri. & Sat. 6–10:30 pm (later during horse-trading season); Sunday dinner, noon–8 pm.

SPECS 1760 Newtown Pike; (606) 231-5152; all cards; full license.

DIRECTIONS From Exit 115, turn left if northbound, right if southbound. Go ½ mile, turning left into driveway for Marriott hotel. Go straight up the driveway instead of turning off toward the Marriott, and you'll come right to it.

South Carolina
North Carolina
Virginia

South Carolina

RAY LEVER'S BAR-B-QUE HUT, *Exit 6, Blythewood*

It's no hut, it's a great brick bunker with a huge sloping roof whose asphalt tiles spell out RAY LEVER'S BAR-B-QUE HUT in letters large enough to be seen from passing airplanes. As is typical of South Carolina pit barbecues, this is an all-you-can-eat affair, but only in the small area around Columbia will you find the meat doused with a tangy, bright yellow, mustard-based sauce. Lever's is as good an example of Columbia-style "Q" that we found, a must for anyone wanting to expand his barbecue horizons.

Those suffering from no more than moderate hunger might just walk around to Ray Lever's Take-Out Room on the side of the building. Here, barbecue sandwiches can be had for as little as $1.45; large combination dinners are $4.25, and anything Lever's serves can be ordered by the pint or the pound. Stock up, then carry your bounty back around to the cafeteria tables and folding metal chairs inside the main dining room.

Or head there right from the start—after all, that's where the fun is. It is quite clear that, despite the ample (if measured) quantities available from the Take-Out Room and the permissibility of consuming them in the dining room, the great majority of Ray Lever's customers avail themselves of the buffet's unlimited portions. On Sunday afternoons, Lever's is an obligatory stop for many folks who come to nourish their bodies after church services have addressed the needs of their souls.

It is with great exuberance that they approach the steam table. On it they find chopped pork barbecue and ribs, both of them variegated with that pungent yellow sauce, along with pork hash (a mixture of all the pig parts that are best disguised), fried chicken, rice, macaroni and potato salads, brown beans, string beans, corn on the cob, and cole slaw. Though the corn was mushy, the peppery slaw was among the best we've found. The cost for all this indulgence is $4.65 per adult, less for children depending on age. Go ahead.

So take your pick—large quantities around the side or unlimited quantities up front. Either way, you get the same quality hickory-smoked barbecue and that beguiling mustard sauce.

HOURS Thurs.–Sun. 11 am–8:45 pm (in summer, until 9:45 pm); closed Mon.–Wed.

SPECS Lorick Rd.; (803) 754-3209 & 754-8408; no cards; no liquor.

DIRECTIONS From Exit 6, head west on Killian Rd. and go about 1½ miles to the stop sign (Wilson Rd.). Turn right on Wilson and go ½ mile to Folk Rd. (big sign for **Ray Lever's**). Left on Folk; it's 1½ miles down, on left.

TAM'S TAVERN, *Exit 66B, Rock Hill*

After working their way through the kitchens and dining rooms of several Charlotte restaurants, brothers Tom, Andy, and Matt Brightwell felt they'd paid their dues. Combining their varied talents and the first letters of their respective first names, they opened Tam's Tavern. Suddenly, for travelers on I-77, Rock Hill was more than just a place to gas up between Charlotte and Columbia.

Unlike the more famous Boone Tavern in Berea, Kentucky, Tam's really is a tavern, but the emphasis is on the food, which is all fresh and homemade. It's a very attractive place, with a subdued coffee-and-cream color scheme, nicely framed art on the walls, and unusual (but comfortable) horseshoe-backed chairs.

While nicely put together, Tam's is comfortably informal in a way that appeals to nearly everyone. Even the Baptist church next door, after objecting to Tam's full-bar status, has opened a house account.

Arriving for lunch, we passed up an asparagus and bacon quiche ($3.25) and a variety of plump burgers on kaiser rolls ($3–$4) to order a chicken salad sandwich ($3.95) that proved to be chunky and moist, seasoned nicely with celery seed, chopped celery, and Spanish onion. It came on a respectable croissant, and on the side—lo and behold!—a fresh-fruit garnish of grapes and orange slices.

Tam's dinner reputation is built around prime rib and its daily seafood specials, for which the fish is usually flown in fresh from the coast. On the night of our visit, however, an indigenous inland species was featured. Fresh mountain trout stuffed with crabmeat in a béarnaise sauce was being chalked up on the board as we finished lunch ($9.25, with rice pilaf and vegetable). Although that price is typical of dinner entrées, you can spend less on a crab and Swiss cheese omelette, or any of the sandwiches from the lunch menu.

HOURS Mon.–Thurs. 11 am–10 pm; Fri. 11 am–10:30 pm; Sat. 5–10:30 pm; closed Sun. There can be a wait of up to 45 minutes between 7 and 9 pm, Fri. and Sat.; closed major holidays.

DIRECTIONS Exit 66B puts you on Route 21 South. Go about 3¼ miles to the light at Oakland Ave. Turn right and shortly pull into a tiny shopping center, called "Olde Towne," on your left.

North Carolina

LA TACHE, *Exit 6B, Charlotte*

Located in the Registry Inn, this plush restaurant with its $7 breakfasts and $17.95 dinner entrées is not a natural candidate for this book. What drew us there were tales of its $6.95 weekday lunch buffet.

Now $6.95 for lunch isn't exactly *bon marché*, especially in the

South, but for the Registry Inn it's quite a bargain. You get a regal atmosphere (pretentious, no doubt, but nevertheless well conceived) and the opportunity to help yourself to some pretty classy cooking on the buffet table.

Every day there are two hot meat dishes (Swedish pork chops and a turkey casserole, for example), cold cuts, cheeses, many fresh fruits, and a great variety of salads. The salads are most impressive: peas with capers, carrot-celery-dill, pickled herring, skins-on potatoes with pimentos and chives, tuna, Waldorf, tomatoes and marinated mushrooms, ham and asparagus, and so on. Those that we sampled were as tasty as they were intriguing. For fruit, we found pineapple, orange, honeydew, canteloupe, and strawberries, all of them fresh even in midwinter.

Best of all for the hungry but discriminating motorist on the run, the Registry Inn is right off the exit ramp, and self-service at the buffet is immediate.

HOURS The buffet described is available Mon.–Fri. only, 11:30 am–3 pm. The restaurant is open for breakfast Mon.–Fri., 6:30 am–11:30 am; Sat. & Sun., 7 am–11:30 am. Weekend lunch served same hours as weekdays, but from the menu only. Dinner every day, 5:30–10:30 pm.

SPECS Registry Inn, 321 West Woodlawn Road; (704) 525-4441; major cards; full license.

DIRECTIONS **Northbound:** From Exit 6B look left and you'll see the Registry Inn.

Southbound: From Exit 6B, the Registry will be directly in front of you. Turn left at light and pull into driveway.

OLD ORIGINAL BARBECUE HOUSE, *Exit 9B, Charlotte*

How, we wondered after four weeks of back-roads barbecue, would a big-city barbecue compare with its country cousins? At the Old Original Barbecue House, a Charlotte institution for 30 years, we had a chance to find out.

The single dark room looked vaguely familiar—its walls covered with the same sheets of ersatz paneling we had become accustomed to and its air filled with the hickory smoke (mixed with tobacco) that marked a genuine barbecue anywhere. Once the food arrived, we concluded that good "Q" is good "Q" no matter where it's served; four lanes of city traffic outside the Old Original Barbecue House had no effect on what happened therein.

Here you have your choice of beef or pork, chopped or sliced. We went for sliced pork on our sandwich ($1.60) and found two pieces of bread widely separated by thick slabs of meat, delightfully charred around the edges. Utterly delicious, even though the sauce was less eventful.

But that wasn't all. Brunswick stew was also on the menu. This southern standby may have lost some of its zest from the days when it was made with squirrel meat, but it wasn't suffering from any lack of character here. Thick with vegetables and the smoky pungency of pit-cooked beef and pork, a bowl of Brunswick stew comes with all combination plates ($3.15–$4.55), or by itself for $1.90 per pint. If you decide to bring home a gallon ($12), you won't be the first.

And then there was also the Old Original's corn bread—a moist and rich-tasting antidote to the compressed Styrofoam that usually passes for this breadstuff.

But as memorable as the above-mentioned dishes may have been, it was the dessert that has etched itself permanently in our culinary consciousness. Owner Ronnie Deese, who grew up in a house on this spot, has received so many compliments on his sweet-potato pie that it's a wonder he continues to accept them with genuine appreciation and an air of modest surprise. Superb it is, with flavors that we simply could not divine. Orange? Honey? Almond? All three and more? It was pointless trying to find out. We already knew that some time ago a fellow from Houston had begged Ronnie for the recipe. No go. Undaunted, the Texan offered him a job—as manager of the restaurant he owned in the Houston Hilton. No thanks, Ronnie said, he was quite satisfied in Charlotte.

You'll be glad he stayed—unless you live in Houston.

HOURS Lunch: Mon.–Sat. 11:30 am–3 pm. Dinner: Fri. only, 5:30–9 pm. Closed Sun.

SPECS 2240 Camp Greene St.; (704) 392-6537; no cards; no liquor.

DIRECTIONS From Exit 9B (Independence Blvd. West), go 1 mile and turn right at Camp Greene St. (just after the light at Remount Rd.). You'll see it immediately on left. Three minutes tops.

PEREGRINE FINE FOOD AND SPIRITS,
Exit 30, Davidson

In the shadow of classy Davidson College, a place called Peregrine Fine Food and Spirits might lead you to expect a faculty lunch crowd, moderate prices, fresh food, and a pleasant decor. But then you learn that it's the students' favorite spot for pizza, and that a popular pizza topping is cukes and sprouts! So what is it, a tasteful café or a college hangout?

Well, it's both. The tones are subdued, the appointments well chosen; during the lunch and dinner hours, the crowd *is* mature. Diners order full-meal salads; deli sandwiches; fancy burgers on kaiser rolls; stuffed baked potatoes; and entrées like lasagna, rib-eye steak, or coq au vin. Pizza is available too, but the kitchen doesn't really start to turn it out until nine or ten at night, when the college kids start to think about shutting their books and feeding study-induced appetites. At about that time the music shifts, and the ambient decibel level rises.

The members of the kitchen staff are quick to reveal their credentials as purveyors of Italian-American cuisine in North Carolina: "None of us are from the South. We're from New Jersey, and do we know from pizza!"

Unfortunately it wasn't quite ready when we came by, so we couldn't verify the claim. We can say without reservation, however, that they know from meatball-sausage subs. Both the garlic- and herb-spiced meatballs and the sweet Italian sausage were first-rate, as was the tangy tomato sauce. This was preceded by a large bowl of French onion soup dashed with tabasco—a little hotter than we might have preferred for this particular dish, but creditable nonetheless.

Prices at Peregrine's are quite affordable, with most sandwiches and light items coming in under $3, salads under $4, and dinner specials $6.95 at the most. The lunch menu is available all day.

HOURS Lunch: 11 am–2 pm, every day. Dinner: 5 pm–midnight, every day. Breakfast may soon be instituted. During Davidson College's Christmas vacation restaurant closes at 10 pm.

SPECS 127 Depot St.; (704) 892-8686; MC/V; beer and wine.

DIRECTIONS From Exit 30, head east for 1 mile to the light at Davidson College. Turn right, and in 0.1 mile, turn right at the blinking light (Depot St.). It's in the first block, on left.

LANDMARK PLACE, *East Broad Street Exit, Statesville*

The Landmark is one of those gentrified brick warehouses. Breuer chairs and plush carpeting have displaced the heat and grime of the workaday world to produce a restaurant at once dignified and trendy, handsome, relaxing, and good. In fact we'll go out on a limb and guess you won't do any better than the Landmark for the 130 miles between Statesville and Black Mountain.

For one thing you can get a few sophisticated dishes here— chicken in phylo pastry ($9.95), veal Jeanette ($12.50), or perhaps fettuccine a la calamari ($6.95). The daily specials tend to be of this order, as owner Joe Sazama tries to take advantage of whatever is best and freshest. We tried a scampi Provençale and found five huge shrimp smothered in onions, mushrooms, black olives, and a good strong tomato sauce. Garnished with grapes and lemon, it was lovely to look at and a joy to eat.

Statesville, though a lovely town, isn't exactly the culinary center of America. Consequently most of the Landmark's menu is given over to steaks, ribs, chops, and good old fried chicken ($6.50). Lunch has the usual burgers and deli sandwiches, though the former also come dressed up "a la Italiano," i.e., on French bread with mozzarella, green peppers, onions, mushrooms, bits of Italian sausage, and topped with a tomato sauce ($3.75). A chicken salad of white meat, almonds, radishes, celery, onion, sour cream, and mayo topped with seasonal fruit ($3.95) will make for a pleasant change of pace, and there are about half a dozen interesting entrées from $2.95 to $3.95.

A perfect choice for rest, relaxation, and variety.

HOURS Mon.–Fri. 11:30 am–2 pm & 6 pm–10 pm; Sat. 6 pm–10 pm; Sun. 9:30 am–2:30 pm for brunch.

SPECS 119 North Center St.; (704) 873-5575; MC/V; beer, wine, and brown bags.

DIRECTIONS Take East Broad St. Exit from I-77 for 1.6 miles to Center St. at the center of Statesville. Turn right and go half-block. On the left, up a little alleyway marked by an awning.

SUB-EXPRESS, *East Broad Street Exit, Statesville*

This is a plain but very pleasant version of exactly what its name suggests. The fluorescent lights and white walls are relieved by local watercolors, some of which were really very good and all of which were better than you'd expect to find in a sub shop. The food wasn't bad either, $1.65 to $3.60 for a whole sub, a little more than half that for a half. Corned beef, pastrami, and kaiser rolls available, and they'll even make up a Reuben for $2.85.

And you get a pretty little town to stroll around in after the meal.

HOURS   Mon.–Sat. 10 am–9 pm.

SPECS   126 West Broad St.; (704) 872-9666; no cards; no liquor.

DIRECTIONS   Take East Broad St. Exit and go 1.6 miles to center of Statesville. One more block brings you to the sub shop, on the right, on the corner.

THE LANTERN, *Exit 93, Dobson*

"Everybody and his brother makes fresh biscuits nowadays," said Clinton Dockery, owner of the Lantern, "but very few know the secret of making *light* biscuits." We had just eaten the Lantern's angelically light version of this southern specialty, and when Mr. Dockery teased us with a reference to his secret, we inched forward to the very edges of our seats. Would he drop the magic formula before we dropped off our seats?

"You can't just roll out the dough and stamp out the biscuits." Ah, here it comes, we thought, and slid back in our chairs. "That makes for *tough* biscuits. You've got to *pinch* them off a ball of dough, one by one."

We haven't put his method to the test, but we stand by his results: the Lantern's biscuits are as light and tender as biscuits come in a region where every restaurant and café gains its pride from the density of its biscuits. The goal is generally something a tad heavier than a helium balloon.

It's not only biscuits that bring folks down to this low-slung brick building. They come from the far side of the Virginia border to eat steaks and seafood; Mr. Dockery says that Virginians order their seafood broiled, while North Carolinians prefer it fried. He doesn't know why, but he's happy to offer it to you either way ($5 or less).

There's also pan-fried chicken and chicken livers, with potatoes and vegetable or a trip to the salad bar for $3.95. Sandwiches and hamburgers are available all day (75 cents–$1.85), but at the lunch hour you couldn't find a much better bargain than the daily special: for a fixed price of $2.50, you can choose one of five or six main dishes such as ham, salmon cake, chicken pie, fried chicken, and barbecued beef tips. We went for the baked country ham, and were delighted to find its piquant saltiness offset beautifully by the sweetness of a smooth raisin sauce. The sauce varies from day to day—you might find pineapple or mixed fruit rather than raisin—but it serves the same function on the palate.

As memorable as the raisin sauce was the dessert that followed it, a dense, fruity pineapple cake baked by Rodney Dockery, the owner's nephew. The young Dockery's kitchen prowess is held in such great esteem around here that our waitress shyly admitted, when we commented on the cake, that her husband is pushing her to ask him for cooking lessons.

HOURS 6 am–9:30 pm, 7 days a week. Closed Christmas, Thanksgiving, and the week of July 4.

SPECS Main St.; (919) 386-8461; no cards; no liquor.

DIRECTIONS From Exit 93, turn right. In 4 quick miles you come to the junction of Business 601. Turn left and you'll see it on the right.

Virginia

MOUNTAIN TOP RESTAURANT, *Exit 2, Fancy Gap*

With a name like Fancy Gap, this town must have something going for it, we figured, and upon inquiry were told that the display of autumn foliage here rivals Vermont's. And then we heard about something else, the home-cured country hams served at the Mountain Top Restaurant.

Some people find that the inherent saltiness of country ham overpowers the many underlying flavors, but it is the salt rubbed into these hams that distinguishes them from the processed variety. In producing run-of-the-supermarket hams, food-processing companies substitute nitrites and a flask of chemicals for salt and time. While country hams are hung to cure for a year, processed hams are ready in days, but the product is vapid by comparison with that of Dallas and Tommy Philips, owners of the Mountain Top Restaurant.

At lunch or dinner, it will cost you $4.75 to find out for yourself how you take to true country ham (price includes two vegetables and salad). If you know from experience that it's your kind of dish, you might want to raise the ante to $6.50 and dig into a thick ham steak. But if ham is not for you, you can get away with spending only $3.65 for a dinner special like stuffed cabbage or chuck-wagon steak (again, vegetables included).

The charms of Mountain Top are more on the plate than in the decor; although the orange booths may compete with fall foliage for honors as the brightest thing around, such colors seem more desirable outside than in. Ersatz brick wall paneling doesn't help either, but the overall folksy tone does fit the restaurant's style.

Our visit was on a fog-thick night in January, so we didn't get to witness the autumnal display. We wondered if it was as good as the ham.

HOURS   Spring, summer, and fall: 6 am–10 pm, every day; winter: 7 am–9 pm, every day.

SPECS   Route 52; (703) 728-9196; no cards; no liquor.

DIRECTIONS   From Exit 2, turn right if northbound, left if southbound, and drive about ¾ mile to the junction with Route 52. Turn right on 52, and go 1 mile; it's on the left, a little past the motel.

I-81

Tennessee
Virginia
West Virginia

Tennessee

LITTLE DUTCH RESTAURANT,
Exits 8 & 12, Morristown

Morristown, Tennessee, is the only town in the United States
(or so they say) with overhead sidewalks. It seems that a flood
ripped through in 1966 washing away everything in its path,
sidewalks and storefronts included. In rebuilding, the architect
wanted to install awnings so that pedestrians could be protected
from future downpours (a large culvert would take care of the
creek); then he figured that it would cost only a little more to
turn the awnings into sidewalks. So now there are two levels of
storefronts and overhead crosswalks linking the two sides of
Main Street; it adds up to a charming sort of storybook quaint-
ness.

We figured that such a nifty town would have at least one
nifty restaurant and the two levels of storefronts would double
our chances, but it didn't work out that way. Just around the
corner from the rebuilt area we found what seemed to be the
only hot spot of Morristown dining. It's called Little Dutch Restaurant, a name that conjured up images of windmill decor and
tulip-toting waitresses. Thankfully, that's not what we found,
although the Muzak and Ethan Allen-style appointments weren't
a whole lot better.

Fortunately our hamburger was. Coming after a bowl of veg-

170

etable soup that tasted like embellished Campbell's, we were surprised to find a plump patty of fresh ground round with bacon, mushrooms, and cheese on a very creditable roll. For this, with a baked potato (french fries also available), we paid $2.95.

Other than burgers, expect Italian-American dishes, steaks, a variety of meaty sandwiches, fried and broiled seafood, Greek and chef's salads, all at prices that rarely rise above $3 or so.

The Little Dutch Restaurant isn't likely to be the culinary highlight of your trip, but it should assuage your appetite reasonably well, your budget even better, and, if you're interested in a little walk after lunch, your curiosity about oddball architecture best of all.

HOURS   Mon.–Thurs. 11 am–10 pm; Fri. & Sat. 11 am–11 pm; Sun. 11 am–2 pm.

SPECS   115 South Cumberland (corner of Cumberland and Main); (615) 581-1551; major cards; no liquor.

DIRECTIONS   **Northbound:** From Exit 8, bear right onto Route 25E North. Go about 3 miles to sign for Route 160 and turn right onto 160 North. Go ¾ mile to the blinking light and bear right toward Morristown. From this point, it's exactly 1½ miles to the restaurant on your right, at corner of Main St.

Southbound: From Exit 12, turn right, go 4 miles to the blinking light, and bear right toward Morristown. From this point, it's exactly 1½ miles to the restaurant on your right, at the corner of Main St.

RIDGEWOOD RESTAURANT, *Exit 69, Bluff City*

Only true barbecue buffs will want to detour this far from the Interstate for a meal, but nobody who takes "Q" seriously will dare *not* to drive the 11 miles of back roads that lead, eventually, to the Ridgewood Restaurant.

Because of the distance (normally well outside the limits of this book) we'll try to resist using too much space to extol the wonders of the barbecue, to ponder the deep, hidden mysteries

of the sauce (secret recipe, of course), or to list the famous gour-
mets and gourmands who have endorsed the Ridgewood as their
number-one choice. Suffice it to say that Jane and Michael Stern,
in their guide to regional American cuisine, *Goodfood*, write, "We
have found perfection, and its name is the Ridgewood Restaurant."

A few months after that book came out, the Ridgewood's
owner, Mrs. Grace Proffit, appeared with the Sterns on ABC's
"Good Morning, America." All of Bluff City's residents gathered
in the restaurant to watch their barbecue hero on TV and then
went back to eating the same pit-smoked ham barbecue they've
been putting away since 1948.

Whether it reaches your table in an oversized hamburger bun
($2.65) or piled on a dinner plate ($6.75), the Ridgefield's barbecue will be bathed in a beguiling ketchup-based sauce. It is a
sauce that works its way slowly to your taste buds (and your
heart), with increasing vigor at each bite, gathering into a storm
of flavor, a mighty crescendo in a barbecue symphony. But we
promised not to get carried away, so we'd better stop here.

HOURS   Tues.–Thurs. 11:30 am–7:30 pm; Fri.–Sat. 11:30 am–2:45
pm and 4:30–8:30 pm; Sun. 11:30 am–2:45 pm and 4:30–7:30 pm.

SPECS   Highway 19E (between Bluff City and Elizabethton); (615)
538-7543; no cards; no liquor.

DIRECTIONS   From Exit 69, turn right if northbound, left if southbound. You'll be on Route 37 South toward Blountville. In just under a
mile, turn left at the light (still Route 37 South) and at the next light turn
right toward Bluff City. In 4 miles, cross under Routes 11E/19 (a large
underpass); keep going straight for another 4 miles. Bear left onto Route
19E South toward Elizabethton, and in 1.8 miles it's on the right.

Virginia

DING'S, *Exits 1 & 2, Bristol*

Ding's is a favorite with local newspaper reporters and business people who arrive considerably better dressed than the decor of this unarguably funky eatery requires. We came in at the tail end of the lunch hour and found most of the tables covered with dirty dishes. Asked if it was the dishwasher's day off, Mr. Ding explained that he was cook, waiter, and bottle scrubber. To handle the lunchtime rush, he just waits for things to die down before clearing the tables.

Fair enough. We slipped into one of the booths covered with old-style textured vinyl and looked up at the lunch menu hanging over the cash register. Pepper steak, sweet and sour pork or fish, egg foo young—that sort of thing. OK, so it wasn't Szechuan or Hunan cuisine; the price tag wasn't trendy either: $2.10, including fried rice and tea. Wonton soup was 50 cents extra.

With Ding's full-flavored broth we were off to a propitious start, and then an immense plate of sweet and sour pork kept our spirits up. Perhaps it was a little heavy in the breading department, but the flavors were clear and fresh, and the meat tender.

Mr. Ding regrets the emphasis on Chinese-American dishes rather than authentic Chinese. It's not that he can't cook the genuine article (which he did in New York's Chinatown before moving south ten years ago), but that he can't get local people to eat it. He tries to tempt them, appealing to their gaming instincts with his "House Special Dinner," described only as "a unique surprise," but few take up the offer. He does consider it progress, however, that more and more people are willing to try loquat litchi duck—especially considering that, at $4.60, it's practically the most expensive thing on his menu.

HOURS Mon.–Sat. 11 am–9 pm; closed Sun. Closed for 7–10 days at Christmas time and for one other week in summer.

SPECS 11 Seventh St.; (615) 968-9512; no cards; no liquor.

DIRECTIONS See **Trainstation Marketplace,** next page.

TRAINSTATION MARKETPLACE, *Exits 1 & 2, Bristol*

You know that the idea of pavilion dining, or "eating malls," as they've been called, has caught on when you no longer have to go to Boston or Baltimore to find it. Here in Bristol, Virginia, is an up-to-date collection of restaurants and snackeries under one roof. As befits the modest community, the Trainstation Marketplace is small compared with Quincy Market or Harborplace, but still it offers the traveler an opportunity to limber up stiff legs while perusing the many possibilities for a meal. Here's an overview:

Pepe's Little Italy serves pizza, subs, lasagna, and the like, fast-food style. At the **Alamo** the cuisine is Mexican, natch, with courtyard dining (indoor) next to potted cacti. **Hot Diggity Dog** has half a dozen variations on the frankfurter, while at **Katharine's Funnel Cake and Juicery** you can watch the proprietress pour batter through a funnel into hot fat to make her crisp Pennsylvania Dutch specialty. **Green's Country Cooking** is an all-you-can-eat buffet with traditional American and southern dishes ($3.50 lunch, $4.50 dinner, children less). No matter where you decide to eat, you might want to conclude your meal with a visit to **Sweets 'n' Stuff,** where sugar-free/salt-free candies are the featured items. They make nice traveling companions, especially because there's no guilt attached.

Actually, we found the most irresistible vendor in the place to be a herbalist named Jim Gray, or, as he prefers, "Catfish Man of the Woods." On the Saturday that we were there, Catfish was set up on a portable cart in the middle of the action. A large handmade sign listed 20 herbs that give his "Special Tonic" its curative powers over at least that many ailments—from blood clots and bad eyesight to "weak sex" and "legs going to come off." If your back aches from all the driving, it's sure to help that, too.

HOURS   Vary according to the vendor; most open around 11 am and close at 8:30 or 9 pm during the week, 9 or 10 pm on Friday and Saturday, and midafternoon on Sunday.

DIRECTIONS   Note: Exit 2 gives the best access to both **Ding's** and the **Trainstation Marketplace,** but at this writing there is no Exit 2 for northbound I-81 traffic. It is under construction, but until open, northbound travelers will have to use Exit 1, as described below.

Northbound: From Exit 1, follow signs for Bristol. In about 1 mile bear onto State St. (big sign) and in about 1½ miles you'll reach the light at Seventh St. For **Ding's,** turn right on Seventh and in one block you'll find it on your left. For the **Marketplace,** don't turn at Seventh but continue straight on State for approximately ¼ mile and you'll see it on your left. Turn left in front of the **Marketplace** for access to parking. Unfortunately the whole drive can take as much as 15 minutes because of the exit situation.

Southbound: From Exit 2 (a left exit), it's exactly 2½ fast-moving miles to the light at State St. (no sign that we could see, but Chevron and First American Bank on the corner). Turn left. It's only 0.1 mile to the light at Seventh St. For **Ding's,** turn right on Seventh and in one block you'll find it on your left. For the **Marketplace,** don't turn at Seventh but continue straight on State for approximately ¼ mile and you'll see it on your left. Turn left in front of the **Marketplace** for access to parking.

MARIMACK INN, *Exit 9, Abingdon*

Marilyn and Mack Murphy have been aficionados of country inns for many years, but they never dreamed that when they opened their own in 1983 it would become an overnight sensation. That happened because they let their son, Matt, in on the act.

During the school year, Matt is a voice major at the Juilliard

School in New York. Heading home to work at the inn after his (and the inn's) freshman year, he decided to bring a few classmates along. They came to wait on tables, but as they served their customers they found it difficult to silence their sonorous voices. Thus was born the idea of singing waiters and waitresses at the Marimack Inn.

As you can imagine, the performance these conservatory students put on is no schlock routine. Working in male/female pairs, they serenade their guests with everything from Broadway show tunes and Gilbert and Sullivan to Schubert *lieder* and *Madame Butterfly*. And on Saturday nights, after dinner, they move into a parlor that's been set up as a miniature auditorium, where they present a variety show. There's no cost to the guests for any of the entertainment, but the waiters say their tips have been enormous.

Unfortunately, we did not get to witness the spectacle because it takes place only when the students are on vacation, and we came by in midwinter. However, we did get to taste Marilyn's cooking, available year round, and we can say that it alone would be worth going out of the way for. (Happily that isn't even necessary, as the restaurant is less than a mile from the Interstate exit.)

For instance, the bouillabaisse. Thick, absolutely thick, with clams, crabs, lobster, catfish, and huge chunks of shrimp, and sparked with bits of bacon, it would hold its own against any, anywhere. We heard another charmed customer say to the waitress, "If I had been at home, I would have licked the bowl." That bowl was served at lunchtime with three types of homemade bread (in case three isn't enough, raisin muffins as well) and an excellent salad that boasted several types of leaf lettuce, fresh broccoli, and a subtly sweet vinegar dressing. Coffee was included in the embarrassingly low $3.25 price tag.

There are also sandwiches and salads; clam chowder and peanut soup; dinner entrées like roast quail, lobster Charleston, veal Alfredo, and Smithfield ham ($5.95–$11.95); and fresh-out-of-the-oven desserts. We tried a marvelous coconut cream pie and heard great reviews of the tipsy pudding.

Lest you think there's got to be a "but" somewhere in our description, we'll close by mentioning that the Marimack's fine food is served in the warm, antique-furnished (but by no means precious) atmosphere of a stately 1812 mansion. Food, decor, entertainment, prices, proximity to the highway—the Marimack has it all.

HOURS   Tues.–Sat. 11:30 am–2 pm and 5:30–10 pm; Sun. noon–8 pm; closed Mon.

SPECS   Route 8; (703) 628-5690; major cards; beer, wine, and cocktails made with port.

DIRECTIONS   From Exit 9, turn left if northbound, right if southbound. In ¾ mile you'll see it on your right.

TALLENT HOUSE, *Exit 16, Marion*

Once called the Beacon, this was a landmark Marion restaurant for as long as anyone can remember, but it's recently been taken over by Warren and Joanne Tallent, who are doing their best to keep the downtown crowd of workers and shoppers fed in the style to which they are accustomed—which is to say, without a great deal of style. Therefore, they are trying to expand Marion's culinary consciousness. So far they've had one success and one failure.

The success is the "Superspud," a large sour-cream-topped baked potato stuffed with ham, green pepper, and onion; it comes with a salad for just $2.25 (at lunch or dinner). Marion was apparently ripe to join the nation in rediscovering the potato, and Superspuds have been a hit. But sesame chicken is another story. Despite the popularity elsewhere of almost anything resembling Chinese cuisine, customers were not willing to wait the 30 minutes required to prepare this dish. The restaurant owners, laudably unwilling to resort to a steam table, dropped it from the menu with regrets.

In addition to the Superspud, we found such lunch items as grilled cheese sandwich with homemade vegetable soup ($1.75), spinach or chef's salad ($2.25), rib-eye steak sandwich with fries ($2.25), and all-you-can-eat pinto beans and corn bread ($1.25). Two favorite dinners are pepper steak ($4.50 with salad bar) and flounder stuffed with crabmeat ($5.95). Breakfasts are the usual

and very low-priced—the "Let's Get Acquainted Special" consisted of one egg, biscuits with gravy, sausage, and unlimited
coffee for 79 cents. In all probability the acquaintance will have
been made and the bargain price raised before you arrive.

It's a spotless, neat and appealing, nothing-special sort of
place, a little on the plastic side. Perhaps the Tallents will find a
few more *au courant* dishes that aren't too exotic for Marion, but
we suspect you'll find things pretty much as we did—simple but
satisfying.

HOURS   Mon.–Fri. 6 am–9 pm; Sat. 7 am–9 pm; Sun. 8 am–2 pm.

SPECS   230 E. Main St.; (703) 783-2100; no cards (yet); no liquor.

DIRECTIONS   From Exit 16, turn left if northbound, right if southbound. Go about ¾ mile to the T (second stop light); it's on the corner,
on left.

THE LOG HOUSE RESTAURANT, *Exit 21, Wytheville*

The previous owners of this building knew it was as old as
the nation to the year, but it wasn't until the Bicentennial, after
stripping off layer upon layer of old plaster, that they discovered
it was actually a log house. Thus, when Virginia Slotter purchased the building a few years later and converted it into a
restaurant, a name immediately suggested itself.

She's done a wonderful job of maintaining the spirit of a
genuinely old place without resorting to *ye olde* decor or
gingham-clad waitresses. The hand-hewn log walls are now
clean and exposed, as is the wide-plank floor. Virginia has added
a tasteful selection of wallpaper, curtains, calico place mats, and
a crackling fire in the fireplace. For such genteel surroundings,
she has kept prices surprisingly low.

At lunchtime, for instance, you can have a smoked-turkey
sandwich on a kaiser roll for $2.20; other sandwiches are less
than $1.50, and a hamburger with blue cheese is $2.60 (shoe-
string potatoes on the side with all of these). We came for dinner
and had a mixed reaction to the stuffed pork tenderloin—the
meat was juicy and tender, but the "Log House dressing," a

bread and apple stuffing, was overwhelmingly bready, rather a disappointment. The parsley potatoes, on the other hand, were quite good. A homemade apple dumpling in cinnamon sauce was so-so.

Dinners at the Log House run $4.25 to $7.50. If ours was any indication, it might be a better bet to come at lunch, when the stakes are lower but the atmosphere the same charming blend of rustic and refined.

HOURS   Lunch: 11 am–5 pm, Mon.–Sat. Dinner: 5–9 pm (till 10 in winter), Mon.–Sat. Closed Sun.

SPECS   520 E. Main St.; (703) 228-5488; no cards; no liquor.

DIRECTIONS   **Northbound:** From Exit 21, turn right, go 1 mile to light at Main St. (Route 11 North). Turn left on Main and go 0.4 mile; it's on your left.

Southbound: There's no exit number; sign says "Wytheville/Route 11 South" (first Wytheville exit). This puts you on Main St. You'll find the restaurant on your right, about 1½ miles from the highway.

VALLEY PIKE INN, *Exit 32, Newbern*

It's not much of a town now, just a crossroads cluster of homes and farms, but until 1893 tiny Newbern was the thriving

seat of Pulaski County. Back then Main Street was called the
Valley Pike, a toll road between Roanoke and the Cumberland
Gap. One of the prominent buildings in town was the porticoed
Haney Hotel, a stagecoach stop that had lodged Andrew Jackson
on more than one occasion. But when the railroad came through,
Newbern somehow got skipped, ending the town's reign as the
New River Valley's wayside stopover. Until Richard Mady came
along in 1977.

That was when the antique shop owner bought the neglected
Haney Hotel and decided to restore it as a restaurant. Tickled at
the idea that their town might be rediscovered, neighbors fre-
quently visited Mady as he toiled all alone; occasionally they lent
a hand, but more often they merely inquired about his progress.
"Oh, I'll be opening the first," he liked to say. "The first chance
I get!" After six years behind the hammer, he went out of the
construction business and into the restaurant business.

When they poured in to share their first meal with Mady and
his wife, Woody June, Newbern residents found a single timber-
framed room built of recycled materials painstakingly chosen for
their authenticity. Unlike so many restored country inns, this one
has no pretenses of gentility: posts, beams, walls, floor, and ceiling are all bare wood, a little stark but comfortable just the same.
It's the kind of place where no one would flinch if you came
tromping through with mud on your boots. Which probably
makes it more authentic than most.

The food and service are modeled after the Homeplace in
Catawba (page 183), and although the Valley Pike Inn hasn't yet
met that restaurant's lofty standard of southern cuisine, we are
willing to predict that it's on its way. As at the Homeplace,
there's no menu; everyone gets fried chicken and a choice of roast
beef or ham; the meats come to the table, along with numerous
vegetables, relishes, and salads, in large platters and family-sized
bowls. The cost is $6.50 per person, half that for kids.

Our notes on the various dishes range from "slightly dry"
(chicken) to "superb" (pepper relish, which, as our waitress explained, gets mixed with the brown beans to create a spritely
taste that was new to us). Also at the high end of the spectrum
was a notation that the blueberry cobbler was "delish" and the
biscuits "remarkably tender"; unfortunately the green beans
were rated as "overcooked" (the rule, we found, for restaurants

in these parts). But nit-picking is inappropriate; the Valley Pike Inn wasn't meant to be fancy. Expect down-home southern cooking prepared with love, and a clientele that is honored to receive it.

HOURS   Thurs.–Sat. 4:30–9 pm; Sun. 11:30 am–6 pm.

SPECS   Main St.; (703) 674-1810; major cards; no liquor.

DIRECTIONS   From Exit 32, turn left if southbound, right if northbound. In about ¾ mile turn left onto Route 611 (sign for Newbern). It's about 1 mile down this road, on the right, in the center of tiny Newbern.

CANTON RESTAURANT, *Exit 35, Radford*

The consensus is clear among restaurant-goers in this part of Virginia: Canton Restaurant has the "worst atmosphere" but the "best food" within miles.

We came in shielding our eyes but were relieved to find that it wasn't all that bad. The paneling, Formica tables, and cafeteria-style chairs are nondescript, to be sure, but unusual light fixtures made from the puffed-up bodies of dried sunfish gave us something to look at.

If the negative description of decor was exaggerated, the positive estimation of Canton's cuisine was not. Here was a restaurant that truly defied our theory that Chinese restaurants worth their soy sauce must be located within shopping distance of a Chinatown.

We'd heard about the Canton's chicken Kew; it's not on the menu, our informant had said, but if you ask for it you'll get it, and you'll be glad you did. Needless to say (after all this buildup), we did and we were. The dish had tender pieces of chicken breast lightly breaded and stir-fried with crisp fresh snow peas, bok choy, broccoli, and black mushrooms; what it lacked was that heavy MSG taste so often associated with mediocre Chinese restaurants.

Chicken Kew isn't the only unannounced star in the Canton's lineup. Although you won't find Szechuan dishes on the menu, owner Chi Chung (Simon) Kwong will be delighted to meet your request. He's from Canton (hence the restaurant's name and menu), but he became versed in Szechuan, Huan, and other cuisines while working his way through Chinatowns in New York, Boston, San Francisco, and Miami.

Not only will Simon accommodate your requests for off-menu dishes, he'll make them up in half-portions at half-price, if you so desire. (Given the size of his full portions, that might be advisable.) If you pay full fare, dinner will run you $4.25 to $6.50; lunch specials start at $1.75, and soups go for 60 cents a bowl. The Canton is worlds beyond the usual small-town Chinese restaurant, but fortunately for the traveler, it still has small-town prices.

HOURS   Tues.–Thurs. 11:30 am–2 pm and 4–10 pm; Fri. 11:30 am–2 pm and 4–11 pm; Sat. noon–11 pm; Sun. noon–9 pm; closed Mon.

SPECS   601 Norwood St.; (703) 639-2345; no cards; full license.

DIRECTIONS   See **BT's,** below.

BT's, *Exit 35, Radford*

Surprised as we were to find the Canton restaurant, we were equally astonished to come upon BT's. The decor here is at the other end of the spectrum, smart-looking and urbane, not what we expected to find in far-southwestern Virginia. With shiny "bent-brass" chairs at the prominent bar, polished hardwood floors, a sporty dining balcony, and waitresses scurrying about in designer T-shirts, we might well have pictured ourselves in

California or New York or, at the closest, the suburbs of Washington, D.C.

The menu is true to type. You'll find thick sandwiches, both meat-filled and vegetarian, some of them in pita pockets, and each with its own cute sobriquet. There are fancy burgers, deep-fried vegetables, nachos, chili, entrée salads, and cheesecake for dessert. Somehow they missed carrot cake, but we're willing to bet a fried potato skin that it'll be available when you arrive!

Although we can't resist poking a little fun at restaurants of this type (we ordinarily call them "bricks-plants-and-oak cafés"), we do find them to be a blessing for travelers in search of light food, low prices, and a pleasant environment in which to eat. And it wouldn't be fair, would it, to describe as "trendy" or "clichéd" a restaurant that offers much needed variety in a part of the country that's drowning in fried chicken and country ham? Especially when the prices are almost all below $3.50, and everything we had there, from homemade cream of tomato soup to Big Lick-brand ice cream, was very good.

So, BT's, lift up your Perrier-and-lime and let's toast to many more years of fried zucchini and pita sandwiches. And please do something about that carrot cake, would you?

HOURS   Sun.–Thurs. 11 am–1 am; Fri. & Sat. 11 am–2 am.

SPECS   218 Tyler Ave.; (703) 639-1282; major cards; full license.

DIRECTIONS   From Exit 25, turn left if northbound, right if southbound and drive 4 fast miles. **BT's** is on the left, directly across from Radford University (immediately after the 7-Eleven store). For **Canton Restaurant,** continue past **BT's** another 0.1 mile until the road ends at a light. Turn right (Norwood St.) and go ½ mile; it's on the right.

THE HOMEPLACE, *Exit 41, Catawba*

To reach the Homeplace you'll have to drive 7 winding miles across the Blue Ridge Mountains, a detour well worth the trouble.

From the Homeplace dining room, pastoral scenes are readily apparent through well-proportioned glass windows, but the inside view of this beautifully restored 1903 house is every bit as lovely. Oak wainscoting, hardwood floors, tasteful wallpaper, mustard-colored tablecloths, and occasional antiques give the restaurant a warm, homey feeling without making the diner feel as if he's in a museum. And on two Saturday nights each month, a local string band, appropriately named the Homefolks, adds its tones.

So much for looks (and sounds). How does it taste? For our money (just $6 of it, per person), the traditional southern cooking you'll find at the Homeplace is as good as you'll find anywhere. There's no menu; the only decision you'll have to make is for a beverage. You're also supposed to choose between roast beef and country ham, but if you can't make up your mind, they'll bring both, along with pan-fried chicken, mashed potatoes, pinto beans, green beans, stewed tomatoes, candied sweet potatoes, creamed corn, cole slaw, homemade biscuits, strawberry preserves, pepper-and-onion relish, and cobbler for dessert.

The only discernible shortcoming of this magnificent feast lay in the canned vegetables. Our experience with southern restaurants has taught us, however, that this is a state of affairs as traditional as gravy on biscuits. Speaking of which, the Homeplace served two entirely different gravies, one for chicken and one for beef; either could have turned the dullest plate of meat into a regal platter. As a matter of fact, chef Paul Horton says the pursuit of his gravy recipes is what keeps the customers knocking on his kitchen door.

HOURS   Thurs.–Sat. 4:30–8 pm; Sun. 11:30–6 pm. No reservations are taken and there is usually a wait on Saturday evening and Sunday, but a new dining room should alleviate the problem.

SPECS   Route 311; (703) 384-7252; major cards; no liquor.

DIRECTIONS   **Northbound:** From Exit 41, turn right and in about ½ mile turn right again onto Route 311 North. ■ Drive about 6½ miles on winding Route 311 as it crosses Catawba Mountain. You'll doubt you're on the right road, but when you reach the Catawba Mercantile Company you're almost there. Keep going; it's just beyond the Mercantile, in the big white house on your left.

Southbound: From Exit 41, turn left and in 0.4 mile, turn right onto Route 311 North. Then, as above from ■.

ROANOKE CITY MARKET PLACE, *Exit 42, Roanoke*

In Roanoke, as elsewhere, the rush is on to revitalize the downtown area, and that's usually good news for hungry travelers. The City Market, several reborn blocks that were once the focus of city commerce, is again burgeoning with produce stands, street vendors, craft and gift shops, and, most of all, restaurants.

With terrazzo floor, bentwood chairs, and a raw bar, **Shucker's Seafood House** is the kind of venerable downtown institution found in nearly every coastal city, and we were glad to find a good one this far inland. The **Market Place Oyster Bar** is a newer arrival, also serving seafood but quiche and salads too, in a woody atmosphere full of plants. **Billy's Ritz** is a steak and seafood house with saloon atmosphere in a landmark building; it's the only Market Place restaurant open Sundays.

If you're more interested in snacking than serious dining, you might start modestly with **Mc's Biscuits,** a tiny luncheonette claiming to have the "best biscuits in town." Mc's biscuits were indeed good, but the slice of dried-out ham we got with one was hardly superlative. If bagels are more your style, try the **Dough Company,** which proudly calls itself Roanoke's only New York-style bagel shop. The emphasis should be on the "style"—sorry, they weren't the genuine article, although a cheese Danish was much closer to the truth.

The **Beef Pitt** has roast beef sandwiches and other fleshy things, and the **Roanoke Wiener Stand** is self-explanatory. At the **B. R. Guest Deli Restaurant,** specials like turkey breast hoagies or tuna salad plates are the daily fare.

What we've described will probably be only half the picture by the time you pull into town. At the center of all the activity we found the City Market Building being gutted and retrofitted with—you guessed it—more shops, stands, and trendy restaurants.

DIRECTIONS Exit 42 puts you on I-581. Go 5½ freeway miles to Exit 5 (Downtown). From the ramp, go straight, following signs for Route 11 South. In 0.2 mile you'll go over a bridge; on the bridge, Route 11 bears off to the right. Don't follow it, but go straight until immediately after the bridge when you should turn right on Salem. In one block the marketplace begins on your left, covering about four blocks. There are many parking lots if you can't find metered street parking.

Note: If you miss Salem as you come off the aforementioned bridge, don't fret. Keep going and turn right on Church; you'll be on the other side of the market (i.e., it will begin to your right).

BUDDY BURGER, *Exits 50 & 50S, Natural Bridge*

Virginia's Natural Bridge is among the seven natural wonders of the world—one of those places you learned about in elementary school but didn't actually think you'd visit. Well, you'll never be any closer, so this is your chance to add a natural wonder to your life list. Of course, your elementary-school teacher never told you that it costs $3.50 to view the bridge. Nor did she tell you about the Natural Bridge Caverns, the Natural Bridge Zoo, the Natural Bridge Wax Museum, or the rest of the tourist pollution that has been dumped in the shadow of this wonder.

That's all right. Your teacher certainly didn't tell you about Buddy Burger either, and, according to one informant, Buddy's chocolate milkshakes aren't merely one of seven wonders, but "the world's best"!

It was therefore one of the sadder moments of our trip when we learned that we would not get to verify her claim. The machine had broken down the night before, while we, alas, were dawdling in Roanoke. We asked what arcane secrets might be employed when the milkshake machine is working but received no satisfaction. The boss (Buddy) wasn't in and the counter attendant didn't seem to know. In fact she thought—though she wasn't sure—that he used a milkshake mix. Oh, heresy!

Since we could not arrange to revisit with the machine on-line, we'll have to leave the mystery for our chocophilic readers to solve.

We can't rate the milkshake, but we can tell you what else we found in this converted Sunoco station right by the exit ramp. There were cream puffs, doughnuts, brownies, fruit pies, and eclairs, all homemade and all quite decent, even if not "the world's best." (We were in the mood for sweets, having suffered so from unrequited milkshake lust.) There was a homemade vegetable soup (overly peppery, but a nice try), as well as beef stew, chili, and hamburgers. If (and only if) you request it, you can get your burger on a yeast roll—quite an improvement over the typical balloon bun. And there are the usual breakfast items, which means eggs, grits, and biscuits and gravy. That's about it. Nothing fancy, nothing especially remarkable, everything fairly reasonable (though a little more expensive than it would have been off the tourist path).

Too bad about that milkshake.

HOURS   Winter: 7 am–7 pm, every day. Summer: 7 am–2 or 3 am, sometimes even later, every day.

SPECS   Highway 11; (703) 291-2222; no cards; no liquor.

DIRECTIONS   Northbound: From Exit 50, turn right and you're there.

Southbound: Exit 50S, a left exit, puts you on Route 11 South; in ¼ mile, it's on your right.

THE PALM PARLOR, *Exit 51, Lexington*

We have long been aware that one effective way of finding good restaurants is to seek educated palates. Head for the nearest university, and in the shadow of academe you're likely to find everything from hamburgers to haute cuisine. With two institutions of higher education in Lexington, we figured we'd doubled our chances. We stopped searching when we found the Palm Parlor, for here were both hamburgers and cuisine that was as haute as any we'd come across in many a mile.

Enough of fried chicken and country ham, grits, and biscuits with gravy! What a pleasure it was to see and smell a wonderfully herby, fresh mushroom soup ($1.50), followed by a large plate of green and white fettuccine sauced with heavy cream, butter, garlic, parsley, Parmesan, mushrooms, and artichokes. Fond as we'd become of the traditional southern standbys, we reveled in the sensuous textures and near-forgotten flavors of such a dish. It cost $8, and came with a leaf-lettuce salad and good French bread. True, the prices were higher than what we had come to expect in the South, but then again the flavors were unexpected too.

While fettuccine has become the Palm Parlor's trademark, the rest of the menu is what we might call northeastern trendy—dressed-up hamburgers; quiche; Reubens, Monte Cristos and other sandwiches; omelettes; meal-sized salads. "Potato Kurls" —whole potatoes curled off a cutting machine and fried—is the favorite appetizer, but at $2.95 it seemed rather a high-profit item. They come at no extra charge with hamburgers costing $2.99 to $3.49, thereby making the burgers themselves seem almost free!

The Palm Parlor's decor fits its *au courant* menu: natural wood with green accents, ceiling fans, café curtains, pressed tin ceiling, a wrought-iron room divider, lots of plants. Attractive as it is indoors, the bistro patio is the most popular place for fair-weather dining.

When we visited, lunch and dinner menus were about to be combined into a single bill of fare and no one was quite sure about future prices, but it seemed likely that they would shake down in the $3 to $5 range at midday, $6 to $10 in the evening. A reasonably priced sandwich menu will be available between lunch and dinner, and from 9 pm until closing.

HOURS Lunch: 11 am–2 pm, every day. Dinner: 5–10 pm, every day. Sandwiches available between lunch and dinner, and until midnight (or later).

SPECS   101 W. Nelson St.; (703) 463-7911; major cards; full license.

DIRECTIONS   Use Exit 51, taking the ramp for Route 60 West. Follow 60 West for about 2½ miles. The third light in the business district is Jefferson Street, and the **Palm Parlor** is on the corner, on your right.

ROWE'S FAMILY RESTAURANT, *Exit 57, Staunton*

The quality of food served inside this wood-frame roadhouse belies its pedestrian exterior, its none-too-intriguing name, its "Lion's Club Meets Here" sign, and its oft-touted motto, "Home Cooking." Rowe's is the epitome of family restaurants, the exaltation of home cooking to an art form. If we really had to limit ourselves to one kind of restaurant, we'd probably choose those that are utterly without pretension but absolutely pleasant throughout; where family recipes have been honed to perfection over many years; where prices are low but quality consistently high; where we could be equally comfortable bringing our dates, our children, or our grandmothers. In other words, Rowe's.

It doesn't matter what you order. As far as we can tell, just about everything's a winner. At breakfast the thick, brown, rich-tasting sausage gravy and fluffy buttermilk biscuits elevate this humble dish to majestic heights. And the homemade cinnamon buns will have you licking your fingers long after your plate is empty. Then, for lunch (or dinner) you can order Mrs. Rowe's pan-fried chicken. If you think you know from fried chicken, try hers. And with it, homemade cole slaw that has real personality,

189

and some of the best french fries—real french fries, hand-cut, the kind you *know* were once potatoes, and not all that long ago. Unfortunately an overly salty bean soup spoiled this lineup of excellence, but we're willing to allow one error in an otherwise perfect game.

Daily lunch specials—solid American grub—range in price from $1.50 to $3.95; dinners of the same ilk are only $2.50 to $4.95.

As good as her entrées are, it is in the dessert course that Mrs. Rowe really struts her stuff. Care for some strawberry pie? If the strawberries aren't fresh, you won't get any. "Doubtless God could have made a better berry, but doubtless God never did," said William Butler of the strawberry, as might also be said of the strawberry pies served here. Even more delectable are Mrs. Rowe's mincemeat pies, served under a drizzle of hot rum sauce. We have our doubts that even God could have made a better pie.

HOURS   Mon.–Sat. 6:30 am–9 pm; closed Sundays and the week of July 4.

SPECS   Route 250; (703) 886-1833; major cards; beer and wine.

DIRECTIONS   From Exit 57, turn left and you'll shortly see it on your right. Half a minute.

THE PAMPERED PALATE, *Exit 57, Staunton*

Should it happen that your palate wishes to be pampered by some flavors more exotic than those offered at Rowe's, Staunton can provide them too. Located in Staunton's oldest commercial building, the Pampered Palate is a tidy little deli-wine-gourmet shop on two levels—six ice cream tables that sport roses in Perrier bottles on the ground floor and a slightly plusher area upstairs. Imported cheeses, New York deli meats, and unusual salads are the trademark items, along with quiche, stuffed potatoes, excellent cream soups, and bagels spread in ways both traditional (cream cheese and lox) and arcane (date-nut-rum cheese).

For sandwiches, there are all the deli standbys (pastrami, corned beef, turkey, etc., $1.75–$2.25) and the nouveau bread stuffers (Reuben variations, roast beef and brie, veggie pita, and the like, $1.79–$3.45). Our chicken salad on bagel was excellent, and we were equally enchanted by artichoke-heart salad on a French roll. If the creative urge strikes, proprietress Karen van Kirk will be happy to accommodate. One regular customer comes in every day for his own invention, a bagel sub: the filling of cream cheese, olives, ham, turkey, salami, Jarlsberg cheese, lettuce and tomato filling measures about 3 inches from crust to crust.

HOURS Mon.–Thurs. 9 am–5:30 pm; Fri. 9 am–8 pm or later; Sat. 9 am–6 pm; Sun. 10 am–4 pm. (Sunday hours were experimental; may be restricted to summers only.) Closed major holidays.

SPECS 26 E. Beverly St.; (703) 886-9469; MC/V; beer and wine.

DIRECTIONS From Exit 57, turn right onto Route 250 West. In about 2 miles, bear right to stay on 250 West as it takes you beneath an overpass. Then immediately turn left toward the business district. In 0.2 mile, turn right at South New St. (second light). Park in the lot and walk up South New St. to the corner (Beverly), turn left, and it's three doors down on the left. It may sound confusing, but it won't be. Five minutes.

THOMAS HOUSE RESTAURANT AND HOME BAKERY, *Exit 62, Dayton*

Whether Mrs. Thomas is the world's greatest cook or merely the world's greatest character is a question that can stir fiery passions between those who have professed unwavering loyalty to her over the past 42 years and those who recognize her as a regional treasure but one with limitations.

Although universally referred to as "Mrs. Thomas's," the restaurant's official name is appropriate, as it occupies two sunny rooms of the owner's house. Her baking is now limited to what bread and pies are needed in the restaurant, but back in the '40s her kitchen produced the only whole-wheat bread commercially available in the Shenandoah Valley ("Even before Pepperidge Farm," she says, with yeasty pride).

Not only is the restaurant located in a house, it *feels* about as homey as restaurants come. You walk up to the open kitchen and announce your selection, chosen off a homemade sign: fried chicken, ham pot pie, barbecue, meat loaf, that sort of thing. You get to pick vegetables too, and bread (whole wheat or white "with no preservatives and that's a promise"). Hand your plate to one of the counter ladies, who takes it over to the oven and unceremoniously piles it with food. Ask for some pear marmalade, and she'll poke through a refrigerator for the mason jar; if it's not to be found, she'll send you out to the dining room to search the tables.

That, we discovered, can be as much fun as swapping tales with Mrs. Thomas. The regulars here take the same kind of pleasure welcoming newcomers to their restaurant as they would to their church. Come to think of it, the atmosphere of pink card tables, folding metal chairs, and religious memorabilia isn't all that far from a church supper, and neither is the $2.50 price tag.

Unfortunately the food tended to be too salty. Oh well, you can't always have top quality with your authenticity. But if you're not on a sodium-restricted diet and your appetite is more for local color than cuisine, you're bound to be sated by Mrs. Thomas.

The receipt we got here was our favorite of the entire trip. The top of the faded green slip of paper read, "Phone 4601," and in the space for the date it said, "_____195__."

HOURS   5 am–11 pm, 7 days a week.

SPECS   222 Main St.; (703) 879-2181; no cards; no liquor ("I don't believe in it and I don't serve it").

DIRECTIONS   From Exit 62 (Harrisonburg), turn left onto Route 11 South. In ¾ mile, turn right on Pine Church Rd. (Route 701). Stay on the main road (701) for 1½ miles to a stop sign at a T. Turn left. In 0.6 mile you'll come to a light (a turkey-packing plant will be on both sides of the road). Go straight through the light, crossing Route 42, and immediately turn right into the driveway alongside a chain-link fence. You won't believe you're anywhere near a restaurant, but Mrs. Thomas's is at the end of the drive.

JESS' QUICK LUNCH, *Exit 64W, Harrisonburg*

It's about a mile and a half through Fast Food Alley to get from the Interstate to Harrisonburg, a neatly groomed little town built around a picturesque square. Lest you even consider stopping before you reach the downtown area, let us quickly tell you that at Jess' Quick Lunch you can get fast food with personality, flavor, and authority (not to mention made-to-order freshness). This is fast food that has pleased Harrisonburgers every day for the past 25 years.

Located right on Courthouse Square, where it rubs shoulders with clothiers, banks, and department stores, Jess' is the kind of downtown institution that in most towns has succumbed to competition from nationwide chains. Perhaps it's the diversity of clientele that has kept Jess' going strong: on any given day, adjacent stools at the mile-long yellow counter are likely to sport a bank president, a wino, a judge, and a college student or professor.

The ambient background sound is the Greek chatter of the countermen, punctuated by waitresses calling out their orders. "Two just chili," comes the cry, and with great dignity (and speed) a white-aproned grillman scoops chili atop one of Jess's locally loved hot dogs. More popular than "just chili" is "one everything," meaning mustard and onions as well. Although these chili dogs, in any of their variations, were perfection within their genus, we were even more delighted by the gigantic hamburgers. Slapped into patties before our eyes, they were grilled until slightly seared on the outside but juicy and plump, then topped with thick slices of rotund tomatoes and onions that could have been plucked right out of a seed catalog. At $1.15, these are burgers to make the fast-food moguls cry in shame.

There are a few other sandwiches like sausage, b.l.t., or ham and cheese, and in the morning there are egg breakfasts (sorry, no McMuffins), but that's about it. Mostly it's chili dogs and hamburgers which, given their quality, are quite enough.

HOURS   8 am–midnight, every day of the year.

SPECS   22 S. Main St.; (703) 434-8282; no cards; beer only.

DIRECTIONS   See **Heritage Family Restaurant,** next page.

HERITAGE FAMILY RESTAURANT,
Exit 64W, Harrisonburg

Yes, Virginia, there are Mennonites in Virginia. We thought we'd somehow stumbled into Pennsylvania when we passed a horse-drawn buggy clip-clopping its way into town but soon learned that Harrisonburg, *Virginia,* is the home of Eastern Mennonite College and a thriving Mennonite community. Instantly we began to think about shoofly pie and scrapple and potato filling. (Clearly our minds rarely wander far from our stomachs.)

It didn't take us long to learn about the Heritage Restaurant. We were a trifle disappointed not to find schnitz und knepp or rivel soup, but the old Pennsylvania Dutch standby, ponhaus (cornmeal-rich scrapple) appeared as "pan hoss," and the homemade sausage was as good as any to be found in Lancaster County. Although Pennsylvania Dutch specialties could be found, the restaurant's menu, decor, and smiling waitresses led us to classify it as all-American wholesome. Meat loaf, chicken and dumplings, and pork tenderloin, for instance, are the kinds of dinners to expect, running $3.50 to $5.00 (vegetables included, mostly fresh) and served in a spotless plain-Jane atmosphere.

There are a few salads of note, including one tasty combination of ham and cheese with fresh peas and a lively dressing ($2.45). We also enjoyed a cream-of-cauliflower soup dotted with pieces of hard-boiled egg.

Although they put three meals a day on the tables, the Heritage specializes in baked goods—wonderful gooey cinnamon rolls, pies (including shoofly, mincemeat, and butterscotch meringue), cakes, and still-warm, yeasty breads that are sold at a counter by the cash register. It's difficult to leave without a bagful of snacks for the road.

HOURS   Mon.–Sat. 6 am–8 pm; closed Sun.

SPECS   350 Waterman Dr.; (703) 433-3911; no cards; no liquor.

DIRECTIONS   Exit 64W puts you on Route 33 West, which you should take for about 1½ miles until you reach Courthouse Square. Traffic around the square is one-way, and you are forced to turn right at this point. However, **Jess'** is three doors down to the left, so you can park anywhere and walk. For **Heritage Family Restaurant,** take the right turn and then two quick lefts, and you'll be on the other side of the square. Turn right onto W. Market St. and go straight for ¾ mile to Waterman Drive (just past Arco station). Right on Waterman, and it's ½ mile down, on right.

SOUTHERN KITCHEN, *Exit 67, New Market*

Whether or not you appreciate the play of flavors that hide behind the pervasive saltiness of Virginia's fabled country ham, you should not pass through this part of the country without experiencing another regional specialty, peanut soup. Now peanut soup may sound a bit arcane, but it's something that must be tried to be appreciated. We admit you've got to like peanuts to begin with, but even the most avid peanut shucker and fan of p.b. and j. sandwiches could not begin to imagine how creamily delicious and nuttily fragrant is the peanut soup at Southern Kitchen.

If we haven't convinced you by now, we're probably not going to succeed, so we'll put the peanut soup on hold and tell you that this pleasant café serves all the other southern standards in generous portions at reasonable prices. Barbecue short ribs ($3.95 at lunch, $7.95 in great quantity at dinner) are perhaps the most popular, their sauce being farmed out, as it were, to a local lady who keeps the recipe a secret even from the restaurant owners. Virginia ham pot pie is a more typically priced lunch, costing just $2.25 with homemade cole slaw. At dinner, you might go for fried chicken livers ($4.25) or sole Florentine ($4.95). The waitresses, who sport black vests and string ties, exude genuine warmth and—we hate to say it because it's so corny—true southern hospitality.

New Market is a beautifully preserved town bursting with Civil War lore. It's hard not to feel a stir of historical passion as you walk down Main Street and consider the famous-name generals who have preceded you. One of them is commemorated in the center of town by the Stonewall Jackson Bank, the walls of which, in case you were wondering, are made of stone.

HOURS Mon.–Thurs. 6:30 am–10 pm; Fri. & Sat. 6:30 am–11 pm; Sun. 7 am–10 pm. Standing room only Saturday evenings and Sunday afternoons. Closed only Dec. 25 and 26.

SPECS Main St.; (703) 740-3514; MC/V; beer and wine.

DIRECTIONS From Exit 67, turn right if northbound, left if southbound, toward New Market. In about ¼ mile, turn right at the light and go 0.4 mile to the restaurant on your left.

THE SPRING HOUSE, *Exit 72, Woodstock*

If you ever thought that those big blue highway signs for GAS, FOOD, AND LODGING were really meant to help you locate good places to eat, you'll retire that notion to your car's litter bag after you find out what happened in Woodstock, Virginia.

"Fast food is colliding with home cooking at Exit 72," reported the *Washington Post* when that paper learned of the troubles that

Dan and Sue Harshman were having keeping their restaurant's name on the I-81 signs. It seems that a berth on the sign is awarded only to the four closest restaurants that meet certain criteria (open 7 days a week, public telephone, etc.). When the Logo Signing Program went into effect, the Spring House was a qualified candidate. But then Hardee's moved in, right by the exit (of course), and all of a sudden the Spring House was number five, a whole mile and a half away.

"It broke my heart to tell her [Sue Harshman] they'd be bumped," Leon Sheets of the state highway department is reported as saying. But rules are rules and programs are programs, and 3,000-signature petitions can't bring mercy or common sense to the letter of the law.

Of course, the Spring House had to command a fair amount of loyalty in Woodstock for the locals to raise the kind of ruckus that would reach the *Post*. From what we could tell, that loyalty was deserved. It's an up-to-date sort of place done in a barny style, and although there may be a few too many artifacts on the wall, it's actually romantic, with candles and tablecloths, subdued lighting, and a host of genteel touches. A very attractive semi-enclosed patio reminded us of more than one place we'd seen on the West Coast.

The Spring House has one of the more imaginative salad bars we've come across. Not merely a colorful display of pickled beets, chick-peas, and iceberg lettuce, it included a delicious green-pea salad, bread pudding, and what's called "Texas caviar" (black-eye peas, jalapenos, onions in a cream sauce). Although the dinners are largely run-of-the-steak-house fare, the Harshmans' imagination has created a few notables like chicken Virginia (chicken breast broiled atop Virginia ham, with a wine and mushroom sauce, $7.99) and Springhouse steak (teriyaki-marinated filet on skewers, $7.35).

If the better part of a ten-dollar bill is too much to spend, you can opt at any time for a dozen thick sandwiches on homemade bread ($1.50–$3.00), hamburgers, omelettes, pizza; breakfasts that would satisfy a trucker; or, for $3.25, the salad bar alone (plus soup).

Let Hardee's and the rest put their logos out on the highway. We've developed a theory that says the number of signs that a restaurant has is inversely proportional to the quality of its food, *especially* if its signs are visible from the Interstate. With a single modest placard over its front door, the Spring House has just the right number of nameplates to suggest the high quality of food found within.

HOURS   Mon.–Thurs. 7 am–10 pm; Fri. & Sat. 7 am–11 pm; Sun. 7 am–9 pm. Closed major holidays.

SPECS   325 South Main St.; (703) 459–4755; major cards; full license.

DIRECTIONS   From Exit 72, turn right if northbound, left if southbound. Go about ½ mile to the light and turn left. It's about 1 mile down, on the right, just before a laundromat.

WAYSIDE INN, *Exit 77, Middletown*

The Wayside Inn is a staple of country-inn books and every guide to American restaurants from Duncan Hines to AAA. We can hardly claim it as a discovery, but neither can we ignore it: the Wayside's accessibility to I-81 makes it as good a stopover for today's motorist as it was for the stagecoach travelers who took respite here years ago.

The guidebooks give coverage enough to the Wayside's origins in 1797, its role as a hostelry for troops during the Revolution and the Civil War, and its abundant collection of antiques ("an antique lover's paradise," they all seem to say—meaning, perhaps, that it's overdecorated). There's no question that this is a remarkable place, but we were more interested in the food.

Other than the hokey Williamsburg-style outfits worn by the waitresses, we found little to criticize. The kitchen has done a remarkable job of living up to its reputation for excellent regional country fare. While breakfasts and lunches that include quiche, salads, and sandwiches are more cosmopolitan than colonial, the unyielding reliance on homemade products, from breads and jams to salad dressings and desserts, makes them worth stopping for. Besides, at this time of day you can buy a visit to Antique Lover's Paradise for as little as $3.00 ($5.00 tops).

But it's the dinner hour that sees regional delights pouring out of the kitchen, and the first thing you should have poured into your own bowl is the Wayside's peanut soup. If you balk at the thought of creamy, liquefied peanut butter, we can understand, but do give it a try, even if that means splitting a cup between two people. Then move on to spoonbread. Though it will cost an extra $2.50 (two servings), this cross between corn bread and soufflé is not to be missed by aficionados of American cookery. It is served in a steaming casserole and eaten (you guessed it) with a spoon.

As a main course you might choose roast duckling with ginger sauce ($11.25), cornish game hen with a cranberry glaze ($10.75), southern-fried rabbit ($9.95), or a dozen other things from pan-fried chicken and country ham to scallops and Virginia mountain trout. But we couldn't resist the dish that most stirred our 19th-century fantasies, huntsman's pie ($10.95). A pot pie of venison, duck, and rabbit with onions and mushrooms in a port wine sauce, it is made in the genuine southern fashion, with pastry on top. While the tastes were undoubtedly tamer than those that might have permeated a genuine game stew, they were still quite a bit more exuberant than what our 20th-century palates have come to expect of meat.

HOURS Breakfast: 7 am–11:30 am, every day. Lunch: Mon.–Sat. 11:30 am–3 pm. Dinner: Mon.–Sat. 5–9 pm. Sunday dinner: noon–8:30 pm. Light fare available continuously in lounge, 11:30 am–10 pm, every day. Dinner reservations advised, especially during peak hours on weekends, and in summer, October, and December.

SPECS 7783 Main St. (Route 11); (703) 869-1797; major cards; full license.

DIRECTIONS From Exit 77, turn left if northbound, right if southbound. Go about ½ mile until the road ends at a T (Route 11). Turn left and in ¼ mile it's on your right. One minute.

TRIANGLE DINER, *Exit 80W, Winchester*

How nice to find an old friend, the stainless-steel diner, complete with arched ceiling, shiny counter stools, and a wall of curtained windows. While nothing in the decor of this diner makes it an especially compelling candidate for John Baeder's photorealistic paintbrush, it is clean and colorful, an altogether pleasant rest stop, and the bright fluorescent lighting will help perk you up for the miles ahead.

As in the Northeast, diners are diners, which is to say that the food is respectable but no better, the prices are low, and the service is quick and friendly. Most items are homemade and, except at the busiest times, it's possible to have your meal on the table as quickly as you could get around to the drive-up window at McDonald's.

What you'll find is standard diner fare—sandwiches like grilled cheese or roast beef with mashed potatoes and gravy (65 cents–$2.25), hamburgers small and plain or huge and smothered in onions (85 cents–$2.75), egg breakfasts ($1.25, including toast, fries, and coffee), and the like.

No great surprises, and nothing that you'll likely request the recipe for. But a place worth knowing about just the same.

HOURS 6 am–9 pm, every day.

SPECS 17 Gerard St.; (703) 667-3541; no cards; no liquor.

DIRECTIONS **Northbound:** From Exit 80, turn right at the light. Go about 1¼ miles on the main road, and you'll see it on your left at the corner of Braddock St.

Southbound: Exit 80W will put you on Milwood Ave. Go 1¼ miles on the main road, and you'll see it on your left at the corner of Braddock.

COALIE HARRY'S, *Exit 81, Winchester*

If pub-style dining is not your cup of tea, don't come to Coalie Harry's. And if the sign at the front door, "Proper dress and behavior required at all times," doesn't deter you, you'll probably have a jolly good time. For Coalie Harry's is perhaps the most authentic—certainly the most enjoyable—British-style pub we've found on this side of the Western Ocean.

Don't expect to be greeted by anyone named Coalie Harry, even though there really is such a person, a salt-of-the-earth cockney coalman who frequents the Spanish Galleon Pub in Greenwich, England, where he came to know Joan and Fraser Scorgie. When the Scorgies moved to America and opened up their own taproom, they named it in Harry's honor because, as Joan put it, "His humor and outlook on life are such that, if a pub could live up to it, it would have to be successful."

Joan, a charming hostess, says she doesn't try to put out gourmet English cooking ("if anybody believes there is such a thing"), concentrating instead on authentic pub fare—hearty meals like shepherd's pie, fish 'n' chips, steak and mushroom pie, Scotch eggs, Cornish pasties, Trafalgar seafood pie, sausage rolls, bangers and mash, and bubble 'n' squeak. OK, OK! We'll back up and do some explaining.

Shepherd's pie and fish 'n' chips you already know about; steak and mushroom pie you can probably figure out. Scotch eggs, which David remembers with great fondness from his

201

undergraduate year abroad at the University of Edinburgh, consist of imported British sausage surrounding a hard-boiled egg, breaded and deep-fried. The Scotch eggs Joan serves are as good a companion to a pint of bitter as any that David can recall from his university days. They are best accompanied by mustard or Crosse and Blackwell's Branston relish, both available for the asking.

Cornish pasties (rhyme with "nasties") were eaten at work by 19th-century tin miners who carried them around all day in their pockets. We're not sure Joan's are quite that rugged, which is just as well—hers are flaky pastries enveloping a tasty filling of ground beef, potato, and onion. As with sausage rolls (similar to Cornish pasties except for the filling), they are actually hors d'oeuvres, although a light appetite could do very well by them.

Moving on to more serious eating, Harry's has Trafalgar seafood pie—a casserole of crabmeat, shrimp, and whitefish filet in a spicy creole sauce. "Bangers and mash," comical as it sounds, is easy to comprehend once you realize that "bangers" is vernacular for the legendary Oxford sausages made with equal parts veal and pork; mash is mashed potatoes. Regardless of which dish you settle on for a main course, you would be remiss not to order "bubble and squeak" from the vegetable list—chopped broccoli and potatoes slapped into croquettes, breaded, dipped in egg, and fried. It's a worthwhile lesson in the creative use of leftovers.

In case your Anglophilia is less pronounced than ours, it's only fair that we mention that there are other possibilities at Coalie Harry's, such as prime rib, strip steak, burgers, French dip sandwiches, cold-cut plates; even lunch specials like chicken curry, lasagna, and Reuben sandwiches. Lunch prices for dishes British and otherwise are $3.50–$4.00; dinners run $4–$5.50 ($6 tops).

Despite the few errant items on the menu, the atmosphere is uncompromisingly English—dark, warm, amply decorated with horse brasses, Bossom statuettes, and pictures of the Cotswolds. There are all kinds of nooks and crannies to hide in, including one quite quaintly called the "snug bar." We were so naive as to ask if there was a dart board and were promptly led to the back bar, where league competition among four teams of dartsmen was in progress.

HOURS Mon.–Sat. 11:30 am–10 pm; light pub fare available until midnight Mon. through Thurs., until 1 am Fri. and Sat. Closed Sun.

SPECS 28 E. Piccadilly St. (how appropriate); (703) 656-0616; major cards; full bar.

DIRECTIONS From Exit 81, head west toward Winchester. You'll be on Berryville Ave., which becomes National Ave. Keep going more or less straight with the flow of traffic, and in about 1¼ miles from the Interstate you'll be forced to turn left. At this point, go 1 short block and turn right on Piccadilly. Go through 2 lights, and it will be on the right, shortly after crossing Cameron St.

West Virginia

AMY'S/LOS AMIGOS, *Exit 16E, Martinsburg*

What's an Egyptian fellow doing running a Mexican restaurant in the middle of West Virginia? That's what we asked Hossein (Henry) Sadeghzadeh, and he gave us a perfectly reasonable explanation. Having immigrated 14 years ago, Henry was working as a cook at Tia Maria in Washington, D.C., when he visited Martinsburg on vacation and discovered that there was not a Mexican restaurant to be found in the three-state area. So in 1976 he bought a declining seafood house and converted it, timing his restaurant's debut perfectly with the wave of popularity that Mexican food has enjoyed in recent years. Now he's constructing an entirely new building to accommodate his steadily expanding clientele. Henry may be Egyptian and his food may be Mexican, but the success story is pure American.

His menu is familiar, not varying greatly from that of most other Tex-Mex establishments. But that didn't bother us—we hadn't seen an enchilada in months. So we dipped into Combinación Numero Ocho—an enchilada, a chile relleno, Spanish rice, and refried beans, with chips and, of course, salsa on the side. While the seasonings may not have been quite as zingy as you'd find in Arizona or Texas, they had Taco Bell beat by a tasty mile. Within the limits of his location in the hinterlands, Henry does everything he can to put out the best in fresh, simple Mexican food: every day he makes the chips and salsa, grates beef for the tacos, stuffs the chiles, and refries the beans. The evidence of his labors is apparent in the tasting.

We don't know what Henry's architect has in mind for the new Amy's, but the old one was a perfectly pleasant, Alamo-esque rendition of family-style Mex-American decor. The 4-foot television screen in the center of the dining room was a little off-putting, but we were assured that it comes to life only for football games.

Most a la carte items at Amy's run $1.30 to $2.60 (taco, burrito, enchilada, etc.), and combination dinners are generally $4–$6.

HOURS   11 am–11 pm, 7 days a week.

SPECS   1211 N. Queen St.; (304) 263-7325 and 263-9113; major cards; full license.

DIRECTIONS   Exit 16E puts you on Route 9 East. We don't know if you'll find **Amy's** in its original location or if it will have moved by the time you arrive. Fortunately both spots are on the same road. Simply take Route 9 East. The new **Amy's** is on the right, about ¾ mile from the Interstate. If you don't see anything going on there, you'll find the original **Amy's** a little further down—just beyond the second stop light, on the left, about 1½ miles from the Interstate.

I-85

Georgia
South Carolina
North Carolina
Virginia

Georgia

THE BEAUTIFUL RESTAURANT, *Junction I-285, Atlanta*

See page 123 for a description of this excellent and inexpensive soul-food restaurant.

DIRECTIONS Turn north onto I-285 and go about 5 miles to the Cascade Rd. exit. Then follow directions given.

THE VARSITY
MARY MAC'S TEA ROOM

Through central Atlanta I-85 and I-75 run together. See pages 126 and 127 for descriptions of these two famous Atlanta institutions. Follow directions given.

JOE DALE'S CAJUN HOUSE, *Exits 27 and 29, Atlanta*

Atlanta is no closer to Louisiana than it is to Washington, D.C., so you can hardly call Cajun cooking a local specialty. No matter—with but a few reservations Joe Dale's Cajun cuisine was excellent, and the bread pudding in bourbon sauce was an experience we will not soon forget.

Cajun cooking is Atlanta's *in* cuisine, with the result that a place like Joe Dale's draws a sophisticated and prosperous urban clientele to its small, comfortable rooms. It's woody and dark inside, a sort of southern *gemütlichkeit* emanating from the bric-a-brac decor that features handsome model ships and antique toys (Joe Dale owns the Atlanta Toy Museum, too). Add red-checked tablecloths and lots of friendliness, and you end up with a warm and very likable place without pretensions.

You can choose any of four Louisiana dishes that get as exotic as court bouillon—fresh fish in a tomato sauce with vegetables, red wine and a bit of brandy ($10.95). The rest of the menu is made up of dishes like whitefish amadine, oysters Rockefeller, shrimp in sherry sauce, or beef tournedos with mushrooms. Prices run from $9.95 to $13.95.

We went for the chicken and shrimp Jambalaya ($10.95) and were delighted with its earthy, mildly spicy flavor, as well as with its generosity—two full breasts and two humongous shrimp on a bed of rice, green onions, and mushrooms. Very good also were the scalloped potatoes with a hint of garlic. The "Cajun house salad," however, was only a pale version of a Caesar's.

Then came the real experience. We were happy with Joe's batting average and almost said no to dessert, when our curiosity (or was it gluttony?) got the better of us. We ordered the bread pudding in bourbon sauce, and waited for the bourbon flavor to overcome the initial impression of cloying sweetness. It did, and suddenly we understood bourbon as never before. It had a flavor that lingered in the mouth like a fine cigar or the rarest brandy, flirting with the boundary of the saccharine but never crossing it, always retreating back into its own deep, rich flavor. It was wonderful, worth four times the $2.50 it cost, and enough to justify a visit for its own sake.

HOURS Mon–Sat. 5:30 pm–11 pm. Closed Sun.

SPECS 3209 Maple Drive N.E.; (404) 261-2741; major cards; full license.

DIRECTIONS **Northbound:** From Exit 27 go under the Interstate and then 2.1 miles north on Piedmont to Peachtree Rd. Left onto Peachtree and then almost immediately another left onto Maple Drive. On the left.

Southbound: From Exit 29 turn right onto Lenox, go 0.1 mile and turn left again onto Marion. Follow Marion 0.8 mile to Piedmont. Right onto Piedmont, and go 2.1 miles to Peachtree Rd. Left onto Peachtree and then almost immediately left again onto Maple Drive. On the left.

THE COLONNADE, *Exit 30, Atlanta*

Some of the best plain southern cooking we came across was here in this popular suburban restaurant, which, despite its name, should not be mistaken for a would-be plantation house complete with pediment, frieze, and ionic columns. No, it's just a long, low, nondescript building plunked down between gas stations and shopping plazas, unremarkable in every way but for its friendly mob of devoted customers. It's their chatter and enthusiasm that provide the atmosphere, not the glitzy wallpaper of plasti-stone decor.

Atlantans dearly love their plain, inexpensive, fast-service, country-cooking restaurants. The most famous of these is Mary Mac's Tea Room, a long-established downtown institution alive with old-fashioned friendliness and new-South bustle (see page 127). But most everyone agrees that the food is better at the Colonnade. Here the tone is set more by older people, who've known about it for years, and a sprinkling of the trendy set for whom it's a recent discovery.

It was at the Colonnade that we discovered what an incredible treat red-eye gravy can be. We ordered the country ham ($5.95

with grits and two vegetables) and were astonished to see arrive so generous a slice that it literally overhung the good-sized platter that bore it. The meat itself was a delight, falling in saltiness somewhere between what Virginians call "country ham" and your ordinary supermarket variety. But the absolute knockout was the clear red-eye gravy, a southern specialty made from ham drippings and coffee (the older the coffee, the better). It didn't just taste good; it was an experience, and ever since, we've been messing around the kitchen trying without success to reproduce it.

A wide variety of dinners, all in the southern vein, are mostly about $6.00; lunch and breakfast are comparably priced, and our guess is you'll be content with whatever your choice.

About the only negative we can report is that you may have to wait in line—the Colonnade is truly popular. But the line moves quickly, and you may well find standing in it an enjoyable experience. People here are extraordinarily friendly, and they love to talk about the restaurant. In the line we met a WW II fighter pilot, and it was he who recommended the ham. He also gave the fried chicken livers ($4.95) high marks. You may want to follow that tip, or see what your own efforts at southern-style socializing can bring.

HOURS   Tues.–Sat. 8 am–10:30 am, 11 am–2:30 pm, & 5–9 pm; Sun. 8 am–10:30 am & 11 am–8 pm.

SPECS   1879 Cheshire Bridge Rd.; (404) 874-5642; no cards; beer and wine.

DIRECTIONS   From Exit 30 go south on Cheshire Bridge Rd. for 1.2 miles. On the left.

KATZ'S DELI, *Exit 30, Atlanta*

Good as much of it was, we were getting a little tired of fried chicken and country ham, and so our pulses quickened when we spotted Katz's sign sticking out above the little shopping plaza. No way were we going to pass up the chance to sample an Atlanta-style Jewish deli.

It was everything such a place should be—up front by the door a deli counter overflowing with pastrami, corned beef, kugel, challah, chopped liver, and a multitude of pastries. And it had the more or less brightly plastic decor without which a corned-beef sandwich just wouldn't taste the same. Except that at Katz's the more common orange, pink, and yellow scheme had yielded to relatively sedate tones of blue and brown.

We feared bland, shoe-leather lox and a bagel the consistency of Wonder Bread, but were delighted with what we got—a big slice of absolutely delicious, not-over-salty, smoked salmon and a bagel that, even if it wasn't the rock-hard authentic kind, had plenty of flavorful crunch. With fine cream cheese, it cost only $2.25, which left us wondering why the same would cost at least $4.50 anywhere up north.

There are 24 other sandwiches in the $4.00–$5.00 range, blintzes with sour cream for $2.95, a quartet of potato pancakes for $2.95, along with smoked fish, stuffed cabbage, stuffed derma, and homemade horseradish. Dinners are a mixture of Jewish and southern dishes and come in three orders of magnitude, "mini," "small," and "full." All include bread and beverage, but the "full" gives you dessert and a choice of three items from a list that includes matzo-ball soup, gefilte fish, cucumber salad, and turkey dressing in addition to the usual vegetables. Brisket dinners run $4.95 to $6.50; short ribs in chicken broth or sweet-and-sour cabbage soup with a matzo ball are the same price, as is a dinner of kosher franks. A dollar less gets the daily

special or any of five other possibilities.

And yes, they do have chicken. But it's baked instead of fried, or more often boiled to make the chicken soup that cures all life's ills.

HOURS Sun., Mon., Wed., Thurs. 8 am–10 pm; Fri. & Sat. 8 am–midnight. Closed Tues.

SPECS 2205 Cheshire Bridge Rd.; (404) 321-7444; V/MC/AE/CB; beer and wine.

DIRECTIONS From Exit 30 go south on Cheshire Bridge Rd. 0.5 mile. On the left.

JIM'S RANCH, *Exit 44, Suwannee*

Jim's has no local charm at all. It's a highway eatery smacked down 100 yards from the road in a Day's Inn Motel. Inside, it's a pleasant enough concatenation of plastic, barnboard, and stills from old westerns—wagon wheels for chandeliers and sheriff's badges pinned to the waitresses' smocks. The food, however, is another story—very good country cookin', with touches that come close to inspiration. And the folks are very friendly.

Jim first impressed us with his handsomely laid-out salad bar that included minced ham, toasted sunflower seeds, hominy, and a pile of garlicky rolls. The first taste of the blue-cheese dressing was shockingly sweet, and we fell into a premature despair. It improved with each succeeding bite, until about half-way through the salad we broke out in praise of the saucier's imagination. Then came the acid test, beef tips in gravy, the latter almost always too thick and cornstarchy. But not at Jim's. The flavor was light and true to the beef stock from which it was born. The biscuits were excellent, and if the vegetable soup wasn't a standout, at least it had big tasty chunks of okra.

The menu is your basic southern affair, the American stand-bys augmented by hushpuppies, cole slaw, catfish, and bar-becue. Most sandwiches are around $2.95. At lunchtime a one-meat, one-vegetable, one-soup and one-salad meal goes for just $3.95. Dinners are in the $6.00–$8.00 range and a lonely hamburger can be had for just $.99.

If Jim's were a tumbledown old place run by the same cook for 30 years, it would be hailed as one of the great roadside discoveries. As it is, you'll just have to settle for just good food. Sports fans, however, can compensate for the lack of atmosphere by the proximity to glory. Suwannee, it seems, is the training camp of the Atlanta Falcons, and you never know who might turn up at the neighboring table.

HOURS Every day 6:30 am–9:30 pm. Closed Christmas Day.

SPECS (404) 945-3475; V/MC/AE; no liquor.

DIRECTIONS 100 yards north of Exit 44, on the right.

CHANDLER'S DOWNTOWN, *Exit 53, Commerce*

All we can really say in defense of this establishment is that it is truly local, that the string beans were full of big meaty chunks of ham, and that the limas were flavored with genuine fatback. Though the flavors were down-home enough, there was nothing to get excited about, and that included the bright, plastic cafeteria decor. Chandler's Steak House is run by the same people and is just a half-mile south of the exit. We didn't try it, but you may want to. Watch out if you attempt the Chinese place at Exit 53. Our smoked duck (which really wasn't half bad) arrived accompanied by a huge mound of french fries presmothered in ketchup.

HOURS Mon.–Thurs. 7 am–3 pm; Fri. & Sat. 7 am–9 pm; closed Sun.

DIRECTIONS From 53, go south on US 441 to first light in Commerce (3.6 miles). Turn left and go 2 blocks to a light. It's on the right, just past the light, on the corner.

South Carolina

ABOUT PENDLETON

Admittedly Pendleton is far from the road—about 8 miles, to be precise—but there are four things to recommend a visit. First of all, we found little we wanted to tell you about between Pendleton and Atlanta. That makes for an 80-mile dry stretch, so southbound travelers may well want to fill up here before pushing on. Secondly, Pendleton is a very pretty place, built around a neatly tended, gas-lamped town square that is entirely pleasing without getting precious about it. Thirdly, there are three restaurants on the square. At least two of them are quite good (the **Farmer's Hall Restaurant** and **Red's Seafood**), and the third looked interesting and cheap, though we were unable to put it to the test (**Miles and Crenshaw Restaurant Cafeteria**). Lastly, there's the hall in **Farmer's Hall**. It's a delightfully odd little building you won't soon forget. All of which seems to make a 20-minute detour well worth the trouble.

RED'S SEAFOOD, *Exits 14, and 19B, Pendleton*

Red's won our hearts with its unique but unpretentious good looks and the thoughtful attention to detail that made our dinner such a pleasant experience. It's owned and run by a husband-and-wife team whose personal touch reaches just about everything in the place, driving the clichés of the restaurant game before it.

To begin with, Red's is woody, but not like your typical bricks-plants-and-oakery. Here things are on the order of good old knotty pine. But what's that Polynesian luau roof doing over a row of tables? And look, there's a mezzanine of tables running along the far wall! Hard to classify this decor, but the result is warm, welcoming, and kinda fun.

Since the seafood is always fresh, that part of the dinner menu is on a chalkboard that adjusts to the vagaries of fisherman's luck. We chose from about ten intriguing dishes that ran from $7.50–$9.75 (sea trout Eugene, snapper Normandie, red bass Bordelaise, as well as just plain fried shrimp). There was a surprising and delightful shrimp salad in the salad bar, and when the house dressing turned out to be an imaginative and tasty version of creamy Italian, we began to realize we'd stumbled upon something good.

Sure enough, the flounder baked with shrimp and mushrooms was a real treat, and there were five (count 'em, five) good-sized shrimp hidden in the parmesan topping. Dubbed a "shrimp cocktail," these crustaceans could have easily fetched $5.00 by themselves. But at Red's, $7.50 bought the shrimp, the flounder, the salad, and a loaf of fresh-baked bread plus a choice of light and tasty hushpuppies, baked potato, french fries, or tame rice sprinkled with a few grains of its wilder cousin. A good deal any day!

You can also get she-crab soup ($1.95 a cup/$2.50 a bowl) or oysters on the half-shell. You can get key lime pie and Kentucky Derby pie, the latter being a sort of pecan pie with bourbon and chocolate chips. It's 2.50 and worth every cent.

For those who simply will not be tempted by seafood, Red's has both pork and beef ribs, a rib-eye steak, and three versions of chicken ($6.25). We wouldn't want to order anything but fish here, since they go to so much trouble to do fish right. But since they do well whatever they try, carnivores are unlikely to be disappointed.

HOURS Mon.–Thurs. 5 pm–9:30 pm; Fri. & Sat. 5 pm–10 pm. Closed Sun. and one week around Christmas.

SPECS 134 Exchange St.; (803) 646-7672; MC/V/AE; full license.

DIRECTIONS Same as for **Farmer's Hall Restaurant** (below). **Red's** is right on the square. Can't miss it.

THE FARMER'S HALL RESTAURANT,
Exits 14 and 19B, Pendleton

We don't want to get too carried away with the building because the Farmer's Hall is by everyone's account a very good restaurant with a more or less continental menu. All the same, we can't resist delighting in this irresistibly squat Greek temple of a building with its four chubby little white columns. It was built in 1826 to house the Pendleton Farmer's Society, and it sits with all the presumed dignity of a country courthouse right in the middle of the town square. For some reason, the architect reserved his arsenal of stately designs for the private homes of the plantation owners and here erected the most endearingly diminutive example of Greek revival architecture we ever expect to see.

The interior renovation of the hall has produced a restaurant with a predominantly early American look, except that here things are lighter and more elegant than those words suggest— all very pretty, with flowers on the tables and nicely framed art on the wall.

At dinner time about $10.00 will buy you a full seven-course meal—hors d'oeuvre, appetizer, soup, salad, and sherbet between the courses. Entrées are on the order of veal cordon bleu, stuffed flounder, and roast pork. Desserts are extra, however, all of them made from scratch on the premises and all with a far-flung reputation for excellence.

Lunch offerings are smaller versions of the dinner fare and run from about $3.95 to $5.95. There's a soup and sandwich deal for $3.95.

We think you'll enjoy it, and though it is far from the road, it's the kind of restaurant that is guaranteed to dispel the fatigue and monotony of the road.

HOURS Tues.–Thurs. 9 am–2:30 pm; Fri. & Sat. 9 am–2:30 pm & 6:30 pm–9:30 pm. Closed Sun., 2½ weeks at Christmas, and Bahai holidays.

SPECS   134 Exchange St.; (803) 646-7024; no cards; no liquor.

DIRECTIONS   Northbound: Take Exit 14 and go north on SC 187 for 6 miles to the junction with US 76. Left on US 76 and go 0.6 mile to the light at the fork with SC Business 28. Bear right onto SC 28 and follow it 1.2 miles to the town square. Quicker and easier than it may sound.

Southbound: Take Exit 19B and go north 6.3 miles on US 76 to light at fork with SC Business 28. Bear right onto SC 28 and go 1.2 miles to the square.

VINCE PERONE'S RESTAURANT, *Exit 48B, Greenville*

It was a great pleasure to find that the Southland can have the kind of family-run Italian restaurant that is so common in the Northeast. Vince Perone began making sandwiches to help pay the bills while a student at Furman University. His efforts grew into a full deli and then a restaurant. En route to success he brought his parents and children into the business. At 80, Mrs. Perone still does the baking, and she's up early every morning to roll out the lasagna.

But don't mistake Perone's for some tiny salt-of-the-earth affair. The restaurant occupies only about one-tenth of an enormous suburban bomb shelter of a building, and Vince is running two other restaurants around town. The rest of the building is his nightclub, of which you are mercifully unaware when in the

215

restaurant. One dining area is slightly on the plastic-posh side of things. The other, however, is quite pleasantly cheerful in a trendy way—butcher-block tables, Breuer chairs, plants, and lots of arched windows.

Perone's is the only Italian restaurant we've come across with a cafeteria setup. At lunchtime you push your tray past a variety of good sandwich fixings ($1.95–$3.95), but you can also choose chicken marsala ($3.50), lasagna ($3.25), or Italian sausage ($3.25). Whatever you pick, it'll come with crusty French bread.

Dinner is by regular table service. Aside from the usual steak and seafood meals that seem absolutely obligatory in the South ($7.00–$12.00), there are eight pasta dishes ($3.75–$5.50), six Italian veal and chicken dishes ($6.00–$9.00), and you can still order some fancy combination sandwiches late at night (about $5.00). Homemade cheesecake, custards, and napoleons offer suitable endings.

HOURS Mon.–Thurs. 10:30 am–10 pm; Fri. & Sat. 10:30 am–11 pm. Closed Sun., Christmas, New Year's.

SPECS 1 East Antrim Drive; (803) 233-1621; major cards; full license.

DIRECTIONS From Exit 48B go 2.4 miles west on US 276 toward Greenville. Turn left at the light onto Antrim and follow it for 0.2 mile through some curves. On the right in small shopping center.

AT LANA'S, NATURALLY, *Exit 48B, Greenville*

At Lana's was closed when we passed through, but we thought some folks would want to know about this tiny vegetarian restaurant and natural-foods store. It's lunch only, and there's nothing very fancy about it—a counter and a few plain bar stools, some tables and metal folding chairs in front of a wall of books aimed at improving your life through diet. Meals are on the order of potato-and-lentil soup, chili, lasagna, soy burger, and salads; they run anywhere from $1.50 to $3.00. Whether or not they will restore your health we do not know, but clearly you won't go away broke.

HOURS Mon.–Fri. 11 am–3 pm. Same on Sat. "if the cook shows up." Closed Sun.

DIRECTIONS Follow directions for **Vince Perone's** (above), but go 0.1 mile farther on Antrim. On the right in an even tinier shopping plaza.

BEACON DRIVE IN, *Exit 70, Spartanburg*

See page 49 for a description of this rather remarkable drive-in restaurant.

DIRECTIONS From Exit 70, enter I-26 East (toward Columbia) for about 3½ miles to Exit 22 (Reidville Rd.). Turn left and in about 3 miles it's on your right.

ANKIE'S DELI DELIGHTS, *Exit 73A, Spartanburg*

Spartanburg was just full of delectable surprises, this one only 2 miles from the exit ramp. It seems the city is a thriving textile center that has attracted numerous foreign firms to the Piedmont. Such, at any rate, is the source of the town's large Swiss/German population, and these are the people you'll find munching bratwurst, wiener schnitzel, and sauerbraten at Ankie's Deli.

Not your typical garden-variety deli by any means, Ankie's is actually a gourmet food store with a German accent, and a full lunch-and-dinner restaurant that specializes in light meals. You can get a sandwich of knackwurst, Westphalian ham, beerwurst, or pastrami ($2.90–$3.95). If you're hungrier than that, try one of the daily luncheons. It might be sauerbraten, Hungarian goulash, or jagerschnitzel ($5.50–$7.00). The roast pork with spaetzle, red cabbage, and salad was just fine. The gravy was deeply flavored and the salad dressing was a light, spicy, delightfully imaginative mayonnaise concoction. Desserts are delicious, varied, and truly homemade—produced for the deli by several different women who work in their own kitchens.

A little of that homemade flavor spills over into the decor. If you take your meal at the big old wooden table down at one end of the deli counter, you may begin to think you're in someone's house. The women who work here eat at this table along with their many German-speaking friends. An earthy brand of humor goes back and forth at all times, and you get lots of mothering attention. All are welcome at the table, but if your Deutsch is rusty you may prefer to eat in the more conventional dining area, an entirely pleasant and informal affair of ladder-back chairs, hanging lamps, and a rainbow of tablecloths.

HOURS   Mon.–Fri. 11 am–10 pm; Sat. 11 am–9 pm. Closed Sun. and major holidays.

SPECS   404-D McCravy Drive; (803) 583-1063; V/MC/AE; beer and wine.

DIRECTIONS   From Exit 73A follow I-585 1.8 miles into Spartanburg. At this point the Interstate becomes Pine St. At the first light turn left onto McCravy and go 0.2 mile to a small shopping plaza on the right (Western Auto sign). It's in there at the far end.

ANNIE OAK'S, *Exit 73A, Spartanburg*

Our dinner at Annie Oak's was quite simply one of the best dining experiences we had in the South, and it would stand up well in comparison to the best we've tasted anywhere on the road. Following the advice of our knowledgeable waiter, we ordered grouper gratinée at $11.95. The delicate fish arrived in a light, subtly cheesy crust that was quite delicious, but modest enough to let the moist fish speak eloquently for itself. A lovely array of greens made up the salad, with pleasing accents provided by summer squash, sprouts, and slivered almonds. The ranch dressing was excellent, and our desert of chocolate silk pie ($1.75) was superb. Wrap up such delights in a tasteful modern decor, and it's hard to do anything but sing the praises of Annie Oak's. The only disappointments were the very ordinary dinner rolls and dilled carrots that just didn't make it. But we're not going to dwell on them.

Annie's opened in 1980, unsure that Spartanburg was ready for a restaurant like this. The original menu was nearly straight American. Bit by bit, though, chicken cordon bleu ($8.95), veal Oscar ($14.95), and shrimp fettuccine ($11.95) found their places next to rib-eye steak ($13.95), lamb chops ($12.95), and sautéed liver ($6.95). The result is an eclectic menu, the completeness of which extends also to lunch. At midday choose between a burger on an English muffin with cheddar cheese ($3.45), a Reuben ($3.95), Polynesian chicken ($4.55—highly recommended by a friend of ours), a croissant stuffed with beef tips in madeira sauce ($5.95), or perhaps crab salad Dijonaise ($6.95).

Annie's tone is one of informal quiet and unmitigated good looks—grass-cloth walls set off by a few chrome-framed prints, green carpeting, white tablecloths, and director's chairs. Here and there shrubbery, but no one tried to turn the place into a botanical garden.

A touch of class, for sure.

HOURS Mon.–Sat. 11:30 am–2:30 pm & 5:30 pm–10 pm. Closed Sun., Christmas, New Year's.

SPECS 464 East Main St.; (803) 583-8021; all major cards; full license.

DIRECTIONS At Exit 73A turn onto I-585, which will lead you right to the center of Spartanburg. After 1.9 miles I-585 ends and turns into Pine St. Continue straight ahead on Pine for 1.5 miles to light at Main St. Left on Main for a half-block. Look for a small sign on the left marked "TOWN SQUARE." Turn into the drive and **Annie's** will be immediately on your left.

KELLY'S STEAK HOUSE, *Exit 99, Blacksburg*

Kelly's has been here for 24 years now, and by all accounts it's the best restaurant between Charlotte and Spartanburg. But that's a lonesome stretch of road. By less regional standards we'd have to class it as just a good steak house, no more, no less.

Charles Kelly cuts the steaks himself. He cuts them thick, and he charbroils them right. Our medium-rare fillet ($11.50) arrived perfectly pink and juicy inside, but crisply golden-brown to the eye. The salad dressing showed imagination, though it was not to our taste; the greens it dressed were just the usual bits of iceberg perked up by a few tomato wedges. The french fries were mushy (order the baked potato). Other steak dinners are $7.00–$14.00. A hamburger plate goes for $4.50, and there are seafood alternatives at $6.75–$10.00. Children's plates are $3.50.

It's a pleasant, quiet, dignified place, almost luxurious with its padded chairs, candles, and carpeting. Three of its four rooms, however, are windowless, and the wallpaper is innocent of discerning judgment. The fourth room, more modern than the others, is the most pleasant of all. It's just as plush as the others, but less kitchy, and it has two walls of picture windows that afford fine views of a lovely pine woods.

Kelly's was begun in 1960 with two employees and an old farmhouse. Room by room has been added as the establishment grew steadily, the just reward for doing a simple thing reasonably well.

HOURS   Mon.–Sat. 5:30 pm–9:30 pm. Closed Sun., 3 days around Christmas, a week around July 4, and for other major holidays.

SPECS   (803) 839-9922; MC/V/AE; full license.

DIRECTIONS   Southbound turn left and northbound right onto SC 5, following signs for Blacksburg. Go 1.2 miles until you see a fish camp/ beer hall on your left and a sign for Tessener's Garage on your right. Turn right, cross the RR tracks, and go 0.9 mile to a stop sign. Turn right at the stop sign onto US 29 and go 0.4 mile to the restaurant, on the right.

North Carolina

TWIN TOPS FISH CAMP
LINEBERGER'S FISH CAMP,
NC 279 Exit, Gastonia

Gastonia is known throughout this part of the South as "that town where all those fish camps are," and a fish camp, for those who haven't experienced this southern institution, is an enormous barn of a restaurant where (but for hushpuppies, potatoes, and cole slaw) the entire menu is seafood, and where (except for the slaw) most everything is fried. To speak the truth, that was a less than appealing invitation, given our high-cholesterol consciousness, but when we heard that the mood in these places is more like a revival meeting than a secular eatery, we were determined to check it out.

What we found one Saturday night at the Twin Tops was a cavernous room whose institutional green walls and fluorescent lighting were relieved only by a seascape mural that ran the entire length of the building, and by the happiness that emanated from the noisy crowd that was obviously loving every minute of it. We plunked down our $5.95 for the "all-you-care-to-eat" special and were both astonished and distressed at the mountain of crispy golden perch, catfish, trout, shrimp, oysters, deviled crab, hushpuppies, and french fries that quickly arrived. Distress gave way to delight when, against all odds, the stuff turned out to be terrific. The fresh oysters were simply delicious; the shrimp (and they didn't skimp on them) were quite good; and all the rest was far better than just OK. Even the cocktail-hot sauce was good, and so was the tartar sauce. It added up to a wonderful experience in local life and good American cooking at bargain prices, well worth the extra miles you must drive to reach it.

If you just can't abide all that frying, the Twin Tops will broil flounder ($5.25 for half an order; $6.75 for the works) or broil up some shrimp ($5.75/$7.25). And they'll bring you an order of fried chicken if you really want it ($3.95/$4.95). But if we ever return we'll focus our energies on the all-oyster dinner and just pig out—unlimited reorders on most full dinners.

American fried just doesn't come any better than this, and for $2.00 you can wash it all down with a full gallon of iced tea.

HOURS   Tues.–Fri. 4 pm–10 pm; Sat. 3–10 pm. Closed Sun. and Mon.

SPECS   (704) 825-2490; no credit cards; no liquor.

DIRECTIONS   Go 7 miles due east on NC 279. **Twin Tops** is on the right. One mile closer to the Interstate and on the left is **Lineberger's,** actually the older and best known of the Gastonia fish camp trio, but it was closed that night due to icy roads.

FANCY FOX TEAROOM AND GIFT SHOP
NC 279 Exit, Gastonia

The only disappointment in our Gastonia fish camp experience was the realization that the distance was far and that neither fish camp serves lunch. Just as we were bemoaning this fact, we spied off under some handsome trees a pretty little building with "Fancy Fox Tearoom and Gift Shop" carefully hand-lettered above the doorway. The dilemma was solved in one swift stroke, but there was no way to sample the offerings since it was far too late at night for a place so genteel as a tearoom.

All the same, we recommend you check it out. We had quite good luck with tearooms throughout the South. They tend to be very pleasant places (even if a bit little-old-ladyish), very friendly (motherly, even), and the food was always far better than anything you'll find in a roadside chainery.

HOURS   Mon.–Sat. 11:30 am–2 pm. Closed Sun.

SPECS   216 S. New Hope Rd.; (704) 867-2411; MC; wine only.

DIRECTIONS   0.6 mile straight east of the exit on NC 279, on the left, just after you cross US 29.

OLD ORIGINAL BARBECUE HOUSE, *Exit 35, Charlotte*

It's not at all difficult, from I-85, to enjoy the wonderful barbecue and unforgettable sweet-potato pie of the Old Original Barbecue House. See page 162 for a description.

DIRECTIONS   **Northbound:** From exit for Route 27 East, turn left, then bear right (sign for Charlotte), then turn right onto Freedom Drive. ■ Go about 1¼ mile to the light at Camp Greene St. Turn right and go about ¾ mile on Camp Greene; you'll see it on the right, just before the stop sign at Independence Blvd.

Southbound: The exit marked Route 27 East puts you directly on Freedom Drive. Follow directions above, from ■.

Note: Our maps told us that this exit (Route 27 East) should have been labeled Exit 35, but the signs had no number.

LANE STREET GRILL, *Kannapolis*

"What's that?" we asked with a suspicious nod at the thin, red-brown, vaguely meaty-looking rectangular slab on the woman's plate. "You must not be from the South," declared our countermate without a hint of indignation in her voice. "It's liver mush." We looked again at the Coke-sign menu, and there it was, "L-mush," which at first we had taken for a North Carolina mushroom concoction. And there too, right under "Have a Nice Day," was the injunction to "Put Jesus First." Yes, indeed, we were in the South.

The Lane Street Grill is a purely rural, purely southern, purely unpretentious little café that is as purely undecorated as it is warm, lively, and friendly. The only thing at all unusual about it is the Gothic lettering on the sign that hangs out in front of the tiny clapboard building, and that is far more endearing than it is distinguished. For food there are only burgers ($.90) and a dozen other sandwiches, a chicken fillet ($1.15), barbecue trays for $2.00–$2.50, a plate of ham or hamburger for $2.87, good homemade vegetable soup ($1.00), breakfast, and just a little more. Like liver mush.

Of course we had to try it ($1.65 with two eggs, grits, and an endless supply of coffee). It was wonderful, a spicy version of what in Pennsylvania Dutch country is called scrapple or pork pudding, made absolutely from scratch and well worth a visit for its own sake. Sit at the counter and start a conversation on the subject with whomever is there. If your experience is as delightful as ours, you'll leave with one more reason to love the South.

HOURS Mon.–Fri. 5 am–6 pm; Sat. 5 am–2 pm. Closed Sun. (of course).

SPECS (704) 938-1066; no cards; no liquor (of course).

DIRECTIONS 1.6 miles west of the Kannapolis exit, on the right. The exit sign says only "Kannapolis" and is not to be confused with another exit further south that will also get you to Kannapolis.

LEXINGTON BARBEQUE, *Old US 64 Exit, Lexington*

It's not just local aficionados who claim that the Lexington Barbeque is the world's best. The *New York Times* food editor liked it so much he recommended it to the White House, and sure enough Wayne Monk was soon serving up his subtle version of the North Carolina specialty at the Williamsburg Economic Summit. Surely the Lexington is the only barbecue joint to have tempted the delicate palate of Giscard d'Estaing.

So is it or isn't it the world's best? In our opinion it's a draw. If the deep hickory flavor is what you like most about barbecue, you'll probably prefer the Fresh Air Barbecue in Jackson, GA (see page 120). But if your special delight is the vinegary sauce that is the North Carolina trademark, there's not much doubt that you'll give the laurels to the Lexington. Here the sauce is spicy and subtle at once, never overpowering the sweet flavor of the meat, but with little peaks of spicy warmth that rise and fall like music. It is a richly textured flavor, each component of which retains its identity and yet blends perfectly with the others. Not just a good taste but an experience, comparable to the very best sorts of Szechuan cooking. And while we can't pour such lavish praise on the cole slaw and hushpuppies, we can say that the minced cabbage was nearly as tasty as the barbecue itself, and that the hushpuppies were light, greaseless, and delicious. Everything about the Lexington indicates painstaking attention to detail and the determination to do with excellence its simple culinary tasks.

It's also a pleasure to report that success hasn't gone to the

Lexington's head. It is and remains the same plain, just-folks place that it's been for 6 years, except that in its simplicity it is never severe or unpleasant, and the "just folks" here tend to dress better than they do at other such eateries.

Nor has success gone to its prices. When your plate of chopped barbecue arrives in its paper box, with it will come slaw, french fries, and rolls or hushpuppies, and you'll be out only $3.60; $2.40 for a barbecue tray; $.75 for an order of hushpuppies. A dozen sandwiches run $.75–$1.60.

They have fried shrimp and fish here, and so impressed were we with the Lexington's general way of doing things that we wouldn't hesitate to try them. But barbecue is what the Lexington is all about, and you should definitely experience it, even if you aren't hungry, right down to the bottled hot sauce they sell to take home. We later discovered that it loses a bit of its fire under broiling but still does wonders for a dieter's drab broiled chicken!

HOURS Mon.–Sat. 10 am–9 pm (until 10 pm in summer). Closed Sun., major holidays, and for a week around July 4.

SPECS (704) 249-9814; no credit cards; no liquor.

DIRECTIONS I-85 was still under construction when we came through, so we'll have to be a little vague. The restaurant is on the west side of US 29/70, just west of downtown. Northbound or southbound, take an exit for Old US 64. Then:

Northbound: At end of ramp turn immediately left onto the service road. Follow it around to a stop sign and turn left. Go 0.2 mile (under a bridge) and then turn left again. It'll be on your left in 0.1 mile.

Southbound: About 2 miles after US 64 joins US 29/70 the restaurant will appear on your right on a hill above the road. You'll have to go to the next exit and double back, which won't be very difficult.

SUNSET CAFÉ, *Exit 125, Greensboro*

One look at this place and you might guess that sometime back in the '70s some hip fellows from out of town took over a fiftyish florist shop and tried to make it go as a gourmet/natural-foods café. No other kind of restaurant could look this funky; no other kind of building was ever made out of just this kind of phony stone; and you'd have to be from New York or California to try this kind of thing in Greensboro.

Marty Goldstein works hard to maintain his standards of affordable quality. We watched him haul in the fresh vegetables through the front door before the Sunset opened for dinner. Partners, wives, kids—everyone helped, and the job got done even if not in the most efficient way imaginable. Soon the chicken paprikash, the chicken Dijon, the quiche, the coq au vin, and four fish dinners were ready. With two vegetables, soup and salad, the average price tag was about $5.85, and the quality was such that you'd happily pay twice that in ritzier surroundings. All of which seem to please the generally well-dressed clientele, who know a bargain when they see it.

Lunch gives you a choice of half a dozen sandwiches in the sprouts-and-avocado genre along with a few regulars like turkey and tuna. Prices are $1.50–$3.20. There's a daily hot sandwich special and a homemade soup du jour for $1.50/bowl. Salads, of course, plus herb teas, and homemade whole-wheat bread.

HOURS Lunch: Mon.–Fri. 11:30 am–2 pm; dinner: Tues.–Sun. 6 pm–9 pm.

SPECS 2503 Spring Garden St.; (919) 855-0349; no cards; beer and wine.

DIRECTIONS See directions for **Spring Garden Bar and Grill,** page 228.

SPRING GARDEN BAR AND GRILL,
Exit 125, Greensboro

We've found for you a handsome, trendy little bar and grill in the shadow of the University of North Carolina. New brass, natural wood, and ceiling fans aplenty, even a floor of those old-fashioned tiny hexagonal tiles. Clichéd, to be sure, but well done and attractive all the same. Most important are the very good sandwiches that are available until late at night and the hearty breakfasts available as early as 7:30 am. An eye-opener of steak, eggs, and cheese goes for just $2.25. We tried a "Cubano" sandwich for $3.75 and thoroughly enjoyed the blend of pork tenderloin, ham, and Swiss with horseradish on a good kaiser bun. Most of the other lunches are a bit cheaper, running the gamut from the plain old 7-oz. hamburger ($2.95), through a variety of deli standbys, to the garden salad that comes in a tortilla shell for $2.25.

HOURS   Mon.–Fri. 7:30 am–1 am; Sat. & Sun. 11:30 am–1 am.

SPECS   1205 Spring Garden St.; (919) 379-0308; no cards; full bar.

DIRECTIONS   From Exit 125 go north on Elm St. toward town. Continue straight ahead on Eugene St. when Elm goes off to the right. (Just follow traffic and signs for University of North Carolina, Greensboro.) Turn left onto Lee and go 0.7 mile to State. Right onto State, two blocks to Spring Garden. Left onto Spring Garden, and go 0.3 mile, just past second light. On the left. For the **Sunset Café,** continue straight ahead on Spring Garden for about 1 mile. On the left.

THE CUTTING BOARD, *Exit 143, Burlington*

The Cutting Board is essentially a good suburban steak house. It's better-looking than most such places, and, according to many, it's the best restaurant of any kind in Burlington. But it is what it is—hamburgers by day and sirloin by night. For anything much more subtle than that you'll have to keep on driving.

The 6-oz. steak wears the unusual price tag of $8.64; the 10-oz. version goes for $10.87. If you want one still larger, you march up to the chef and tell him exactly how you'd like it cut.

This he then does before your eyes (to the tune of $1.25/oz.), and in seconds the meat is turning a sizzling, bubbling, juicy golden brown.

There's not quite so much fanfare connected with the humble hamburgers, but the Cutting Board's owners seem determined to give their customers an active role in designing the meals. The plain, simple, and very good chuckburger comes for $4.16 (including tea). Then you can start with the options, and for $.40 an item you can be as creative as you like.

The restaurant itself is handsome enough, in a slightly over-decorated, suburban sort of way—too many Tiffanies, a gratuitous greenhouse, a little too much bare wood, and so forth, but it's all pleasant enough.

HOURS   Daily, 11 am–2 pm & 5 pm–10 pm.

SPECS   2619 Alamance Rd.; (919) 226-0291; AE/MC/V; beer and wine.

DIRECTIONS   One block north of Exit 143, on the left.

HAM'S SOUTHERN STYLE DELI, *Exit 145, Burlington*

OK, bargain hunters, have we got one for you! How about a 40-store shopping center composed entirely of manufacturers' outlet centers? Even though Burlington Mills now makes only socks and sweaters in Burlington, NC, Alamance County still boasts of itself as the outlet center of the world (as do a few other counties we've been through). But whatever brings them here, the effect of these stores is always the same. You no sooner get out of the car than visions of bargains dance through your head —maybe a discontinued stereo for next to nothing or a suit with imperfections so tiny it would take an old-world tailor to spot them.

Find what you can or ignore the whole business. But, in any case, eat at Ham's, the discount deli. Most restaurants raise their prices in the evening, but after 4 pm Ham's slashes them to the bone! Reductions up to 20 per cent! The regular $2.30 pastrami sandwich is just $1.91! The bagel and cream cheese are reduced from an already low $.99 to an incredible $.79! Subs, salad, beer, and Coke—everything in stock is down 20 percent!

What's more, the food's not bad. We took seriously the words "southern style" in the deli's name and didn't try the corned beef ($2.15) or the lox and bagel ($2.07). Instead we went for a combo of roast beef, corned beef, turkey, slaw, and Russian dressing on rye. For $2.55 it was fantastic. Even the thick-cut french fries were good. At such prices we ask no more, not even from the absolutely undecorated, bright, plastic interior.

Subs, salads, cakes, and about 40 sandwich choices. Ham's is fast, cheap, convenient, and tasty. If you can find a better deal, make it. Or better, tell them about it at Ham's. They'll probably match any advertised price.

HOURS   Mon.–Thurs. 11 am–8 pm; Fri. 11 am–9 pm; Sat. 11 am–7 pm; Sun. noon–6 pm.

SPECS   2398-D Corporation Parkway; (919) 229-0829; no cards; beer and wine.

DIRECTIONS   From Exit 145 go north one block to the light and turn left into the Burlington manufacturers' outlet center. Go to the far end, turn left, and you'll soon see **Ham's** on your left.

THE COLONIAL INN, *Exit 164, Hillsborough*

Despite all the historic hoopla on the highway, Hillsborough really is a lovely old town, and you would do well to forget the road while meandering its ancient streets and examining its architecture. A good bit of it comes from the 18th century, and one such building is the Colonial Inn, America's oldest, in operation since 1759.

You just have to love the massive fireplaces, the wide-board floors, the antique tables, and the warm tavern feel that pervades the entire restaurant. We could have done without the waitresses' colonial dress and the few other points on which the inn makes too many concessions to the tourist trade, but there weren't enough of them to be really bothersome. It is, after all, a genuine inn, and that makes *all* the difference.

No surprises on the menu, however. Just good, solid, southern cooking from pan-fried chicken to roast beef. But we did make one discovery here—Cornwallis yams, a tasty and unusual blend of coconut, pineapple, and sweet potatoes, named for the man who lost at Yorktown. Prices run from $.95 to $6.95 at lunchtime, from $4.50 to $10.95 at dinner.

HOURS   Mon.–Sat. 11:30 am–2 pm & 5 pm–9 pm; Sun. 11:30 am–9 pm. Closed Dec. 23–Jan 1.

SPECS   153 W. King Street; (919) 732-2461; MC/V/AE; beer and wine.

DIRECTIONS   From Exit 164 go 1.3 miles north to the third light (King St.) in the center of tiny Hillsborough. Turn left, 1 block, on the left.

BAKATSIAS CUISINE, *Hillendale Road Exit, Durham*

We think we've found a true "Casa de la Maison House." At least Bakatsias had most of the symptoms: a waitress who seemed determined to recite every overwritten menu description; a quiet, dignified, plush, heavily draped dining room that went about three steps too far to make a point; and above it all a humble acoustic tile ceiling that seemed to belie the whole business.

But we don't want to quibble. Even though Bakatsias is in a shopping center, it was rather handsome and rather good. Everyone said it was the best place in town, and we recommend it to you as a polar opposite antidote to the reality of travel. Come in a slightly campy mood, and you won't be put off by anything. If the decor is a bit overwrought, no apologies at all need be made for the lovely, light vinaigrette house dressing. And if the chicken amandine was only good, the zucchini and summer squash were simply wonderful.

Dinners run $10.95–$17.95, mostly continental, but not without a wide selection of steaks. There are five salads for lunch ($2.95–$5.75), five light antipasto type dishes ($4.95–$6.95), nine sandwiches ($3.75–$5.50), and half a dozen or so entrées from $5.95–$9.95.

HOURS   Mon.–Fri. 11:30 am–2:30 pm & 5:30 pm–10:30 pm; Sat. 5:30 pm–10:30 pm. Closed Sun.

SPECS   1821 Hillendale Rd.; (919) 383-8502; major cards; full bar.

DIRECTIONS   One block north of the Hillendale Rd. exit at the south end of a small shopping plaza (Loehmann's Plaza).

SOME THYME, *Guess Road Exit, Durham*

Some ten years ago, Mary S. Bacon played around with her favorite ingredients and came up with a fresh idea: avocado, tomato, sprouts, and a sprinkling of herbs atop a fried egg and a slice of whole-wheat bread; then, a layer of mozzarella and a brief visit to the broiler. Voilà! The creation was christened with her initials and the MSB has since become the *pièce de résistance,* the cornerstone, of her restaurant.

Its recognition in Durham is well deserved. The MSB is a sandwich event, an absolutely remarkable combination of flavors, each delicious on its own, from the homemade bread straight up through the cheese, but the combination is even greater than the sum of its parts. It was the best sandwich we ate in six weeks of solid eating. But in all fairness we must say that the Sprouted Mushroom, another Mary Bacon original, was a very close second. Who knows what else we could have found had we the time (or the room) to try the many others, like the Delancy Street Special—pita stuffed with smoked bluefish, cream cheese, and a "special" dressing—or the multigrain Beanburger with melted blue cheese.

The setting for these outstanding sandwiches—as well as a wide selection of homemade soups, salads, and entrées—is rather on the earthy side. This is where young Duke University students go to see what a hippie is supposed to look like, although they're likely to be disappointed (or misinformed) because most everyone we saw here fit quite reasonably into the present decade. True, the decor incorporates barnboard and whole tree trunks (used as posts), but it's clean, light, and quite pleasant overall. Perhaps it's the bulletin board, where you can read announcements of yoga courses, folk concerts, old movies, and women's self-defense classes, that gives the place that '60s feel.

The menu is entirely vegetarian, loosely interpreted for the '80s to include seafood. Sandwiches, snacks, drinks (including some luscious yogurt-based smoothies), and bagels made by a subway-token-toting New Yorker are available all day, and at dinner time an eclectic selection of entrées appears: Middle Eastern tabouli and falafel, Indonesian curried shrimp, Oriental stir-fries, Mexican burritos, and more. Teas, both black and herbal, and coffee variations, from Cafix to cappuccino, finish you off in fine style.

Sandwich prices run $2.65 to $3.95 (halves available), full-meal salads are around $4, and dinner entrées average $5.

HOURS   Lunch: Tues.–Sat. 11:30 am–2:30 pm. Dinner: Tues.–Thurs. 5:30–9:30 pm; Fri. & Sat. 5:30–10 pm; Sun. 5:30–9 pm. Sunday brunch: 10 am–2 pm.

SPECS   1104 Broad St.; (919) 286-1019; no cards; full license.

DIRECTIONS   From exit marked Guess Road/NC School of Science & Math, turn left if southbound, right if northbound, onto Guess Road. In about ½ mile, at a five-corner intersection, take a gentle right onto Broad. In 0.4 mile, cross Club Blvd., and you'll find **Some Thyme** near the end of the first block, on left, before the florist. It doesn't jump out at you, but you'll see it if you look.

ANOTHER THYME, *Gregson Street Exit, Durham*

We enjoyed Some Thyme so much that we wanted to experience its younger, uptown sister, Another Thyme. What we found was an urbane café that attracts Durham's smart set and emanates an air of culture and charm. Smooth hardwood trim, handsomely mounted black-and-white photography on salmon-colored walls, and a slickly finished bar contrast markedly with the homemade decor of Some Thyme, but the food carries on the tradition of excellence.

You won't find beanburgers on the menu at Another Thyme, but MSB's, Sprouted Mushrooms, Vegetarian Pockets, and most of Mary Bacon's other sandwiches and dinner entrées are to be found at her newer restaurant. The decor may be tonier, but the prices are just as reasonable.

In addition, Another Thyme cooks up a few exotics to expand the culinary horizons of even the most cosmopolitan Durhamites. Trekokker is perhaps the most unusual, an appetizer that many are afraid to try. We can't really understand why: the deep-fried pieces of Camembert, garnished with apple slices and strawberry preserves, are as gorgeous to the tongue as to the eye.

You'll eat well at either place; just pick your decor.

HOURS   Lunch: Mon.–Fri. 11:30 am–2:30 pm; Sat. noon–2:30 pm. Dinner: Sun.–Thurs. 5:30–10 pm; Fri. & Sat. 5:30–10:30. Limited menu between lunch and dinner (except Sun.) and after dinner until midnight or later (every day).

SPECS   109 N. Gregson St.; (919) 682-5225; V/MC; full license.

DIRECTIONS   **Northbound:** Use Gregson St. exit; at the light, go straight and in about 1¼ miles, it's on your right, after the light at Morgan.

Southbound: From Gregson St. exit, turn right and follow signs for Gregson St. Go about 1½ miles; it's on your right, after the light at Morgan.

Note: Travelers on I-40 who enter I-85 in Durham should follow directions given on page 74.

SYBLE'S RESTAURANT, *Creedmore Exit, Creedmore*

Syble's Restaurant is one of those truck stops with a far-flung reputation, distinguished from other such establishments by the fact that here the food is really good. We might have guessed it from the outside when we noticed that all the trucks in the parking lot were pickups with local plates, but the new, clean, dark, and plastic interior gives no tip-off to the good cooking.

It was early in our southern travels when we visited Syble's. We were still anxious to experience the North Carolina barbecue mystique in all its manifestations—even in a truck stop that didn't look at all like the authentic country shack of our imagination. Again we learned that authenticity doesn't count for all that much in the world of barbecue. Our soft bun of minced pork, liberally doused in a pungent vinegar sauce, was really quite delicious, and it left us wondering how a place with so ordinary a menu could produce such smoky delights. Weeks later we learned that it's common for an "authentic" local pit to supply the smoked meat to pitless restaurants, with no apparent loss of flavor.

Most of Syble's menu is straight southern cooking at very reasonable prices. A dinner of country ham and red-eye gravy goes for just $3.25; fried chicken for $3.95. You can spend $7.95 for a rib-eye steak, but you can also get a sandwich for as little as $.75 ($1.75 tops). If Syble tends to the other details as well as she manages those we tested, you can be assured of more than your money's worth whatever you choose.

But to get back to barbecue, it was at Syble's we learned that cole slaw does not come on the side with a barbecue sandwich. To our initial horror we found the tiny bits of minced cabbage right in there between the buns, all mixed up with the meat! We munched bravely onward and soon realized the foolishness of our Yankee prejudices. Delicious—with or without the slaw.

HOURS   24 hours daily.

SPECS   (919) 528-9998; V/MC; beer and wine.

DIRECTIONS   0.2 mile east of the NC 56 exit, on the left.

SKIPPER'S BARBECUE,
Parham Road & US 158 Exits, Henderson

There are two well-established barbecue joints in Henderson, and much debate over their relative merits. Since the competition was closed when we passed through, Skipper's won by default.

Now folks here say that Skipper's just isn't the same since it moved from its original shack to a new (but hardly fancy) building. Could be, but what we found in the new environs was certainly tasty enough to justify a stop, and far better than anything you'll get from the chains. Whether you choose a barbecue and cole slaw tray ($2.35/$2.95/$3.35), half a barbecued chicken ($3.85), Brunswick stew, or a good thick vegetable soup, you can't spend more than $4.25. You'll be fed quickly, and you'll probably go away satisfied.

At the left turn on the way to Skipper's you'll pass the competition, Nunnery-Freeman's. If you'd like to cast a vote in the great Henderson debate, have half your meal at each, and pay special attention to the hushpuppies that seem to be the special bone of contention.

HOURS   Mon.–Sat. 10 am–9 pm. Closed Sun.

SPECS   (919) 438-5228; no cards; beer only.

DIRECTIONS   **Northbound:** Exit is labeled US 158E (Bypass). At the light at the end of the ramp go left and continue 0.6 mile. On the right.

Southbound: Exit is labeled Parham Rd. Go left at the end of the ramp, 1 block to a stop sign. Turn left and go 0.6 mile. On the right.

MIDDLEBURG STEAK HOUSE,
Fleming Road Exit, Norlina

Don't come to the Middleburg Steak House in search of subtle cuisine. It is exactly what its name implies, an all-American meat-and-potatoes restaurant to the core. The only alternatives to beef are a couple of lobster tails and a child's chicken fillet. Rib eyes are the house specialty ($8.75 for 6 ozs. and a dollar for every 2 ozs. beyond that). Then comes an 8-oz. fillet for $10.25, beef kabob for $8.95, a N.Y. strip $10.25, and barbecued beef ribs for $7.25. Take your pick. The price includes a trip to the salad bar, baked potato or steak fries, a chunk of Texas toast, and coffee or tea. That just about exhausts the menu, but what the Middleburg does, it does well. You can be assured that if such plain but hearty fare is your mood, you won't do much better in this part of the world.

The lack of imagination in the Middleburg's menu is partly made up for by its wonderful old building. It's the only log cabin we know to have been built with Depression era relief funds, and like many such public works, it was done on a grand scale (for a log cabin). The horizontal lines of gray weathered logs are interrupted by vertical columns of handsome stonework, which is a touch we'd never seen before. It's not Chartres, by any means, but it was built to be a community hall, and in its modest way it's an interesting monument to civic pride.

The setting is quiet, rural, and lovely, while on the inside all is quite pleasantly rustic—fireplace, log ceiling beams, red-checked tablecloths, plain wood chairs, and candles. There's an unnecessary touch of old-time decoration, but nothing offensive at all. Quite a pleasant little spot for a quiet meal.

HOURS　Wed.–Sat. 5:30 pm–10 pm; Sun. 5:30 pm–9 pm.

SPECS　(919) 492-7088; beer and wine.

DIRECTIONS　Northbound exit is marked US1/NC 158/Fleming Rd. Southbound exit is marked Fleming Rd./Middleburg. In either case just go 0.9 mile east toward Middleburg. On the left.

Virginia

BRIAN'S STEAK HOUSE, *Exit 2, South Hill*

Central South Hill boasts two flea markets, a religious bookstore, and not much else. For eats there's only a pizza joint that was as run-down as any we've seen and a burned-out diner.

Thus, almost by default, Brian's is *the* local restaurant even though it nestles in happily among the fast-food places at Exit 2.

It's new, clean, and plasticky, distinguished by a large greenhouse dining area and a ceiling thoroughly hung with a forest of plants and fans. It is also friendly and inexpensive. It has liquor-by-the-drink, good hours, and it's close to the road. Unfortunately its virtues don't extend to its cooking. The ribs and hash browns were mediocre, and the salad dressing was just OK. And what can you say about a slab of Texas toast, a 1½-inch-thick chunk of buttered Wonder Bread that grew up in the Lone Star State and could well have stayed there?

Brian's will do in a pinch, but don't go out of your way.

HOURS   Daily 6 am–10 pm.

SPECS   (804) 447-3169; AE/V/MC; full bar.

DIRECTIONS   On US 58, 0.6 mile north of Exit 2. On the right.

THE NOTTOWAY RESTAURANT, *Exit 8, Warfield*

For some reason there is fixed in our minds a certain image of a middle-class, rural Virginia restaurant—a vaguely colonial affair put together with conventional good taste, slightly stuffy, entirely local, specializing in fried chicken, and inhabited by people who always look as if they're on their way to church. This image the Nottoway fulfilled in every detail. Except for a few men in cowboy hats, the clientele consisted mostly of older women who gossiped quietly and pleasantly at the Formica tables and obviously enjoyed their pan-fried chicken, bland vegetables, and soft rolls, all the while maintaining an air of dignity that seemed just a bit too grand for the surroundings.

Let there be no mistake about it—the chicken was very good. The pan frying seems to make it less greasy than a dip in a vat of hot oil. The result was a flaky, mild product that left us licking our fingers and chewing the bones for every last morsel of flavor. At $4.95 for half a bird with two vegetables, it's a fair deal.

Other specialties include numerous variations on Virginia ham and a local oddity—a cold plate of sardines, sweet onions,

239

potato salad, sliced tomatoes, and crackers ($3.95). Sandwiches are as inexpensive as $.75. An 8-oz. fillet tops the reasonably complete menu at $9.25.

While you won't find any really rare culinary treasures at the Nottoway, it's quite perfect in its own way and you'll have to go far to do any better. It is what it is, and it's been here for 50 years, run by the Harrison family for the last 25.

HOURS   Mon.–Sat. 6 am–9 pm; Sun. 7 am–9 pm.

SPECS   (804) 478-7875; V/MC/AE; beer only.

DIRECTIONS   0.1 mile north of Exit 8, on the left. Can't be missed.

KING'S BARBEQUE, *Exit 13B, Petersburg*

North Carolina friends told us to have no truck with Virginia barbecue, so it was with some trepidation that we entered this, the northernmost "Q" establishment of our Southland tasting tour. The wonderful aromas that rose from the fireplace right behind the counter put us quickly at ease. There were the crusty chunks of pork smoking temptingly away, and the moment we tasted the sauce's pungent blend of vinegar and tomato flavors, we knew we were going to be happy whether or not this was the "real thing." One month and a hundred barbecue joints later, we felt qualified to declare with authority that King's offerings were good stuff by anyone's standards.

King's has other advantages, too. For one thing, you get to

eat in a quite pleasant (even if innocuous) new building, sort of colonial-looking on the outside and knotty-pine-warm within. For another, it was one of the few barbecue places we found that offered anything besides its savory specialty. If you want a hamburger, King's can take care of you. All of which means that a barbecue joint doesn't have to be authentic-looking to be good. Or to be cheap—barbecue sandwiches at $1.05 and $1.80, a full dinner for $3.75.

For those who insist on authenticity, the tumbledown J. J. Rawlings Pit-Cooked Barbeque is right next door, outdoor seating and all. But only King's has french-fried sweet potatoes.

HOURS   Tues.–Sun. 6 am–9 pm. Closed Mon. & Dec. 25–30.

SPECS   (804) 732-5861; no cards; no liquor.

DIRECTIONS   From Exit 13B go north on US 1 for 1.6 easy miles. On the left.

I-95

Florida
Georgia
South Carolina
North Carolina
Virginia

Florida

JOE'S STONE CRAB RESTAURANT,
Exit 5, Miami Beach

Among legendary Florida restaurants, Joe's Stone Crab has few peers. It dates from 1913, a year that may not seem ancient to Yankees accustomed to dining at colonial inns and Victorian hotels. But when a waiter named Joe Weiss opened Miami Beach's first restaurant, Miami proper was still a swamp and the Beach a pelican roost.

Ten years later Joe added to his menu a seafood delicacy that was virtually unknown outside Dade County—the outsized claws of Miami's resident crustacean, the stone crab. Back then, wrote Damon Runyon, these critters "were so numerous that a man could dip a foot anywhere in Biscayne Bay and come up with a stone crab hanging on each toe." It must have been a painful way to go crabbing, and other, even more effective, methods were devised, much to the detriment of the crab population. Now the crab harvest is carefully regulated; only one claw can be taken from each animal, which is then thrown back in the water to regenerate the missing limb, a process that takes about 2 years.

Very little kitchen wizardry is applied to the claws from the time they leave their original owners until you find them stacked in a handsome heap upon a pewter platter at Joe's. Because the

242

firm, sweet flesh is highly perishable, the claws are steamed right at the dock, then buried in ice. They will never again be heated, for stone crabs are eaten cold. For condiments, expect drawn butter, mustard, and lemon wedges. We preferred a squeeze of lemon alone, but had great fun experimenting with all the combinations.

Stone crabs really are delicious, a South Florida experience you wouldn't want to miss unless you're the type that visits Maine without eating lobster. Unfortunately, as with many South Florida experiences, stone crabs don't come cheap. "You want a delicacy? You gotta pay for it," said our waiter with perfect candor (and snobbery). What you gotta pay is $15.50; for that you get five foot-long claws, beautifully peach-colored and black-tipped, and a basket of wonderful breads—salt rolls, onion rolls, rye bread, pumpernickel, and black raisin—all of it the highest quality. If picking at crab claws doesn't appeal, you can get the same crusty bread with other local seafood entrées that include red snapper, frogs' legs, yellowtail, Spanish mackerel, pompano, and some more familiar names. These run $5–$10, lunch or dinner. And no matter what you order, you'll want to try Joe's fried sweet potatoes, a costly ($2) but worth-it variation on home fries.

Key lime pie is the dessert of choice; whether or not they use real key limes at Joe's we do not know. These perky little yellow-colored limes are said to be unavailable to anyone who doesn't grow them himself. Regardless, the pie at Joe's ($1.95) had a pleasantly bitter undertaste, a delightful contrast to the sugary meringues that most restaurants pass off for this dish. (Because the southern limit of this book was the end of I-95 in Miami, we did not have a chance to compare Joe's key lime pie with that served at Manny and Isa's on the Florida key of Islamorada. According to absolutely *everyone*, Manny and Isa's has the last word in key lime pie.)

Joe's is classy and suave, but not in the least bit cushy or plush. Like one or two venerable seafood houses in nearly every coastal city, it has a certain virile charm and authenticity that simply can't be ordered out of a catalog. Always a pleasure to find, restaurants of this ilk are especially rare in Johnny-come-lately Florida. Joe's sets a high standard for the others.

HOURS Open only during the crab season, mid-October to mid-May. Lunch: Mon.–Fri. 11:30 am–2 pm. Dinner: every day, 5–10 pm. Reservations advised during peak lunch and dinner hours.

SPECS 277 Biscayne St. (corner of Washington); (305) 673-0365; major cards; full license.

DIRECTIONS It's a 10-minute drive from I-95, more during rush hour. From Exit 5 (of I-95), enter I-395 East, which becomes the MacArthur Causeway. Get in the right lane. In 4 miles, immediately after crossing the bay, bear right onto Alton Road South. Go about ½ mile until Alton ends. Turn left onto Biscayne St. and go 1 block. On left.

LA ESQUINA DE TEJAS, *Exit 6, Miami*

How's this for the American dream? Wilfredo Chamizo leaves behind his restaurant and everything else he owns, takes his family, and flees Cuba for the United States, arriving on Thanksgiving Day 1961. Working as a dishwasher, and moonlighting at a factory job, he saves enough money to buy a small restaurant in Miami's Little Havana. The restaurant thrives. Then, on Cuban Independence Day 1983, he is paid a visit by no one less honorable than the President of the United States, who comes to lunch with complete entourage and press corps. *¡Muy, muy bien!*

President Reagan being about as popular in Little Havana as General Eisenhower was in France on D day, the visit spurred business even more, leading a *Miami Herald* columnist to suggest that a surefire way to boost the Miami economy would be to take the President on a whirlwind tour of every business in the city. So far, Chamizo is the only Miami restaurateur to benefit from this approach, and he knows a good thing when he owns it: the silverware, dishes, chair, even the table that Reagan used are now locked safely in a bank vault. "You wouldn't believe some of the offers we've had for them," said the owner's son, Will. We didn't have a chance to disbelieve because he wouldn't reveal any figures.

Now there's an immense red-white-and-blue bouquet in the spot where Reagan dined, and the menus are printed with his signature, seal, and message of good wishes. Everything he ordered is available as a combination plate called "The President's Choice." Of course we had to order it, and we found ourselves treated like heads of state. The food just kept coming and coming (no, they didn't know we were writing a book!), beginning with Cuban water bread, then a plate of pollo asado (half a roast chicken), moros (mixed black beans with rice), and fried platanos (Cuban bananas), followed by flan de coco (coconut flan, a velvety smooth custard), and café (potent Cuban-style coffee). We loved the sweet, chunky plantains; the chicken, mildly seasoned, was tender and juicy throughout. Politics aside, we were grateful to Ronald Reagan for enabling us to obtain such a prodigious quantity of food for only $5.40.

What the expatriate Cubans who frequent this authentically glitzy two-room restaurant eat, and what American Presidents (and guidebook authors) order are not one and the same. There are about 30 entrées on the bilingual menu (most $4–$6.50), and while some are as tame as T-bone steak or fried-pork fillet, a few others are exotic enough to discourage even our adventuresome palates: breaded brain, pickled kingfish, and tongue stew, for example. Although we were too stuffed from our presidential meal to even consider another dish, the favorite dessert, torreja ($1.20), sounded enticing—it's something like a sweet, uncooked French toast, the bread being soaked in cinnamon-and-anise-flavored honey syrup instead of egg. There are also sandwiches in the $1.50–$3.00 range.

But for entrées, the biggie, especially on a Saturday night, is Valenciana paella, an immense bowl brimming with seafood over saffron rice; its $24 price tag is steep, but it's meant for two. According to Chamizo, three can share it and still leave with doggie bags.

The restaurant's name, by the way, is a famous corner in Havana, literally "square of the roof shingles." A menu designer assumed that *Tejas* was Spanish for "Texas," and for that reason you'll find a map of the Lone Star State incongruously gracing every menu. It is not meant to suggest that LBJ got there before Ronald Reagan.

HOURS   8:30 am–midnight, every day of the year.

SPECS   101 S.W. 12th Ave.; (305) 545-5341; major cards; beer and wine.

DIRECTIONS   From Exit 6 enter Route 836 West, but almost immediately take the first exit for N.W. 12th Ave. Turn left and in exactly 1 mile you'll see the restaurant on the left side at the corner of S.W. 1st St. (It's 2 blocks past N.W. 1st St., which has a sign, whereas S.W. 1st does not.)

MARIO THE BAKER, *Exit 14, North Miami*

Mario Scinicariello *is* a baker, and a darn good one, but he's also an all-around Italian cook who runs a happy, noisy, little

Italian restaurant—noisy more because of its unsoftened surfaces than a rowdy clientele, and not exactly tiny but too small for its obvious popularity. The line of customers waiting to be seated regularly pokes its tail out the front door, but we were assured that the wait would be only 10 to 15 minutes. It was.

Mario's garlic rolls alone make the trip worth it. Toasty and crisp as a bagel on the outside, soft and chewy and slightly sweet within, they literally drip with garlic-infused olive oil. Make sure to tuck a napkin in your collar before you lift even one—we didn't, and our shirts still have the spots to prove it.

You won't get any garlic rolls if you order pizza, of course, and although the pizza is locally adored we didn't want to pass up the rolls, so we can't describe Mario's tomato pies. We can tell you, however, that it won't cost you very much to try them for yourself; even the largest pizza, with two items (all fresh) and great globs of mozzarella, costs only $6.25. (There are also submarine sandwiches in the $3 range.)

We accompanied our garlic rolls with eggplant Parmesan and baked ziti (both, $3.75) that we found hugely proportioned and redolent with all the herby flavors expected of tomato-based southern-Italian cookery. That's what you'll find here—solid red-sauce stuff, what we used to think of as Italian cuisine before fettuccine primavera and its chic northern cousins began displacing lasagna. We were happy to be reunited with our old tomato-topped friends.

HOURS Mon.–Thurs. 11 am–midnight; Fri. & Sat. 11 am–1 am; Sun. 1 pm–11 pm.

SPECS 13695 West Dixie Highway; (305) 891-7641; no cards; beer and wine.

DIRECTIONS Use Exit 14. If northbound, turn right at the bottom of the ramp onto 135th St. If southbound, go straight through the light at the bottom of the ramp, and turn left at the next light onto 135th St. Either way, take 135th for about 2 miles to the major intersection with West Dixie Highway (Route 909). Turn left and in 0.1 mile you'll see it on your right.

SAGE BAGEL AND APPETIZER SHOP,
Exit 21, Hallandale

The story, perhaps apocryphal, is that after the seventh brick in one year flew through the window of his Queens bagel shop, Milton Fuerst threw up his hands and said to his wife, "It must be a sign from God."

"To stop baking bagels?" she asked.

"No, to bake them in the Promised Land."

And so the Fuersts packed up their suitcases and their bagel shop and moved to Florida. Their baggage included a 14-foot-long brick-lined oven that had to be reconstructed brick by brick. But Milt Fuerst's bagels have to be made right or not at all, and that means they're baked in contact with hot bricks. Otherwise the result isn't bagels but doughnuts with rigor mortis.

Before he was ready to leave he picked up some more company for the trip, his friend Sid Eichen whose New York appetizer shop had sold many a spread that ended up on Milt's bagels. In Florida, the two men combined their talents into the Sage Bagel and Appetizer Shop, a commissary just as well stocked, just as well loved, and just as much of a madhouse as their New York paradigms.

As soon as you walk in, your eyes blink from the visual overload: hundreds upon hundreds of commercially produced items displayed in cans, jars, boxes, bags, and sundry other containers large and small. Equally impressive is the assortment of smoked fish, salads, and spreads, and ten bins of bagels that are constantly replenished from their place of origin behind swinging metal doors.

There are two serving counters, each staffed by half a dozen white-aproned men. Over their heads hang four or five dozen salamis, each proudly wearing its seal of kosher authenticity. After spending a few minutes getting oriented, we noticed that everyone waiting up front was holding numbered tickets while those at the side counter were not. A large sign instructed: "Numbers are not needed for deli only." Hmmm. Since a list of bagel sandwiches (simple cream cheese, $1.00, to roast beef, pastrami, corned beef, etc., $3.75) was posted behind the side counter, we queued up there without pulling a number.

Our turn finally came. "One bagel with pastrami, please . . ."

"Bagel with pastrami??!!" cried the counterman, in chorus with two of his coworkers who didn't even look up from their work. "You're in the wrong line." The others muttered corroboration.

We eventually got our sandwich, although we never did figure out how the place was supposed to work. Our advice is to be safe and take a number, and if there are two of you, strategically place one on each line.

Although most of Sage's business is takeout, there are chairs at a long skinny counter that faces the window. But it's kind of a shame to sit there, with the fun and craziness behind your back. The pastrami, in case you were wondering, was the real thing—lean, warm, and Hebrew National. On the side we had gefilte fish—homemade gefilte fish like we never had at home. And pickled herring (of which there were three kinds to choose), and a little whitefish. And rugalah, those wonderful, crispy, almond-flavored cookies. And . . . well, it's a good thing we arrived just before closing time or we'd probably still be there, not halfway through all of the possibilities.

HOURS   Mon.–Fri. 8 am–6:30 pm; Sat. 8 am–7 pm; Sun. 8 am–6 pm.

SPECS   Sage Plaza, 800 E. Hallandale Beach Blvd.; (305) 456-7499; no cards; no liquor.

DIRECTIONS   From Exit 21, head east on Hallandale Beach Blvd. In about 1½ miles cross US 1, and at the next light (N.E. 8th Ave.) turn right into Sage Plaza. You're there.

GRAPEVINE PUB, *Exit 29, Fort Lauderdale*

With 165 watery miles of navigable canals, it's been boosted as the "Venice of America"; with the nation's college campuses vacationing on its beaches and in its bars each March, it's earned the nickname Fort Liquordale; with 3,000 hours of sunshine in an average year, it claims to be the fastest-growing city in America. Whatever you want to call it, Fort Lauderdale is a vibrant, modern, cosmopolitan place, and we couldn't think of a better way to get a quick fix on this town than by stopping at the Grapevine Pub.

If the weather is calm (it almost always is), you will want to sit on the brick patio under a bower of grapevines. The restaurant's owner, Dr. Scot Wilson, is a physician by profession and a horticulturist by passion; a sign over the patio entryway reads, "Wilson's Botanical Garden," and that it is—a showcase for his collection of potted greenery. Everything that's not rooted in the ground is up for sale—ferns, zinnias, orchids, pencil plants, Scheffelera, crotons, and other flora both native and exotic.

Already overburdened with excess baggage, we didn't dare purchase anything we couldn't eat on the spot, much as we might have enjoyed the company of a four-foot crown-of-thorns in the backseat. And while the food wasn't quite as extraordinary as the setting, we quite enjoyed the combination lunch special ($3.75)—most of it, anyway. After a cup of mediocre vegetable soup came two charming mini-sandwiches on finger rolls, with an applaudable potato salad and a luscious fresh-fruit garnish on the side. It was served, unfortunately, on a plastic plate with plastic pouches of mayonnaise sitting unceremoniously on top of what would otherwise have been a very attractive presentation.

At dinner time, the plasticware gives way to china, and the menu changes from quiche/salads/sandwiches in the $4–$5 range to chicken/ribs/seafood in the $6–$11 area. Shrimp is popular, especially when stuffed into a half-pineapple along with tropical fruit ($8.95). At the low end, there are croissants de soir, sandwich style (under $4.00); and at the other side of the spectrum are all-you-can-eat seafood specials, like stone crab claws ($22.95) or you-peel-them steamed shrimp ($17.95).

HOURS   Mon. 7:15 am–3 pm; Tues.–Fri. 7 am–10 pm; Sat. 5–10 pm; closed Sun.

SPECS   309 North New River Drive East; (305) 462-6495; MC/V; beer and wine.

DIRECTIONS   From Exit 29, head east on Broward Blvd. (Route 842) toward downtown Fort Lauderdale. Go about 1½ miles to S. Andrews Ave. Turn right, go 0.2 mile to the second light, and turn left onto E. Las Olas Blvd. Just 1 block on Las Olas and then turn right on S.E. 1st Ave. Follow it around the curve; as soon as you've passed under the bridge, pull into the restaurant's parking lot on your left. Five minutes tops. (Although they put out bumper stickers that say GRAPEVINE PUB —TRY AND FIND US, it isn't difficult, *if* you know where to go. And now you do.)

TOM NORRIS' PLACE FOR RIBS, *Exit 32, Tamarac*

It's about 6½ miles out of your way for some of the best ribs around. See description on page 317.

DIRECTIONS   From Exit 32, head west on Commercial Blvd. In roughly 6½ miles, you'll reach the light at University Drive. Turn right on University, and in one block, **Tom Norris'** is on your left.

YE TOWER RESTAURANT, *Exit 46, Lantana*

Lantana is known to the outside world as point of origin for one of America's least respected but best circulated newspapers, the *National Enquirer*. But the *Enquirer* is the new kid on the block: far more venerated is Ye Tower Restaurant.

Paul Dunbar opened his doors in 1925, and although he now locks them at night, little else has changed since then. His is the oldest existing business in Palm Beach County, a relic from the days when prospective real estate buyers arrived from New York by the trainload. Paul was with them, but instead of staking out his parcel, he started a barbecue stand to feed the others. He picked a choice location at the base of a 55-foot tower climbed by the land hunters in order to view the plots. A few years later the tower was creamed by a hurricane, but Paul retained the name and has since built a 5 foot facsimile on the roof.

With a shock of white hair that would blind an Eskimo, the octogenarian has a twinkle in his eye and a kind word to say about any subject under the Florida sun. At one time he was mayor of Lantana, and through his efforts, a 3,000-foot strip of pristine shoreline has been preserved in perpetuity—quite the exception on Florida's overdeveloped Gold Coast. Now Paul keeps out of politics, but you'll still find him in the kitchen of his restaurant, where he flips the burgers and bakes the pies six days a week and plays golf on the seventh. "It's all the recreation I need," he remarks, clearly implying that the word retirement is not in his vocabulary.

Paul is not at all reticent about discussing his cooking techniques, and he'll even show you the 1919 edition of the *Fanny Farmer Cook Book*, from which he takes some of his recipes. Obviously we were charmed by him and his tiny stucco building, and we weren't disappointed by his simple all-American fare.

Prices have gone up 1,000 percent since the old days, but at $1.50, we couldn't call his barbecue sandwiches expensive. Cheese and egg salad sandwiches, and hamburgers, are 60 cents! But hoisting ourselves up onto shiny stools at the old-fashioned soda fountain, we couldn't resist ordering milkshakes and chocolate malts. Our sweet teeth satisfied, we settled down to a tasty, dripping barbecue sandwich and then Paul's rib-sticking corned-beef hash ($2.95 as a dinner with two vegetables, bread and butter). None of it is likely to receive *Florida Trend* magazine's Golden Spoon award, but we found it hearty and satisfying just the same.

HOURS   Mon.–Sat. 8 am–3 pm and 5–9 pm; closed Sundays and holidays.

SPECS   916 South Dixie Highway; (305) 586-9607; no cards; beer.

DIRECTIONS   From Exit 46 (Lantana Road/C.R. 812) head east. Go about 1 mile to US 1 (Dixie Highway) and turn right. In about 3/4 mile it's on your left (corner of Central Blvd.)

HAMBURGER HEAVEN, *Exit 52A, Palm Beach*

In Palm Beach, where blood runs true blue and driving the Rolls yourself is a sign of hard times, we knew we'd have to find an affordable perch from which to conduct some discreet voyeurism. That proved simple: everyone we asked—millionaires and mortals alike—suggested Hamburger Heaven.

As we learned from the bulletin board entitled HAMBURGER HEAVEN MEMORY LANE, the original angels of this particular heaven were Mr. and Mrs. William McDonald who opened their gates after eating at every restaurant Duncan Hines had recommended between their home in Connecticut and Palm Beach. That was in 1945, and within one year Hamburger Heaven itself was recognized by the traveler's Bible, Hines's *Adventures in Good Eating*.

Hamburger Heaven still provides the earthly pleasure of burgers that are out of this world. Made from the very leanest cuts, ground daily on the premises, they are served on kaiser rolls or English muffins, and cooked to order. Our Everglades Burger came open-faced, topped with a mountain of onions, mushrooms, and melted cheddar cheese. A Vegetable Burger is crowned with ratatouille, while the popular Palm Beach burger comes with melted Swiss and cheddar over bacon. All of these cost $3.75.

Hamburgers aren't the only candidates admitted to this

253

heaven. Breakfasts include a few fancy things (eggs creole, for instance), in addition to familiar omelettes and two eggs over light ($2 and up). There are lunch and dinner specials too—chicken and broccoli in cream sauce, for example, served in a popover alongside salad and a beverage ($5.95, including beverage). For the figure-conscious, there is a plethora of diet plates, but any gains made by eating tuna salad on melba toast are imperiled by a counter stacked with gorgeous desserts.

Pert and pretty, Hamburger Heaven doesn't look much different than any other well-put-together luncheonette except that the tables are adorned with Perrier bottles and fresh flowers. Although the *Wall Street Journal* can be seen at half the customers' tables, there are no displays of sartorial splendor. But out the front door and off to our Toyota, any class distinctions that may have blurred came right back into focus.

HOURS   7:30 am–9 pm, every day.

SPECS   314 South County Rd.; (305) 655-5277; no cards; no liquor.

DIRECTIONS   Exit 52A puts you on Okeechobee Blvd. East, which you should take for about 1½ miles until you've crossed the drawbridge into Palm Beach. (You'll *know* when you're there.) The second light over the bridge is South County Road. Turn right; it's on the right at the end of the block.

ENRIQO'S MEXICAN KITCHEN, *Exit 65, Fort Pierce*

While he was a seagoing carpenter in the merchant marine, Gene Seissiger visited nearly every port of call in Mexico, and he took with him his penchant for hearty eating. Now he's stateside again, cooking up some of his favorite Mexican discoveries. Having experienced the real thing, Gene won't limit his menu to the typical Tex-Mex dishes that Americans love, so along with the tacos, burritos, and chiles rellenos, Gene puts out less familiar machacas, carnitas, and mamuts.

No matter which side of the menu you order from, you'll find the food fresh and homemade. He mixes his own salsa, marinates fresh chiles in his own kitchen, and rolls the tortillas into taco shells. The tortillas, in fact, are quite literally homemade—

by a Mexican friend of Gene's who lives in Lake Worth and ships the cornmeal rounds by Greyhound bus every morning. When they arrive they're still warm.

We wanted to check out both the familiar and the unfamiliar, and so we went for a chile relleno and a plate of carnitas, the latter being cubes of pork, seasoned to tongue-tingling piquancy and served with refried beans, rice, and tortillas. Our plaudits went to both dishes.

The most you can spend for a complete dinner at Enriqo's (not counting appetizers) is $5.35; many items are a dollar or more below that. Lunch specials run $2.50 to $3.50. It's not overly atmospheric, but oil lanterns on barnboard walls emanate a warm, ruddy glow that is reflected off red-checked tablecloths.

HOURS Lunch: Mon.–Fri. 11:30 am–2 pm. Dinner: Mon.–Thurs. 4–9 pm; Fri. & Sat. 5–10 pm. Closed Sun.

SPECS Center West Plaza, 3215 South US 1; (305) 465-1608; no cards; beer, wine, and homemade sangria.

DIRECTIONS **Southbound:** From Exit 65, bear left onto Route 70 East toward Fort Pierce. Follow Route 70 (Okeechobee Rd.) for about 1½ miles. ■ At the fork across from the Orange Blossom Mall bear right onto Virginia Ave. In 2½ miles, turn right onto US 1 South. Go about 1¼ mile to Center West Shopping Center on the right; **Enriqo's** is to the right of the movie theater.

Northbound: Northbound travelers will be on Florida's Turnpike because I-95 is discontinued at Fort Pierce. Take Exit 56 off the Turnpike, and follow signs for Route 70 East (Okeechobee Rd.). In 1½ miles, you'll pass under I-95; keep going straight for another 1½ miles, and then follow directions above, from ■.

THE FISH MONGER, *Exit 66A, Fort Pierce*

When 2,500 gold doubloons were recovered from a 1715 Spanish shipwreck off Fort Pierce a few years ago, city boosters immediately dubbed the region Florida's "Treasure Coast." Rather than exploit the sunken-booty motif, however, this restaurant is more interested in boosting its own treasure—well-prepared, unfailingly fresh seafood.

With only a very small number of exceptions, the menu is entirely original. Owner/chef Jim Longstreet loves to play with recipes, borrowing a little from one and grafting it onto another, substituting this for that or that for this, and coming up with something he can call his own. His Grouper a la Oscar, created by tampering with a famous veal and asparagus dish, won "Best in Show" at the first annual "Foodarama" competition involving restaurants from a four-county area. You can order it ($12.95) for your dinner; having come at the lunch hour, we could not.

Of the many sandwiches on the midday menu, a grouper club sounded most tempting, and we weren't disappointed by its three layers of fried fish and fixings. We also ordered the day's lunch special, although it wasn't seafood at all: chicken salad with pineapple, banana, and grapes in a sour-cream dressing. Stuffed in a half-pineapple and garnished with chopped pecans, it made a stunning presentation and a spritely meal.

Both the grouper club and the chicken salad cost $4.95, including soup, french fries, and salad from a handsome buffet laid out on a fishmonger's cart. Like everything else served in this attractive nautical-style family restaurant, the salad bar's bounty suffers from no unwelcome additives, artificial sweeteners, or fresheners. Jim, who could hardly be called a health-food nut, is deeply concerned that his food be as pure and healthy as possible and has thus banned from his kitchen all products that contain preservatives or other chemicals. Because animal fats may turn into carcinogens under high temperature, all frying is done in vegetable oil, and the oil is changed, not filtered, daily.

Lunches, as many of them meaty as fishy, run $3.95–$6.95, and all include access to the salad cart. Dinners lean more heavily on fruits of the sea, ranging from $8.50 to $15.95. Child's portions are $5.95.

HOURS Tues.–Sun. 11:30 am–11:30 pm; light meals in lounge until 1:30 am. Closed Mon.

SPECS 21 Fisherman's Wharf; (305) 465-8620; MC/V; full license.

DIRECTIONS From Exit 66A you will be on Route 68 East. In about 4 miles turn left onto US 1 North. Go about ¾ mile to the light at Fisherman's Wharf. Turn right, cross the railroad tracks, and in about 500 feet it's on your right.

Note: Approaching Fort Pierce, only southbound travelers will be on I-95; northbound travelers will be on Florida's Turnpike. They should use the Turnpike's Exit 56 and enter I-95 for about 2 miles to the first exit, Exit 66A; then use directions given above.

THE ATHENIAN, *Exit 71, Melbourne*

Sitting proudly behind a blue and white canopy and a window full of plants, the Athenian has been serving breakfast and lunch in downtown Melbourne for longer than most of the city's current residents have been around to eat it. No one seemed to know just when it opened, but this neighborhood luncheonette wears the luster of age, and it wears it with the kind of grace and dignity that we find irresistible in a restaurant. Verifying our hunch that the clientele was purely local, our waitress apologized for neglecting us as newcomers. Since she hadn't ignored us for more than a minute, we could only wonder what kind of service the regulars receive.

As expected, the culinary emphasis is on things Balkan, but we found more Greek travel posters on the walls than dishes on the menu. A Greek salad is available every day ($2.75), and each weekday finds a Greek special (moussaka, spanakopita, etc., generally around $3). Otherwise, it's an unfettered American menu with sandwiches, burgers, and the like, all under $2.

Low as the lunchtime prices are, breakfasts are half as much. Two eggs with handcut home fries and a remarkably fluffy homemade biscuit cost $1.15; coffee adds but 15 cents to the bill!

Once all towns had places like this, but competition from franchise and chain restaurants drove most of them into history. Downtown Melbourne's neighborhood lunchroom has survived, although you'll have to drive through 6½ miles of fast-food jungle to get there. We think you'll find the detour worthwhile.

HOURS   Mon.–Fri. 6 am–4 pm; Sat. 6 am–1 pm. Closed Sun. and holidays.

SPECS   1904 Municipal Lane; (305) 727-8066; no cards; no liquor.

DIRECTIONS   From Exit 71, turn onto Route 192 East toward Melbourne. In about 5½ miles (moves fairly fast), the road forks. Bear left with Route 192. About ¾ mile later, turn right onto Municipal Lane (1 block after the light at Waverly Place). It's on your right in the middle of the first block.

CORKY BELL'S, *Exit 72, Melbourne*

We faced an immediate dilemma as we entered this year-old no-nonsense stucco hut of a seafood restaurant. Arriving at 6 pm on a Friday evening, we discovered a line that had already doubled back upon itself. Should we even consider writing about Corky Bell's? Would our readers be willing to brave such a queue? One conclusion was inescapable: either Melbourne was suffering from acute seafood deprivation or Corky Bell's was doing something right. After consultation with a few of the contented, surfeited customers, it was easy to see which was the case.

But how long would we have to wait in order to prove it? The hostess, who was entering names into a bulging spiral notebook, said 20 minutes. We didn't believe her. Off we went to peruse shop windows in nearby stores, blithely returning 40 minutes later.

"Schwartz?" she said as we walked in the door. "I called you twenty minutes ago."

When we (finally) could observe the action, it became clear that at least part of the attraction of Corky Bell's is the prodigious quantities of food bestowed upon the diners. They heap (and we mean *heap*) the food on huge (and we mean *huge*) round metal trays and serve it family style to each table or booth. As at any self-respecting southern seafood house, all meals include hushpuppies, cole slaw, and french fries (or baked potato). Choose among four fish dinners (catfish, snapper, trout, and flounder, $5.25–$7.25) or about a dozen combinations of shellfish ($7.50–$11.50). It's not cheap, but you sure won't go hungry, and there is no charge for sharing, a practice that we would recommend to all but the most ravenous. Lunch specials are more modest both in quantity and price (around $4.00).

Having raised our cholesterol levels well above recommended limits long before arriving at Corky Bell's, we first decided upon a platter of boiled shrimp. It arrived, in the gargantuan proportion described, and it tasted—well, it tasted like boiled shrimp. What else can we say? Nice-sized, meaty, fresh boiled shrimp. The cocktail sauce was nothing to write books about and the hushpuppies were a little too salty, but the cole slaw, made with both green and red cabbage, was tangy, crisp, and obviously homemade.

Of course, the great majority of Corky Bell's customers go straight for the fried seafood, and we had to try some before we left. So a "medium" fried trout dinner (nothing called "small" is offered here) came next, sweet, succulent, and cooked to suggest crispness but not desiccation.

We weren't at all sorry to have stopped here and waited (twice); we only wished we had someplace to bring the doggie bag.

HOURS Mon.–Thurs. 11 am–9 pm; Fri. 11 am–10 pm; Sat. noon–10 pm; Sun. noon–9 pm.

SPECS Sarno Plaza, 2088 Sarno Blvd.; (305) 259-7230; MC/V; beer.

DIRECTIONS From Exit 72, turn right if northbound, left if south-bound, onto Sarno Blvd. Go 3 miles and you'll reach Sarno Plaza on your left. It's at the far end of the shopping center, in a separate building.

THE BLACK TULIP, *Exit 75, Cocoa Village*

Cocoa Village is a gussied-up community of shops with names like the Strawberry Patch, the Pear Tree, Potpourri, and the Village This or the Village That (Men's Shop, Book Store, Country Store, etc.). For nourishment, choose between several deli-style sandwich shops, a juice bar, an ice cream parlor, and a low-priced crêperie. Or get serious about your meal and head straight for Cocoa's celebrated restaurant, the Black Tulip.

Arriving without reservations, you may find yourself waiting on line to be seated, but maitre d' Tom Hietpas assures that even that will be a pleasurable experience. "Anyone who has the courtesy to wait," he declares, "receives a glass of wine or a cocktail on the house." Since the Black Tulip has only a limited liquor license, a cocktail here is not your run-of-the-gin-mill highball, but an original creation that will linger on the tongue long after the dessert course. We heartily commend Tom's "Tulip Delight," a spritzer of plum wine, club soda, and Dry Sack sherry. Any misgivings about pausing for a leisurely meal dissolve with the first sip.

The wait also affords you the opportunity to drink in the warm essence of the Black Tulip's decor, an unusual (and successful) blend of gallery and bistro, with slightly baroque trimmings and a tulip motif that is carried off with subtlety and good taste.

While Tom oversees the customers' happiness on the floor, his partner Daniel Colzani holds sway in the kitchen. Dill is clearly Dan's favorite herb, and its aromatic signature is imprinted in almost every sauce and dressing. There's plenty of it in the mushroom barley soup that has been featured in *Cuisine* magazine; we passed that by in order to sample a remarkable conch chowder that was also flavored by the versatile herb, but even more by delectable morsels of Florida's State Mollusk. On Fridays, Tom told us with unbridled pride, people call in to reserve it.

The cuisine is Continental and *nouvelle;* expect dinners like fettuccine primavera ($7.75) or fillets of beef with an artichoke sauce ($9.95); there's also an emphasis on fresh Florida seafood, so you'll see the likes of grouper with toasted almonds and sautéed shrimp in hollandaise ($9.75). Lunches, most in the $3.50–$4.00 range, run from burgers and chicken salad to quiche and omelettes—less exotic than dinner, to be sure, but very well prepared and beautifully presented in copious quantities.

Though more than satisfied, we could not resist a poached pear for dessert. Served cold, this whole Bosc pear came in a light cinnamon-spiced Burgundy sauce that, on its own, could have made an elegant cocktail.

HOURS   Lunch: Mon.–Sat. 11:30 am–3 pm. Dinner: Mon.–Sat. 6–10 pm. Sundays, usually closed but occasionally open; call to check. Reservations a must for weekend dinners.

SPECS   207 Brevard Ave.; (305) 631-1133; major cards; beer, wine, and aperitifs.

DIRECTIONS   From Exit 75, turn right if northbound, left if southbound, onto Route 520 East. In about 4 miles go straight through the light at US 1. Two lights later (Brevard Ave.), turn right and it's immediately on the right. Parking lot around the corner to your right.

SAND POINT INN, *Exit 80, Titusville*

Should you arrive at Sand Point Inn by sailboat, the restaurant will shuttle you from your moorage directly to the back door of the dining room. Cantilevered out over the Intracoastal Waterway, this striking wooden building gives all of its patrons—whether they arrive by land or by sea—a chance to try out their sea legs without getting seasick. Sand Point Inn is a study in how a seaside restaurant can make its orientation clear without cloaking its walls with fishnets, floats and lobster traps.

Owner Jack Baker is no small-time restaurateur; in fact, he also owns a fishery solely for the purpose of supplying this and his dozen other restaurants up and down the eastern seaboard. Nevertheless, Sand Point Inn is one of a kind, unlike anything else in Baker's restaurant stable.

Naturally, everything is fresh (from your table you can even watch shrimp boats approaching their dock), but it is also thoughtfully and carefully prepared. Unless you request it, your seafood will not be fried—baked, broiled, and casseroled preparations are far more popular. We feasted, for instance, on a plate of rock shrimp broiled in their shells, basted with butter and garlic. Rock shrimp are just little guys, but their taste is as sweet and their texture as firm as lobster (*Maine* lobster, that is, which, incidentally, is the only kind served). Here, they're split lengthwise, and arrive with a wee fork for the extracting and a bowl for the shuckings. On the side are a baked potato and a most welcome variation on hushpuppies. Made with creamed corn and fried in a beer batter, these pups were moist, textured, and ever so edible; you may wish to request them without the powdered-sugar garnish that they ordinarily wear.

Sand Point's low-priced lunch menu remains in effect until 6 pm. Thus, early birds can get dinner for midday prices. Our afternoon rock-shrimp meal, for instance, cost $4.95 at 5:30 pm, but it would have doubled half an hour later. Although early birds get slightly less to eat, they can supplement any quantitative deficiencies by paying an extra 95 cents to visit the U.S.S. *Salad Boat,* whose booty is attractively displayed on lush beds of romaine lettuce. In addition to its greens and vegetables, the salad bar has crackers which are often taken out to the deck where they end up in the mouths of nonpaying seagulls and pelicans.

It is also worth noting that the clam chowder we had here (95 cents/$1.25) would hold its own against Boston's finest; that sandwiches ($2.25–$3.95) are available before the 6 o'clock witch-

ing hour; and that pre-6 pm meal prices generally run $4–$6, with evening costs twice that. We should also direct your attention to the resin-topped collages of shells, driftwood, plants, and other coastline collectibles that have been frozen in place upon every tabletop. No two of them are alike, and each has its own unifying theme. A little gimmicky, to be sure, but we were impressed just the same with the variety of beachcombers' treasures on display and the fascinating geometries in which they appeared.

HOURS   Every day, 11:30 am–10 pm. Closed only for Thanksgiving.

SPECS   Marina Road; (305) 269-1012; all cards; full license.

DIRECTIONS   From Exit 80, turn right if northbound, left if southbound, onto Route 406 East. It's about 2¾ miles to the junction with US 1, at which you should turn left onto 1 North. Get in the right lane and in 0.2 mile, turn right, as if to enter the marina (this is just where US 1 curves off to the left). Immediately after turning toward the marina, take a left onto Marina Road. Go ½ mile on Marina Road and you'll see **Sand Point Inn** on your right.

KLAUS' CUISINE, *Exit 87, Daytona*

For 2 weeks that come around once in 4 years, the world's attention is bestowed upon a select corps of athletic performers who assemble at the Olympic Games. At about the same time, an equally talented cadre of performers gather to compete in games of a very different sort, the Culinary Olympics. In 1980, the head coach of America's gastronomic athletes was a Floridian named Klaus Friedenreich. His culinary prowess can be witnessed and tasted year-round in Daytona.

Klaus's cuisine is purely American, but not in the way that most people envision American food. To this chef, American cuisine means the finest native ingredients and a heavy dose of Yankee ingenuity. In 1980, it was that combination that resulted in medals for two Friedenreich entrées, Turkey Breast Oklahoma and Sea Bass Saint Augustine. At our own meal, we saw gold before we even got to the entrée.

"It's just sour cream, puréed strawberries, a dash of soda, and a dash of rum," volunteered our flowerily dressed waitress when she heard our oohs and aahs over Klaus's cold strawberry soup. With her wide-brimmed straw hat and basket of popovers, she was the very picture of cheeriness, and she fit right into the informally elegant decor. We hadn't asked her for the recipe, and even with it we doubt we can reproduce the wildly joyous flavors of this dish. We'll not soon forget them (nor their price tag, $2.75 per cup).

The house salad, heavy on iceberg, did not approach the strawberry soup, and our popover came out overbaked. (It was replaced.) Eventually we were ready for the Big Dish, Klaus's gold-medal-copping Turkey Breast Oklahoma. Technically it is a warm galantine: finely ground turkey is rolled flat, topped with Virginia ham stuffing, then rolled up, baked, and sliced. This happy marriage of compatible flavors comes with almond-sparked green beans (hooray—crisp, dark-green beans for a change) and a stuffed yellow squash.

All dinners include crackers with cheese spread, vegetable plate with dip, salad, popover, vegetables, and potato or wild rice; they run $9.25 (chicken cordon bleu) to $17.95 (rack of lamb); the two famous prize winners are both $9.50, and a sampler plate with three dishes is $14.95. Quantities are ample—we took some of our dinner away with us, wrapped in aluminum foil that had been crafted into a swan. At Klaus's, even the doggie bags have class.

HOURS Tues.–Sun. 5–10 pm; closed Mon. Reservations virtually essential weekends between 7 and 8:30 pm.

SPECS 144 North Ridgewood Ave. (actually in Holly Hills, just north of Daytona); (904) 255-7711; all cards; full license.

DIRECTIONS **Northbound:** From Exit 87, turn right onto Route 92 East. In 5 miles turn left on US 1 North. Go 1.2 miles; it's on your left.

Southbound: From Exit 89, turn left onto US 1 South. Go exactly 10 miles and it's on the right in the block after 2nd St. If you come to the light at Mason Ave., you've gone too far.

Note: This is not as great a detour as it might seem. After eating, do not retrace your steps, but reverse the instructions given above for travelers coming from the other direction. This is especially important if you are southbound. (If unclear about returning to I-95, ask at the restaurant.)

BRIDGETENDER INN, *Exit 91, Flagler Beach*

Appropriately enough, the Bridgetender stands sentry over a drawbridge on the Indian River, but the real draw here is the Bridgetender's nightly buffet. It's an all-you-can-gorge orgy of roast beef, roasted chicken, barbecue ribs, shrimp creole, seafood casserole, steamed rock shrimp, fried clam strips, baked trout, catfish, grouper fingers, crab patties—all of these and more, for $6.95.

It was really quite a spread, and for steam-table fare it was excellent. We especially liked the robust Manhattan chowder; if the sea were as thick with fish as that chowder, we'd all be able to walk on water. Other standouts were grouper and trout, but after a short while the multiplicity of piscine tastes began to merge.

The buffet is offered daily between 5 and 9 pm, and on Sundays a brunch buffet goes out from 11 am until 3 in the afternoon. (It's similar, but a little lighter on the seafood, which is replaced with waffles, grits, ham, home fries, and other breakfasty things.) If you miss the Bridgetender's buffet you won't go hungry, but you'll have to order from the sandwich-oriented lunch menu ($2–$3) or the mostly steak and fried-seafood dinner list ($6 and up).

As appropriate as the Bridgetender's name is its dockside decor. It's a very comfortable nautical-theme restaurant with an abundance of swordfish and ship models adorning rough wooden walls. Most of the decorations fit into the "seen it before" category, but we were enamored with the lighthearted wood carvings of birds, fish, and crusty old salts. When the weather allows, the best place to sit is under a sun umbrella on the riverside deck, among free-flowing fountains and free-flying seagulls. Boats of every ilk churn the water, and someone is bound to tell you that the Indian River is part of the Intracoastal Waterway that goes "all the way to New York." Not a bad way to travel, we thought, especially if there are restaurants like this all along the way.

HOURS   Every day, 11 am–11 pm.

SPECS   820 Moody Blvd.; (904) 439-3764; V/MC; full license.

DIRECTIONS   From Exit 91, turn right if northbound, left if southbound, onto Route 100 East. In 3 miles you'll cross a drawbridge, immediately after which you'll see the **Bridgetender** on your left.

ABOUT SAINT AUGUSTINE

"Old" and "oldest" are the bywords in Saint Augustine, America's first city. It was a half-century young when the Pilgrims immortalized a certain boulder on the coast of Massachusetts.

Saint Augustine's premier tourist attraction is the Castillo de San Marcos, known locally as the Old Fort. A block or so away is the Old City Gate. Also competing for antiquarian honors are the Oldest Wooden House, the Oldest Wooden Schoolhouse, and even the Oldest (continuously operated) Pharmacy. We fully expected to turn the corner and find the Oldest Restaurant.

That didn't happen, but what we did find in Saint Augustine was, if not the oldest, the highest concentration of quality restaurants we'd come across south of Washington, D.C. Finding a good meal in Saint Augustine isn't much harder than finding a tourist at Disney World. We've narrowed down the restaurant possibilities to a manageable trio of sure bets, but we will not claim that ours are the best. To satisfy your own culinary curios-

ity, we suggest you wander around town to explore the gastronomic turf. The chances are good that within minutes you'll have
discovered for yourself more worthy eateries than you could
sample in a week.

LE PAVILLON, *Saint Augustine*

Claude and Giselle Sinatsch are Swiss and German respectively, and it is not surprising to find that the menu of their
engaging restaurant, Le Pavillon, features fondue alongside hasenpfeffer as well as a few tasty items culled from the cuisine of
neighboring France.

As is often the case, what stands out in the memory of a fine
restaurant is not necessarily an elegant entrée or a divine dessert,
but a much less elaborate course; here it was the bread. Home-
baked sourdough rolls, they were sliced, garnished with butter
and Parmesan cheese, and toasted to a golden crustiness. For
these alone we would come back, but of course there was much
more.

The shrimp salad garni, for instance, arrived as gorgeous as a
Japanese still life arranged on the plate. There were wedges of
tomatoes and hard-boiled eggs, julienned vegetables, German
potato salad, and a luscious, satiny smooth shrimp spread. When
it left the table our dish was hardly a picture to paint, as we had
zestfully consumed every delicious morsel. A tender, full-flavored lamb shank was another lunch special, and it came with
homemade spaetzle, those delicate butter-dripped noodles that
are the pride of Swiss and German cooks.

These lunch specials were both $4.85, about average here,
although sandwiches come with potato salad for only $2.70. Din-

ners are more, of course, generally $9–$11 for an entrée, although light appetites can be satisfied with crêpes ($4.50,
including salad and those irresistible Parmesan rolls). Swiss
minced veal in cream sauce, bouillabaisse, hasenpfeffer, and
other preparations of game meats (including venison) come
highly recommended.

Not really a pavilion, this building is actually a century-old
house that's been lovingly restored by the Sinatsches. Enter
through an enclosed porch, and if you like its light, airy feel, seat
yourself at one of the tables centered around a small fountain.
Or proceed to an inside dining room with floral wallpaper, lacy
curtains, and an overall "French country" charm. Wherever you
sit, you'll be attended by personable suspender-clad waiters who
add a charm of their own.

HOURS   Every day, 11:30 am–2:30 pm and 5–10 pm. Closed month
of August. Reservations advised on weekends.

SPECS   45 San Marco Ave.; (904) 824-6202; major cards; beer and
wine.

DIRECTIONS   See Directions for Saint Augustine Restaurants,
pages 270–71.

GYPSY CAB COMPANY, *Exits 92 & 95, Saint Augustine*

A Gypsy cabbie is a maverick taxi driver, not affiliated with
any chain or large company, and Ned Pollack is a maverick restaurateur. He started in the business before he even graduated
from college, and this is his fourth restaurant. With each he's
achieved the impossible, selling out at a profit within 2 years.
His previous endeavor, the Malaga Street Depot, appealed to a
mix of counterculture and moneyed types, and quickly became
the hoppingest breakfast spot in town. Now, as he approaches
the grand old age of 30, Ned is turning his attention to lunch and
dinner.

From what we can tell, Gypsy Cab will be another success
story. With partner Paul Hayden-Hinsley, Ned has put together
a tasteful, if somewhat starkly decorated place in a glass-walled,

shed-roofed structure not much larger than a two-car garage. Well-framed modern art gives an urbane touch. The menu is an even mix of trendy (frittatas, fancy sandwiches, full-meal salads, stir-fried vegetables) and classical (chicken marsala, Hungarian goulash, beef tortellini). Absolutely everything—soup and salad dressing to pasta and pastry—is made by his own hands. You can taste it.

Our dinner, for instance, started with a wonderful romaine-based salad glazed with a mysterious, deep-flavored dressing. ("It's got brewer's yeast," he said *after* we'd made our compliment.) Excellent French garlic bread, a lively ratatouille, and a herby cheese-stuffed baked potato came alongside scrumptious chicken marsala. The cost for this amply packed dinner plate was a most reasonable $6.95; shrimp scampi over fettuccine was the most expensive item on the dinner menu at $8.25, while lunches and Sunday brunches are all $3.50 or less.

It was only Gypsy Cab's first month of operation when we stopped by, and we asked Ned what he intended to do differently with this restaurant. "Not go crazy," he answered without a moment's thought.

HOURS Lunch: Mon.–Fri. 11:30 am–3 pm. Dinner: Mon.–Sat. 6–11 pm. Sunday brunch: 11 am–3 pm.

SPECS 828 Anastasia Blvd.; (904) 842-8244; V/MC; beer and wine.

DIRECTIONS See Directions for Saint Augustine Restaurants, pages 270–71.

HARBORSIDE RESTAURANT,
Exits 92 & 95, Saint Augustine

This is the closest thing we found to a workingman's restaurant in Saint Augustine, but its location on the Comachee Cove Yacht Basin makes it no ordinary roadside hashhouse. The clientele is, in fact, a diverse mix of those who arrive by pickup truck and those who step off their yachts. It's a sweet little place, mildly nautical in theme, with an unbeatable view of the small harbor that is filled with sailboats, motorboats, and charter fishing craft. Eat inside and watch them through a wall of windows or sit out on the deck.

Our breakfast was a wonderful early-morning eye-opener. Peppery, herby, hand-cut home fries and fresh-out-of-the-oven sticky buns stole the show. Since crab-salad sandwiches are the Harborside's specialty, we couldn't leave without one: a large triple-decker with a creamy, chunky filling, we found it irresistible, and only the reminder of our work ahead discouraged us from having another. Subs, burgers, and a few other sandwiches (chicken salad, b.l.t., corned beef on rye) round out the basic menu; champagne brunches on weekends are the closest the Harborside comes to getting fancy.

Unless you opt for the bubbles on Saturday or Sunday, you'll have a hard time spending much more than $3 here on your meal; our first-rate breakfast was just $2.29, and the crab sandwich extravaganza was $2.99.

HOURS   Wed.–Mon. 7 am–4 pm. Closed Tues.

SPECS   A1A North, Comachee Cove; (904) 824-1976; no cards; beer and wine.

DIRECTIONS FOR SAINT AUGUSTINE RESTAURANTS

Northbound: Although there are I-95 exits closer to Saint Augustine, Exit 92 is the simplest, quickest one to use; it puts you on US 1, a 4-lane freeway that takes you directly into town in 16 miles. (Consult a map to see why this isn't really out of your way at all.) As you approach downtown Saint Augustine, you'll see a sign directing you to turn right for Route A1A/Historic Sites/Downtown. Northbound directions to the three featured restaurants are given below, *from that sign.*

Le Pavillon: At the sign, do not turn but go straight for about ¾ mile to Castillo Dr. Turn right on Castillo, and go 1 long block to the light at San Marco. Turn left and **Le Pavillon** will soon be on your right. See **Note,** below this **DIRECTIONS** section.

Gypsy Cab Company: Turn right at the sign, and in ¾ mile cross the Bridge of Lions (sign for Beaches). Restaurant is 1¼ miles past the bridge, on left. See **Note,** below this **DIRECTIONS** section.

Harborside: At the sign, don't turn but continue straight for about 1½ miles to W. San Carlos Ave. Turn right on W. San Carlos, go 1 long block to stop sign; left at the stop sign, and then almost immediately turn right onto Route A1A North. From this turn, it's just under a mile to Comachee Cove on your left just before the bridge over North River (big sign for Clam Shell Restaurant). You'll find **Harborside Restaurant** around the right side of the first building. See **Note,** below this **DIREC- TIONS** section.

Southbound: From Exit 95, turn left onto Route 16 and drive 5.4 quick miles to the light at Ponce de Leon Blvd. (US 1). Cross it, and 500 feet later you'll reach a stop sign at San Marco Ave. Southbound directions to the three featured restaurants are given below *from that point.*

Le Pavillon: Turn right onto San Marco, and in about 1¼ miles, the restaurant is on your left. See **Note** below.

Gypsy Cab Company: Turn right onto San Marco, and in about 2 miles turn left over the Bridge of Lions (obvious). Restaurant is 1¼ miles beyond the bridge, on left. See **Note** below.

Harborside: Turn right onto San Marco, and in about ½ mile turn left onto Route A1A North (sign for Vilano Beach). In just under a mile, you'll see Comachee Cove on your left just before the bridge over the North River (big sign for Clam Shell Restaurant). You'll find the **Harbor- side Restaurant** around the right side of the first building. See **Note** below.

Note: Under no circumstances should you backtrack to return to I-95. Continue along US 1 (Ponce de Leon Blvd.) North or South, and you will eventually see signs directing you onto I-95. In this part of Florida, US 1 moves along quite nicely, and a detour to Saint Augustine will cost you very little extra driving time.

BEIGNETS, *Jacksonville*

Beignets serves beignets. We're not sure if beignets were what happened when the French tried to make doughnuts or if doughnuts were the result when Americans tried to make beignets, but we know which we prefer. Truly delicious, these sugar-dusted fritters are the ultimate in empty calories. But we're getting ahead of ourselves—we recommend you eat your beignets after, not before, lunch.

When sisters Pat Sheffield and Lois Harrell decided to open a breakfast shop in Jacksonville, they intended to serve only the favorite breakfast pastry of their native New Orleans. But their customers wouldn't stand for such a limited menu, and the two ladies soon moved on to full lunches—genuine creole dishes like red beans and rice, shrimp creole, redfish court bouillon, crab gumbo, and chicken jambalaya. So now Beignets is a full-fledged breakfast and lunch restaurant; even dinners have crept in, so far on Fridays only.

For starters, it's an adorable little place. Once inside, you'll forget you're on a busy street of gas stations and shopping centers. Hand-quilted place mats rest on white tablecloths, and color photographs of New Orleans street scenes are displayed in wrought-iron frames. But the real atmosphere is provided by the menu and the food.

We couldn't resist trying that creole standby, red beans and rice, which includes a generous quantity of sausage even though its name implies strict vegetarianism. It's a simple, comforting dish made fiery more by the application of hot sauce at the table than by inherent spices ($2.95). The shrimp creole was marvelous, seething with a complexity of flavors that leaves a slight, but not overwhelming, tingle at the back of the throat ($4.50). Another lunchtime favorite is the court bouillon, a soup of vegetables and red snapper (broiled separately to stay firm). A muflatta sandwich is ham and Swiss on French bread with an olive sauce.

Friday's dinners are similar to lunch, costing a dollar more (and including a salad), although one or two special entrées like shrimp etouffé or deviled crabs come in at $7 or $8. Breakfasts are simple, featuring strong creole coffee to accompany the beignets. Soon to be added is "lost bread," a puffy New Orleans version of French toast.

Finally we were ready for the restaurant's namesake, the addicting, irregularly shaped fluffs of fried dough. To describe the taste it is necessary to evoke doughnuts, an unfortunate comparison. Suffice it to say that beignets, with their delicate flavor and soft texture, are doughnuts that have grown up. They are served with a canister of confectioner's sugar. Almost as much fun as eating them is the accepted process of thumping out a cloud of fine sugar that coats the pastries, and everything else at hand.

HOURS Mon.–Sat. 7 am–3 pm. Dinner Friday only, 6–9 pm. Closed Sun.

SPECS 2930 W. University Blvd.; (904) 731-1788; no cards; no liquor.

DIRECTIONS From University Blvd. West exit (no number when we were there), go about 1 mile to the light at Saint Augustine Rd. Straight through the light and almost immediately pull into the small shopping center on your left.

JACKIE'S SEAFOOD KITCHEN, *Exit 123, Jacksonville*

We recommend this locally popular, just-folks seafood place more for its ambience than its flavors. Surely a wonderful view of the Trout River and some dilapidated piers would provide a welcome break from the traffic, and the cats that romp around outside preying on stray hushpuppies only add to the atmosphere. Inside, white vinyl tablecloths, some barnboard, and draperies of seashell-studded fishnet do only a little to relieve the essential plainness of Jackie's. No matter, the Mercedeses and BMW's pull up regularly for fresh Apacaloola oysters, either done up as a stew ($3.95), steamed, fried, sandwiched, roasted, Parmesaned, or simply on the half-shell ($4.25/dozen).

Perhaps we should have gotten the message and tried the oysters, but the mullet roe sounded more exotic. A mistake, pure and simple, unless this local dish is an acquired taste. So then we tried the broiled trout—acceptable but unmemorable—which came with hushpuppies and two vegetables for $4.25. Other dinners are $3.25–$9.95, and aside from the usual, you can choose one of three creole dishes for $5.00 or $6.00. Sandwiches are $1.25–$3.95.

HOURS Daily 11 am–11 pm.

SPECS   531 Trout River Drive; (904) 764-0120; V/MC; beer and wine.

DIRECTIONS   From Exit 123, northbound turn right and south-bound left onto Englewood Ave. East (FL 116). Go 1.3 miles to a T and turn left onto Main St. Go 0.6 mile on Main, and just after the RR tracks (before the bridge) turn right onto Sycamore, which will almost immediately put you on Trout River Drive. Continue 4 blocks. On the left.

Georgia

ANGELO'S, *Exit 2, Saint Mary's*

Italian restaurants aren't all that easy to find in the South. The thought of Angelo's lasagna ($4.75), chicken cacciatore ($5.75), or eggplant parmigiana ($5.25) was therefore enough to tempt us into this windowless bomb shelter of a building. Even the thought of a good pizza ($3.65) would have been sufficient. Which makes it all the more remarkable that once inside we passed over the entire Italian menu and ordered crawfish stew over rice with a salad bar and garlic bread. Maybe it was the proximity to the sea, or maybe it was the price—a mere $3.95. Or perhaps it was because we just didn't expect much in the way of Italian cuisine from a strip-development-style building. (We confess to our prejudices.)

Whatever the reason, we were lucky. Though the first taste was unimpressive, the flavors came through more clearly with every bite, and by midmeal we were delighted with the dish's subtle spiciness. Then came the aftertaste, which was even better, and we resolved that if this was what Angelo did with Cajun cooking, his native fare just *had* to be worth the trouble of a six-mile drive.

Another good sign was that the place was absolutely packed with local people, and everyone seemed to be having a wonderful time. The plain and simple interior was filled with good cheer, and on the way out we felt very good about life.

HOURS   Mon.–Sat. 11 am–10 pm. Closed Sun.

SPECS   1813 Osborne Rd.; (912) 882-3636; V/MC; beer only.

DIRECTIONS   From Exit 2, Go 3.2 miles east on Saint Mary's Rd. to a blinker at GA 40. Turn right onto 40 and go 2.8 miles. On the right. Very light traffic.

PLAZA RESTAURANT, *Exit 4, Woodbine*

The plaza has just got to be the center of local life in tiny Woodbine, and a visit here might provide you with an edifying lesson in sociology. It's a clean and pleasant place that won't offend your eyes, and there's an old soda fountain to be enjoyed. More than that we cannot tell, since everyone had gone to bed when we passed through at 9 pm. But how much can you lose when one meat, two vegetables, and a beverage go for $3.50?

HOURS   Daily 6 am–8:30 pm.

DIRECTIONS   From Exit 4 go 2.4 miles west to Woodbine. Turn right and go 0.6 mile. On the left.

THE GEORGIA PIG, *Exit 6, Brunswick*

It's not often you find a good restaurant that's colorful, handsome, inexpensive, and sits a mere quarter-mile from the exit ramp, but such is the Georgia Pig, absolutely the best-looking barbecue shack we came across, and in the judgment of many, the best-tasting anywhere.

If you like your barbecue just a mite on the sweet side, you may well agree. Here the smoked and vinegar flavors share the spotlight with a touch of sugar to produce an excellent mild sauce, and the Georgia Pig was the only place we found that went to the trouble of finding a better bun than you can buy at the A & P. To our minds that justifies the $2.95 price that is higher than usual for this southern specialty. Good ribs too ($6.50/lb.), but not quite so good as the shredded-pork sandwich. A few cents more will get you barbecued beef instead of pork, and for about $6.00 you can get any of these treats on a dinner plate.

Unlike the vast majority of new buildings made to look old, the log-cabin architecture of the Georgia Pig actually succeeds. It's plain and simple inside, containing a huge fireplace in which the meats sit smoking, filling the air with their wonderful aroma. There are long tables of century-old yellow pine and bark-covered log beams overhead. Two older women run the place, one handling the orders, while the other minces the meat with a deftly wielded cleaver.

And we have to congratulate whoever landscaped this restaurant. Though obviously meant for the highway trade, all temptation to garishness has been resisted. Instead, the Georgia Pig nestles modestly and almost invisibly into a grove of pines. There's hardly a sign to be seen, and a path of cypress shavings leads you gently from parking area to porch.

And that's about as good as an interstate oasis can be.

HOURS   Daily 10 am–8 pm.

SPECS   (912) 264-6664; no cards; no liquor.

DIRECTIONS   Quarter-mile east of Exit 6, on the left.

EMMELINE AND HESSIE'S, *Exits 6 & 8, Brunswick*

It's a 13-mile detour to reach Emmeline and Hessie's from I-95, but if you're looking for good food and a complete change of pace, it's well worth the trouble. Not only is the restaurant a fine example of California-style architecture; not only is it built out over the marshes of Glynn, with fine views in every direction;

and not only do they offer an excellent selection of seafood and light meals; but the restaurant is on Saint Simon's Island (almost), which is a very beautiful and uncluttered resort area unto itself. You may prefer to stay on the island for the night and forgo the pleasures of another dreary motel.

Beneath criss-crossing redwood and cedar beams that bear abundant cascades of foliage, we sampled an excellent beef chimichanga ($3.95), one of four Mexican dishes on the lunch menu. This was ground beef and tomatoes in a tasty but mild chili sauce, served on a lightly fried flour tortilla and topped with sour cream and chives; it was as interesting as it was ample. There was a fine salad bar (with fresh spinach) and a chicken gumbo that tasted quite wonderfully more like scallops than chicken ($1.95/cup). Though fully spiced, the seasonings never overpowered the ingredients. Sitting there gazing into the marsh and tasting these good flavors, we entirely forgot about the road and the weariness of travel. Seafood of course is Emmeline and Hessie's specialty, the menu an informally eclectic collection of dinners that run from $8.95 for the catch of the day, chicken béarnaise, and teriyaki, to $11.95 for coquille Saint Jacques combination plates. The three steak dinners they offer run higher.

At lunchtime they'll sell you a plain hamburger for $3.50, but it would be a shame not to take advantage of the restaurant's unusual touches, like the Mexican burger that adds guacamole and sour cream to your basic cheeseburger and gives you some salsa on the side ($4.50). Four versions of potato skins, salad bar for $4.50, chili for $1.75/cup, and oysters on the half-shell for $1.95. Lots more, tending toward the trendy, but, if our sampling is any indication, always rather good.

HOURS   Daily 11:30 am–10 pm.

SPECS   Saint Simon's Causeway; (912) 638-9084; AE/V/MC; full bar.

DIRECTIONS   **Northbound:** Take Exit 6 and go east on US 17 toward Brunswick. Turn left in about 5 miles, remaining on US 17. About 10 miles from the exit you will see signs for the Saint Simon's Causeway. Turn right onto the causeway and go 3.6 miles to the restaurant, on the right in the Golden Isles Marina.

Southbound: Take Exit 8 and go east on GA Spur 25 (N. Golden Isles Parkway). In about 5 miles turn right onto US 17. In about 5 more miles you will see signs for the Saint Simon's Causeway. Turn left and go 3.6 miles on the causeway to the restaurant, on the right, in the Golden Isles Marina.

ARCHIE'S, *Exit 10, Darien*

Archie's is a local favorite, but it's also well known to travelers on the New York-to-Miami corridor. In deference to this swell of popular opinion, we're willing to grant that it might have been just a bad day when we passed through, but, frankly, the sour-grease smell that permeated this unrelievedly bright and barren place did little to sensitize us to its virtues. Indifferent service and quarreling between kitchen and serving staffs did little to help the situation.

On the plus side, we did overhear some cracker conversation on populist politics. And even though our plate of fried shrimp did not seem especially noteworthy at first, we have to admit we kept right on eating the little golden curls until the plate was as bare as the building. In the "finger-licking, American fried" category, we guess that warrants good marks. The chicken gumbo was OK; the fries and hushpuppies were about what you'd expect.

Archie's is a seafood joint, and though its basic approach to cuisine is to fry anything that once lived, they will boil the shrimp ($5.85) and broil the flounder ($5.50). Hamburgers are just $.95, steaks $5.00–$9.00, and a quarter fried chicken goes for $2.95.

Because Archie's is near the road and has good hours, it managed to get its logo on the exit signs. You need have no fear of its being a chain, however. We assure you, it's absolutely local.

HOURS   Mon.–Sat. 6 am–10 pm. Closed Sun.

SPECS   Highway 17; (912) 232-5997; no cards; no liquor.

DIRECTIONS   From Exit 10 go east 1 mile to a T. Turn right and go half-mile. On the left.

CHEROKEE RESTAURANT, *Exit 13, Midway*

The Cherokee is a well-tended and quite wonderful old highway restaurant from the days before McDonald's, a place where the food is good to very good, where prices are reasonable, and where the waitress is so friendly you start to think about moving in. Especially recommended are the excellent fried oysters and the handsome salad bar that includes, besides the usual, spinach, pineapple, okra, broccoli, cabbage, and three flavors of pudding.

We tried the $7.95 seafood platter and immediately looked in on those fresh osyters, as rich tasting and sensuous as any we've known, and if you order a plate of them alone we guarantee you'll leave feeling sinfully happy. So good were they we hardly noticed the excellent hushpuppies, the fish, the shrimp, and the deviled crab, all of which were good or better. Catfish dinners are $5.95; half a fried chicken is $5.50. Oyster stew for $2.95, and ten ordinary sandwiches at very modest prices.

Though clean and pleasant, there's nothing unusual about the Cherokee except for the skill of its cooking. As if to prove its down-home character, the mayor of Midway came in for lunch, and we listened in as he and the owner discussed that eternal subject of rural politics—whether city folks moving in would raise or lower the tax rate. The building itself is a long, low turquoise affair with more windows than wall, and there's a wonderfully '40s-ish sign out front that ought to be in the Smithsonian.

279

HOURS   Sun.–Thurs. 11 am–9 pm; Fri. & Sat. 11 am–10 pm.

SPECS   Highway 17; (912) 884-9988; no cards; no liquor.

DIRECTIONS   From Exit 13 go 3.6 miles west on GA 38 to town of Midway. Then left onto Highway 17 for 0.2 mile, on the right.

THE ISLANDER, *Exit 13, Halfmoon Landing*

It's about 8 miles from the Interstate to this restaurant, but once you're there, anything resembling traffic or noise or the pace of modern life will seem hundreds of miles away. A more beautiful setting would be hard to find, especially in the evening when the Islander's wall of windows gives an unencumbered view of Halfmoon River's skiffs and dories profiled against a setting sun.

Sometimes owner Lamar Carter can be seen bringing his own catch to shore; it will be in the frying pan just a few minutes later. If the number-one ingredient of seafood is freshness, the Islander has few rivals.

There are no real surprises on the menu. It's the usual bounty of fish and shellfish—trout and flounder to shrimp and oysters —but we were surprised to learn that the Islander breaks with local custom and broils more seafood than it fries. Another surprise was the flounder—a whole fish, not mere fillets, stuffed with crabmeat and baked to perfection ($8.95).

These dishes (along with a couple of meaty ones) are available in various combination plates, beginning at $5.95 and culminating in the Captain's Platter at $9.50. All come with a huge baked potato, better than average hushpuppies, and a trip to the salad bar (undistinguished, except for wonderful horseradish-laced cole slaw). The $19.95 dinner for two is commonly shared by three, and no one walks away wanting.

The building itself is clean and pleasant, but generally nondescript. That's all right—there's plenty to look at on your plate and out the window. Talk of condominiums is in the air, so don't waste too much time in getting here.

280

HOURS Spring through fall: Wed.–Sat. 5:30–10 pm; Sun. 4–10 pm; closed Mon. & Tues. Winter: Thurs.–Sat. 5:30–10 pm; Sun. 4–9 pm; closed Mon.–Wed.

SPECS (912) 884-3500; V/MC; beer only.

DIRECTIONS From Exit 13, turn right if northbound, left if southbound onto Route 38 East. In about 7½ miles start looking on the right for a small sign for Halfmoon Landing/Islander Restaurant. Just after that sign, the road forks; bear right. In 1.2 miles, at the fire department, follow the paved road as it veers sharply to the right. In 0.1 mile, you come to a T. Turn right and in 100 feet you'll see water in front of you and the restaurant on your right.

LOVE'S CATFISH RESTAURANT AND FISHING CAMP, *Exit 16, Savannah*

Absolutely the best catfish we found in 14,000 miles of southern driving are yours to be had on the banks of the Ogeechee River just three minutes from the Interstate. In fact, it wasn't until we found Love's that we understood what catfish was all about. Little did we know that these oft-maligned, bewhiskered little fish could be cooked to rival the very best of southern fried chicken. Larry McLendon, whose family has run the place since 1949, told us that the secret was the Ogeechee River itself. It is absolutely unpolluted, he said, and since a catfish tastes like the water it lives in, everything depends on *where* the fish is caught. A Love family member hauls them out of the river daily, we were told, and to prove it he pointed out some huge nets hanging out to dry just beside the restaurant.

We have no reason to disbelieve this theory, and in fact we heard it from another great catfish spot in Tennessee (see page 143). But we have to give a good share of the credit to the wonderfully seasoned, almost spicy batter they use at Love's, and to the fact that they manage to cook the fish to a greaseless, crunchy perfection without drying it out. You're almost sure to love it, either at the $4.95 price tag for the fish with salad bar, hushpuppies, and potato, or on the $7.95 all-you-can-eat house special.

But for a lonely hamburger ($1.95 with french fries), the menu is all seafood and almost entirely fried—Georgia white shrimp, oysters, and trout for $5.95; scallops for $1.00 more. Shad (in season) and scallops are $7.95. A pound of boiled shrimp with Love's own special seasoning is $9.95. Child's plate (under 12 and over 65) is $2.95.

If Love's were the kind of place that sold ambience instead of food, its view of the cypress-studded Ogeechee River would add $3.00 to the cost of dinner. Instead, hold on to your money and steep yourself in country-western music (played softly), Formica tables, plain-paneled walls, and very friendly people. The sun sets directly across the river from Love's. If your timing is right, it will make for the perfect end of a long day's drive.

HOURS   Tues.–Sat. 5 pm–9 pm; Sun. 12 noon–9 pm; Mon. & major holidays, gone fishin'.

SPECS   Highway 17S at King's Ferry; (912) 925-2232; V/MC/AE; beer only.

DIRECTIONS   From Exit 16 go 150 yards east and turn at the first right, between two gas stations. Go one block and then bear left at the fork. (At this point you'll see a sign for Love's on the left. It says 1 mile, but don't believe it.) Go 0.8 mile to Basin Road. Turn right on Basin and go 1.9 miles. On the right, at the river.

MAMMY'S KITCHEN, *Exit 16, Savannah*

Thick, juicy ribs, crunchy on the outside and tender within, loaded with true hickory flavor, and so good by themselves it would be sacrilege to use the sauce. That's what we found at Mammy's Kitchen, along with a good vegetable soup, a wonderfully tangy three-bean salad, and homemade pies. All this is wrapped up in a pleasantly homey version of knotty pine, wooden tables, and red-checked curtains; reasonable prices are the finishing touch.

Frankie Sapp, who started Mammy's 20 years ago, sat rocking near the fire behind the curved wooden table that serves as a counter. What, we asked, was the secret of those ribs? "The basting sauce," she said. And what was in the basting sauce? "Oh," said Frankie, eyes atwinkle, "a little of this and a little of that." We could learn only that "this and that" included vinegar, soy, and Worcestershire sauce. The critical ingredients that gave the ribs their special flavor remained a secret, but we'd never have been able to duplicate them at home even if we knew them. Mammy has her own smokehouse outside, and we doubt our landlord would approve.

Around Savannah Mammy's is known for good, inexpensive food. The menu is not large or exotic—pretty much a straight steak-and-seafood affair, augmented by barbecue items ($1.85 for a sandwich; dinners of barbecued pork, sausage, beef, and chicken from $3.95 to $5.95; $6.95 for a little of everything). Steaks are no higher than $7.95; four pieces of fried chicken are $3.95; about 20 straightforward sandwiches, $.95 to $1.95.

Despite its name, the place isn't kitschy or touristy—we spotted only three Mammy dolls for sale. If you don't want catfish and you don't want to go into Savannah, Mammy's is definitely the place to go at Exit 16.

HOURS Mon.–Wed. 11 am–9 pm; Thurs.–Sat. 11 am–10 pm; Sun. 11:30 am–7:30 pm. During summer, until 10 pm. on Mon.–Sat. and until 9 pm on Sun.

SPECS 5794 Ogeechee Rd.; (912) 925-6007; V/MC; no liquor.

DIRECTIONS From Exit 16 go east on GA 204 for 2 miles to the exit for US 17. Take US 17 (Ogeechee Rd.) north for 1.1 miles. On the left.

ELIZABETH ON 37th, *Savannah*

Once dubbed "the pretty lady with the dirty face," Savannah has scrubbed up and blossomed into a beautiful woman. Most brilliant of all the flowers in her bouquet of restaurants is Elizabeth on 37th, a turn-of-the-century mansion now turning out nouvelle and continental entrées that are the rage of Savannah gastronomes and newspaper reviewers who've come from as far as New York.

The decorations are exquisite, impeccably researched for period authenticity down to the Scalamandré wallpaper and the historic Savannah colors. Happily the air of formality falls short of snobbery, and an affable staff makes everyone feel at home.

And the food lives up to the decor. After a heady aperitif of white wine and cassis, we began dinner with a hunter's soup—pork-tenderloin stock with big chunks thereof, oriental mushrooms, barley, and celery. To call this exemplary broth delicious would be an understatement; its deep meaty flavor addresses the tastebuds head-on. Unfortunately $2.50 buys only a cup; clearly no one should come here on a budget.

Cassis finds its way into the glaze used over the lamb chops, too, resulting in lamb as good as any we've ever had. Just as exceptional were the large butterfly shrimp, split and stuffed with crab meat, sautéed in butter, and served on a bed of mixed carrot, spinach, and egg fettuccine. Of course the pasta, as well as the shrimp, are blushingly fresh. These two entrées are $16.50 and $15.50, respectively. If neither sounds quite exotic enough, how about parchment-wrapped poached shad stuffed with roe, chervil, and mushrooms? Or flounder Elizabeth—broiled with a topping of fresh crab in cream and sherry?

We could continue in this vein because the menu and the list of specials read with suspense, but we'll move on to desserts. Elizabeth calls itself a Restaurant and Dessert Café, an appellation earned by the sizable list of seductive diet wreckers. We limited ourselves to one, crisp nut meringue: vanilla Häagen-Dazs on a shell of hard meringue under mixed chopped nuts and caramel ($2.75).

While the luncheon menu is not as elaborate, it is by no means commonplace. Spicy beef roulade, shrimp and mushrooms in puff pastry, Cornish turnovers, and crab salad are typical examples. Entrée prices run $5.50–$7.50, salad included.

Elizabeth and Michael Terry came to Savannah from Atlanta where they ran a wine and cheese shop; as the story goes, Elizabeth, who'd had no formal culinary training, found herself entertaining dinner guests six nights a week. Now she does the same thing, except that the guests are paying. Which is just as well for those of us who otherwise wouldn't have been invited.

HOURS Wed.–Sat. 11:30 am–2:30 pm and 6–10:30 pm. Closed Mon. and Tues. No reservations; expect a wait if you arrive between 8 and 9 pm on Friday or Saturday.

SPECS 105 East 37th St. (corner of Drayton); (912) 236-5547; major cards; beer and wine.

DIRECTIONS Exit 17A puts you on I-16 East. It's about 7 miles to Exit 35, which you should take. At the bottom of the ramp, go straight through the light, bearing left at the next light onto 37th St. (heading east). In 0.7 mile, you'll reach the restaurant on the right at the corner of Drayton. Parking is across the street, in the lot beside Merriwicke House (make a U-turn at the light past **Elizabeth).**

MRS. WILKES' BOARDING HOUSE,
Exit 17A, Savannah

From I-95 it's a ten-mile detour to Mrs. Wilkes' Boarding House, so we were more than just disappointed to learn she had closed it down for the holidays when we came by to check it out. But such is the reputation of this venerable establishment that no collection of oddball restaurants would be complete without at least a mention.

Word has it that Mrs. Wilkes serves up just about the best there is to be had in the way of home-cooked southern meals—turnip greens, fried chicken, biscuits, gravy, creamed corn, black-eyed peas, and that sort of thing—$4.50 for a full lunch. These things we heard from so many different people in all parts of the South, we'd bet our last meal that it's the truth.

Now you can't usually judge a book by its cover, but what we learned from the outside tended to confirm Mrs. Wilkes's reputation. No tumbledown vestige of the Depression, this. The restaurant (no longer a boardinghouse at all) is located smack in the middle of Savannah's historical district on an oak-shaded block of fine old Federal-style houses. The signless restaurant is in the basement of one such, and a peep through the window revealed a charming, comfortable room furnished with seven or so neatly set tables. One wall was brick, another was papered, and the whole effect was entirely inviting.

Frankly, it's worth the detour just to have a look at this part of Savannah. It's one of the country's unsung wonders—the largest historical district in America, with gardens, squares, statues, and memorials in the middle of every other intersection and superb architecture everywhere. The roots of ancient live oaks push up against the mossy brick sidewalks, and the pace of life slows to a dignified stroll.

HOURS   Mon.–Fri. 11:30 am–3 pm.

SPECS   107 W. Jones St.; (912) 232-5997; no cards; no liquor.

DIRECTIONS   Take I-16 east 8 miles into the heart of Savannah. Take the last exit (Montgomery St.) and go straight on Montgomery 2 blocks to the first light (Liberty St.). Right onto Liberty, and go 3 blocks

to Banard. Right onto Banard, and go 2 blocks (around the square) to
Jones St. Left on Jones, half-block, on the right.

South Carolina

CHIC-A-PLENTY, *Exit 5, Hardeeville*

Chic-a-Plenty is an ancient vestige of preinterstate roadside
America. Picture, if you can, an old refrigerator made into a play-
castle and topped with a badly peeling plywood cutout of two
roosters and a hen up to God only knows what mischief. "If I
fixed up the building, I'd get more tourists, but then I'd lose the
local trade." Indeed. To judge from its looks, the residents of
Hardeeville would find a Burger King intimidating.

No matter. Step right up to the window and read the menu.
It's scrawled on cardboard and taped to the wall: 2 pieces of
chicken for $1.50, 3 pieces for $2.10, 4 for $2.80, or 18 for $12.34.
With or without the rolls and french fries that can be had for a
few cents more, you'll soon taste the juiciest, most tender fried
chicken of your life. Even if it's not the tastiest, it's very good.
The secret, we learned, is half a day's marination before cooking
and double breading to keep the meat from drying out.

Side orders of red rice, corn on the cob, fried okra, vegetable
sticks, and fried cheese are available for very little, and if you're
adventurous, try an order of livers and gizzards for $2.60. The
barbecue ought to be good since it comes from a well-known
local pit, but we'd advise you to pass on the pizza.

HOURS   Sun.–Thurs. 10 am–10 pm; Fri. & Sat. 10 am–11 pm.

SPECS   Highway 17; (803) 784-2250; no cards; no liquor.

DIRECTIONS   From Exit 5 go 0.8 mile straight west. On the left.

THE PALMS RESTAURANT, *Exit 22, Ridgeland*

We could find nothing to rave about or complain about at the
Palms, and we'll promise only that a stop here will taste better

287

and be more interesting than a visit to any exit-ramp tourist trap pushing everything from fireworks and bath towels to "factory outlet" oil paintings.

The Palms is a respectable southern-style restaurant, distinguished only by a surprisingly formal-looking dining room and a pair of fancy, gilded chandeliers in the shape of palm leaves. The lunch buffet offers a meat and as many vegetables as you want, plus beverage, for $3.65. There's always fried chicken. Other possibilities might be liver and onions, chicken liver and gizzards, or hamburger patties. Dinner holds no surprises and runs from $4.00 to $10.95.

HOURS   Daily 7 am–10 pm.

SPECS   106 Highway 17; (803) 726-5509; MC/V/AE; beer and wine.

DIRECTIONS   From Exit 22 go 1.7 miles toward Ridgeland. On the right. Plenty of signs.

KEITH'S RED BARN, *Exit 53, Walterboro*

One of the great misfortunes of traveling in this part of the South is that the local barbecue places are open only three days a week, thereby robbing the weekday tourist of the best sort of cheap roadside food there is. Keith's, unfortunately, is one such. Though it is by all accounts the best barbecue in the area, and though he ships it out for several counties in any direction, it'll have to be Thursday, Friday, or Saturday if you want to sample it in its own spanking new environment of knotty pine and red-checked tablecloths.

HOURS   Thurs.–Sat. 11 am–9:30 pm; closed Sun.–Wed.

SPECS   104 Hayden St.; (803) 549-5141; no cards; no liquor.

DIRECTIONS   From Exit 53 go 3.3 miles toward Walterboro on Alternate 17. Turn right at the first light and go 1.5 miles to a left turn just past an Amoco station. One block, on the left.

CLARK'S RESTAURANT, *Exit 98, Santee*

We weren't expecting much when we entered the plasticized chalet of a building that is Clark's. Had we known it's been in the same family for 36 years, and that for the first 25 of them it was a comfortable old roadside eatery, our surprise at finding good home cooking here would not have been so great.

The long and short of it is this: terrific vegetable soup with a deep, full flavor; good baked (not fried) chicken; rice that showed imagination in the seasonings; and absolutely wonderful sweet-potato patties—the best version we came across of that southern standby. Add an acceptable apple crisp and turnip greens that were as good as that humble dish gets. That was our meal, and with it we were very happy. Good straight southern cooking, prepared with care and a bit of inspiration. You may not go off raving about its exquisite subtleties, but you'll have to go to Charleston to do much better. Whereas Clark's is 30 seconds from the exit ramp.

Nor is the place at all offensive. The dining room is more innocuous than painful, and its 20-foot ceilings and white tablecloths tend to make for something like a touch of class. It's certainly relaxing enough, and the people are very friendly. Ten lunches (with three vegetables) go for $3.25 or less; sandwiches are $.85–$2.15, and there's a chef's salad for $2.85. Dinners are about $6.95 with salad, potato, vegetable, dessert, rolls, and beverage.

HOURS   Daily 6 am–10 pm.

SPECS   Highway 6 and I-95; (803) 854-2101; V/MC/DC/AE; full bar.

DIRECTIONS   Just west of Exit 98 in a thicket of motels and junk food.

JERRY'S MENAGERIE TRUCK STOP
D & H BARBEQUE
CENTRAL COFFEE SHOP, *Exit 119, Manning*

Our luck in Manning was not so good, but we've reason to suspect yours could be much better. First we tried Jerry's Menagerie, all decked out in stuffed fish and aquaria. Though the place had won several truck-stop awards, we noticed that none was more recent than 1978. After tasting the food we knew why.

Then we drove the 2 miles to town in search of the D & H Barbeque, about which we'd heard some pretty good things. But, alas, it is one of those Thursday-to-Saturday places. We can tell you only that it is plain, new, and clean, with a menu that includes fried chicken and barbecued turkey in addition to the usual barbecue fare.

By now it was late, and we trudged desperately around the center of Manning in search of something to redeem our efforts. And then we found it—a true village coffee shop with '40s-ish-looking signs and a great old soda fountain. The Central Coffee Shop was pure Norman Rockwell, what with its venetian blinds, its genuinely old ceiling fans, and even an art deco metal awning out front; absolutely pleasant, clean, and peaceful. Unfortunately it keeps Norman Rockwell hours—closed at 8:30 pm. So lovely was the place that we encourage you to stop in for its looks alone, but more than that we could not learn.

HOURS   **Jerry's:** 24 hours; **D & H:** Thurs. 10 am–8 pm, Fri. & Sat. 10 am–9 pm; **Central Coffee Shop:** unavailable.

DIRECTIONS   **Jerry's** is right at Exit 119. For the **D & H** go 1.8 miles into Manning on SC 261 to the second light. Turn right and go half-mile. On the left. For the **Central,** go 1.9 miles into Manning on SC 261 to the third light. Turn left, quarter-block, on the right.

CARRIE NATION'S, *Exit 160A Florence*

See page 40 for a description of this popular restaurant.

DIRECTIONS   Exit 160A puts you on I-20 into Florence. In about 2 miles, go straight through the light and immediately turn left into Florence Mall. Drive past Penney's; the restaurant is midway down the length of the mall.

THUNDERBIRD MOTOR INN, *Exit 164, Florence*

We probably don't have to tell you about the Thunderbird. It's already a very well-known stopoff on the Florida run, and even if you've never heard of it, you won't fail to notice its flashing neon thunderbird sign, eminently visible from both lanes of the Interstate. So many north-south travelers mentioned the Thunderbird (usually in terms as glowing as the sign) that we wouldn't have dared to avoid it, even if it didn't exactly epitomize what we're searching for.

It was clear as we entered this motel's dining room that value was one of its strong points. There's a buffet every day, changing in composition and price from breakfast ($3.50) to lunch ($3.95) to dinner ($5.00), but offering at all times an unlimited quantity of a seemingly unlimited number of dishes. We came on a Saturday night, and although business was brisk, there was no waiting on line. This kind of turnover has its advantage in that the food isn't out long enough to get that stale steam-table taste. But then again, there's no escaping the fact that it *is* steam-table fare.

They call the Thunderbird's dining room the "Country Kitchen Restaurant," and it does show evidence of regional awareness well beyond that of your usual highway motel. Fatback flavors the spinach and the peas, for instance, but unfortunately another regional practice, overcooking the green vegetables, is found here too. The moist and tasty corn bread, however, was beyond reproach. While the roast beef was overdone and the mashed potatoes entirely forgettable, the fried chicken was juicy and the stuffed peppers very nice indeed. That's the way we found the buffet throughout—so-so dishes next to far worthier ones. And since there were plenty to choose from—over 30 dinner-time items—the overall experience was not at all regrettable.

So we give the Thunderbird credit for doctoring up convenience foods and generally improving upon the usual. With its tremendous reputation and a location just feet from the exit ramp, the kitchen might easily get away with less. And while we could hardly agree with the man who called his meal here, "Best I ever ate!" we might admit what we had was among the best we've found within a mere biscuit's throw of the Interstate.

HOURS   Open every day 6 am–9:30 pm (until 9 pm on Sundays). Here's the breakdown: breakfast, 6–10:30 am; lunch 10:30 am–4 pm; dinner 4–9 or 9:30 pm. Closed only Christmas Day.

SPECS   US 52; (803) 669-1611; major cards; beer and wine in dining room, liquor in lounge.

DIRECTIONS   **Northbound:** From Exit 164, bear right. At light turn left and look to your left.

Southbound: From Exit 164 go straight through the light and look left.

North Carolina

THE PINK RESTAURANT, *Exit 2, Rowland*

It is a great pleasure for us to tell you that here on the border between the two Carolinas there is an alternative to that bastion of tourism whose name we don't have to mention because you've already seen it plastered on 40 (exactly—we counted!) billboards for the past 100 miles. A darn good alternative, too.

The Pink Restaurant has been a neighborhood institution in Rowland for as long as anyone can remember. Its blue-plate specials have won a clientele of such devotion that when the long-standing owner died in August 1983, the entire town anxiously followed the search for a new proprietor. Ever since Mrs. Martha Smith took over in December of that year, she's been reassuring customers that she won't close the restaurant; they in turn tell her that she's doing just fine.

It's really a delightful place, true to its name both inside and out. Once all the dishes were pink too (those that remain are reserved for Sunday dinner). The old-style paneling and ceiling beams wear a patina of age that cannot be reproduced by new restaurants trying to appear old. But of course the true character of the restaurant comes from its clients, the villagers and tobacco farmers of the eastern Carolina border area. This is their gathering place, and whether they simply grab a coffee and run or hang their hats all morning depends entirely on the weather and the time of year.

Mrs. Smith, who is as warm and welcoming to outlanders as she is to locals, types up a different menu every day. The one we found for lunch was typical: fried fillet of flounder, deviled crab, chicken pot pie, liver and onions, etc. These come with a choice of two vegetables as well as beverage, dessert, and rolls or hushpuppies. The cost for all that food, cooked to order, is always $3. But value and atmosphere aren't all the Pink Restaurant offers: the food is good. The liver, for instance, is strictly calves' liver—fresh, juicy, and well proportioned. Devotees of this specialty call in advance to see if it's in before coming down for lunch.

Sandwiches, hamburgers, and a few salads are also available, all of them well under $2. Dinners, currently served only on weekends, are more typical of steak and seafood houses than neighborhood lunchrooms: 10-oz. rib-eye steaks are the biggest seller ($8.50), although plates of fried shrimp and oysters may please lighter appetites and wallets ($3.50–$4.50 for small; $4.50 - $6 for large).

The Pink Restaurant couldn't hope to compete with South of the Border (and we doubt it would want to), but gradually the word is getting out. A healthy contingent of folks from Charlotte and Greensboro make this a regular stopoff on their way to Myrtle Beach, and it is with great self-satisfaction that they introduce themselves to the new owner and tell her, "This is our fifteenth time here, and you'll see us on our way home, too." You'll see us next time we're in the neighborhood also, Mrs. Smith.

HOURS   Breakfast and lunch: Every day, 6:30 am–2:30 pm. Dinner: Fri. & Sat. only, 5:30–9 pm. Dinner hours may be expanded to other days.

SPECS   West Church St.; (919) 422-9919; no cards; no liquor.

DIRECTIONS   From Exit 2, turn left if northbound, right if southbound, toward Rowland. Go about 1¼ miles to the first light and turn left. In 0.1 mile you'll see the sign for **Pink Restaurant** ("Home-Cooked Meals") pointing you to the restaurant, to the right (down West Church St.).

JOHN'S, *Exits 20 & 22, Lumberton*

John's is the most talked-about dinner house in Lumberton, a postindustrial mill town that isn't exactly a gourmet's mecca, but owner John McLelland tries hard to please the sensibilities of those who want more than a burger to go. It's a difficult restaurant to classify. After some thought we tentatively pegged it as a steak and seafood house without the blood-red carpet or the salad bar. But not quite. Black-vested waiters and low lighting provide touches of class, but these are undermined by plastic plants and overbearing Muzak. And while the menu is heavy on steak-house fare, you'll also find cream of artichoke soup and fettuccine Alfredo. So call it what you will; we can confidently call it the best fine-dining-style restaurant a traveler is likely to come across in this part of North Carolina. (The French Country Inn, up the road a piece in Selma, came highly recommended, but the maitre d' mustered up his snottiest tone of voice to inform us that no one *ever* eats there without a reservation, thus rendering it a poor candidate for this type of book.)

At any rate, that cream of artichoke soup at John's was quite lovely ($1.25/$1.75)—rich, tangy, sparked with many small morsels of artichoke heart. As an entrée, veal Louise (we're not sure if that's a misspelling or if Louise had her hand in this dish) was nicely done in a wine and mushroom sauce but fettuccine Alfredo on the side was undistinguished (except by an overenthusiastic sprinkle of dried parsley); the bread was no better than mediocre. This cost $7.95, which is near the high end of a menu whose entrées run $5.50 to $10.50. In addition, a complete dinner, soup to dessert, is featured each evening at around $10 or $11.

We quite enjoyed John's dessert specialty, peanut pie, although a knife had to be pressed into service to sever the ¼-inch crust. The filling of peanut butter and cream cheese topped with chopped nuts proved to be much more delicious than we doubting Yankees had imagined.

HOURS Mon.–Sat. 5:30–10 pm; closed Sun.

SPECS 183 Kahn Drive (I-95 Service Road North); (919) 738-4709; MC/V; beer and wine.

DIRECTIONS **Northbound:** From Exit 20, go straight through the light at the end of the ramp; this puts you on a service road that curves around past the Ramada Inn (don't reenter the Interstate) and then runs parallel to the highway. In about 1¼ miles, it's on your right.

Southbound: From Exit 22, turn left, cross over the Interstate, and immediately turn right. In just a few feet, turn left onto the service road that runs parallel to the highway. It's ½ mile down the service road, on your left.

SMITHFIELD BAR-B-Q, *Exit 95, Smithfield*

This was our first exposure to the barbecue of eastern North Carolina, a unique style found nowhere else in the country. What makes it unique is the pungent, peppery, vinegar-based sauce. This infusion is totally devoid of tomatoes or tomato products, even though the peppers render it bright red. You'd never guess its composition when you see it dispensed from recycled ketchup bottles!

The pork, here broiled on electric cookers, is chopped and doused with sauce to take on a tangy taste that at first seems incongruous but soon grows into an addictively delicious experience. The closest thing to it is sweet-and-sour sauce, but comparing the two is like comparing fettuccine carbonara with spaghetti and meatballs. We heartily recommend the barbecue found here and at Parker's (below); if you can free yourself from a mental association between tomatoes and "Q," we think you'll enjoy it too.

The Smithfield is an unassuming but clean cement-block bunker wearing a fresh coat of Indian-red paint and shiny new wax on the linoleum floor. The Formica tables all boast a pitcher of "tea" (meaning iced tea in the South, invariably sweet). A first for us was the lavatory sink right out in the dining area, adjacent to the front door.

There are all kinds of pork, chicken, and combination plates available in prices ranging from $2.50 to $4.35; barbecue sandwiches are less. A few things of interest: Unless you specify otherwise, it will be assumed that you want your chicken fried rather than barbecued. If you'd rather find out how broiled chicken tastes in the same tangy sauce that's used on pork, speak up. Second, be sure to try the potato salad; it was among the best we found anywhere, embellished with diced red peppers and little bits of sweet pickle that made every bite as unusual as the barbecue.

Whether or not you'll be tempted to order it, you may enjoy knowing about the Smithfield's biggest combination offering. A large sign announces: "FAMILY PACK FOR TAILGATING: 1 lb. pork, 1 lb. slaw, 8 pcs. fried or bbq chicken, 1 doz. hushpuppies. $8. Feeds 4–6. A quick meal for Mom. Give her a break. She is special."

HOURS Every day, 9 am–9 pm. Closed only Christmas.

SPECS 920 Selma Rd.; (919) 934-8721; no cards, no liquor.

DIRECTIONS From Exit 95, head west toward Smithfield. In about 1 mile, turn right onto Route 301 North. It's about 1 mile down, on the right.

PARKER'S BARBECUE, *Exits 116 & 121, Wilson*

In a region where debate on matters pertaining to barbecue is never taken lightly, two itinerant Yankees should hesitate to pass judgment. Just the same, we'll venture to say that much as we enjoyed the Smithfield, we were even more enamored of Parker's. We're not sure if Parker's gets the edge because it grinds crispy bits of pork skin into the meat, resulting in a pleasantly varied texture, or because it applies fiery red pepper seeds with a free hand. Whatever the reason, this was barbecue with zip, barbecue that spoke directly to our taste buds.

Parker's is a low, white wood-frame building that could almost pass for a New England chowder house if it weren't for the outlandish canopy over the entrance that makes it look more like a miniature wedding palace. Inside, an abundance of ruddy wood gives a lodgelike feel that is quite pleasant.

While nary a hint of tomato flavors the barbecue sauce, you will find some in the Brunswick stew; if native southeastern cuisine is new to you, be sure to try this wonderful chicken and vegetable dish, even though you'll never find it in its original form—where squirrel was the featured meat. At Parker's, Brunswick stew accompanies all dinners, and they are most reasonably priced between $2.50 and $3.25. Also on your dinner plate will be a zingy cole slaw and boiled potatoes. We asked if the reddish glaze over the potatoes was barbecue sauce. Oh no, our waiter explained, it's paprika. Not just a shake of paprika, he added, but a measured quantity that's actually boiled with the spuds. How much? we wondered. Not much, he said, just a *pound* for every 10-gallon batch of potatoes.

We left with our taste buds dancing. And we'll be back.

HOURS   Every day, 10 am–9 pm. Closed last full week of June.

SPECS   Highway 301 South; (919) 237-0972; no cards; no liquor.

DIRECTIONS   Northbound: From Exit 116, turn right onto Route 42 East; go 5¾ miles to light at Forest Hills Rd. Turn right and go through 1 light to stop sign at T. ■ Turn left, and go ½ mile to the stop sign and blinking light at US 301. Don't turn onto 301, but look left and you'll see your way into **Parker's** parking lot.

Southbound: From Exit 121, turn left onto Route 264 East. Go about 3½ miles to the first light and turn right (Forest Hills Rd.). Go 3 miles, through 2 lights, to a stop sign at a T. Then, as above from ■.

Note: Return to the Interstate by reversing the directions given above for people traveling in the opposite direction (i.e., northbound travelers take Forest Hills Rd. all the way to Route 264 West; if southbound take Forest Hills Rd. to route 42 West).

CAROLINA CAFÉ, *Exit 138, Rocky Mount*

It's always a joy to sing the praises of a thoroughly delightful, entirely local, low-priced restaurant with good honest food—the kind of Mom and Pop place that is all too rare nowadays due to

competition from the nationwide chains. But it's a special pleasure to tell the world about such a restaurant when, like a mouse
in a cat's lair, it stares defiantly at the home office of one of the
nation's biggest fast-food operations. Rocky Mount, North Carolina, is home to Hardee's, and the Carolina Café, just down the
road from the chain's sprawling headquarters, is the very kind of
place that Hardee's and its kin have driven into history. But not
here—Rocky Mount residents love their café too much to let that
happen.

The Carolina Café opened up in 1942, long before anyone had
ever heard of McDonald's, let alone Hardee's. It barely shows
the march of time. Sure, it's gotten a little frowzy around the
edges, but it doesn't seem at all decrepit, and we'd sooner take a
place with a few blemishes and genuine character than something spanking new and sterile. The booths are of black-painted
wood with deep maroon, Formica-topped tables—Formica from
an era when that word did not imply sterility and plasticity. An
old sideboard holds family pictures, and behind the front counter
is an ancient Hamilton Beach milkshake machine, still whirring
away. Holding court back there is a gentleman who wears a
blazer and a string tie; his may not be the most efficient outfit for
the job, but it adds to the café's gentle dignity.

The Carolina's menu unabashedly lists four soups as Campbell's and one as homemade vegetable. They all go for the same
price ($1.05/bowl). On the luncheon menu choose two vegetables
(black-eyed peas, collard greens, candied yams, etc.) and one
main course (the likes of sirloin steak, pan-buttered shrimp,
country ham steak, and—get this!—*kosher* knockwurst) from
$2.60 to $3.95. But the day's special is the real deal; a plate of
braised beef short ribs was the best and biggest such serving
we've had for anywhere near $2.55. That's right. $2.55, including
the vegetables.

Sandwiches run all the way up to $1.50, available at lunch or
dinner; dinner entrées reach $5.25 for filet mignon, but at $3.75,
sugar-cured pork chops are closer to the average.

If the Carolina Café has any particular claim to fame, it's the
meringue-topped peanut-butter pie. At first the thought of peanut butter metamorphosed into a slice of pie had us clearing our
throats in despair, but our doubts were instantly dissolved by
the pie's silken texture and subtle nutty flavor. Momentarily, we

wondered why Hardee's hasn't mimicked its neighbor's brilliant dessert, but we realized that no mass eatery would dare expose American palates to something they haven't known since early childhood. Those of us who prefer a little adventure with our coffee will thank places like the Carolina Café for providing it.

HOURS   Mon.–Fri. 11 am–8:45 pm. Closed Sat. and Sun.

SPECS   9906 North Church St.; (919) 446-9976; no cards; no liquor.

DIRECTIONS   From Exit 138, take Route 64 East for about 5 miles (fast) to Church St. exit. Turn right and go 0.3 mile. It's on the right.

PEKING RESTAURANT, *Exit 173, Weldon*

Robert Lee is a rare bird. Having migrated from Peking to New Jersey, he eventually folded his wings in North Carolina, far from the nearest Chinese community. We have rules about avoiding Chinese restaurants that are beyond shopping range of a Chinatown, but the Peking is the exception that proves the rule: Lee actually goes to the trouble of ordering fresh Chinese vegetables from New York, an expensive practice that can be detected on the plate but not in the price tag.

Every day the Peking Restaurant offers a lunch buffet for the astonishing sum of $2.88. We'd heard it was worth a drive from Richmond, but by the time we got there it was too late for lunch. So we cannot say from first-hand experience whether the Peking's spread of egg-drop and hot-and-sour soups, pepper steak, chicken chow mein, sweet-and-sour pork, fried rice, and egg rolls is better than average for Chinese-American fare. But we can report that the prices at dinner time climb only modestly (most items are around $5), and the food becomes less Chinese-American and more Chinese.

What you'll find is the light, wine-sauced, noodle-prone cuisine of Lee's native city (although egg foo young does sneak in). The "Peking Delight," a creation of chicken, beef, shrimp, and vegetables, was truly delicious—the snow peas fresh and crisp, the meat ever so tender, and the overall flavor untainted by chemical taste enhancers. The trick, Lee explained when queried, is to use only fresh meat and to marinate it a full 24 hours. As for MSG, he spurned it with contempt.

Lee has put together an extremely pretty place out of modest materials and an abundance of charming touches. Red napkins folded like flowers sit in wine goblets on each table, giving the entire room a springlike ambience.

When he first came to North Carolina, the restaurateur was called Chao Rien Lee, but he didn't lose any time in changing his first name to create a time-honored southern handle. We doubt, however, that anything more than his cooking ability was needed to gain him the respect of his neighbors.

HOURS Lunch: Tues.–Fri. 11:30 am–2:30 pm; Sat. & Sun. noon–2:30 pm. Dinner: Tues.–Thurs. and Sun. 4:30–9 pm; Fri. & Sat. 4:30–10 pm. Closed Mon.

SPECS 815 Roanoke Rapids Rd.; (919) 536-3655; MC/V; beer and wine.

DIRECTIONS From Exit 173, head east on Route 158 toward Weldon. Restaurant is about 1 mile down, on the right.

Virginia

KING'S BARBECUE, *Exit 3, Petersburg*

See page 240 for a description of a perfectly pleasant barbecue with a more-than-barbecue menu.

DIRECTIONS   Northbound: Use exit labeled Petersburg/Norfolk/ Route 301/Route 460, and follow signs for Petersburg and Washington St. Left on Washington, and go about 3 miles; it's on right.

Southbound: From Exit 3, follow signs for Washington St. Right on Washington, and go about 3 miles; it's on the right.

HALF WAY HOUSE, *Exit 6W, Chester*

Hanging on the stone walls in the cellar dining room of this pre-Revolutionary inn are half a dozen framed restaurant reviews, the most recent of which was written in 1948. It seemed time for a new look at the old place.

Strategically located midway on the stagecoach route between Richmond and Petersburg, the 1760 building breathes with a rich and colorful history that has seen presidents, generals, and foreign heads of state pass through its five-foot portals (watch your head). With the help of two large fireplaces, a warm sense of antiquity glows in the dining room, which has been authentically, but not prissily, preserved.

Adding immeasurably to the atmosphere is James Burton, the prepossessing black waiter who has held court here for 30 years. Wearing a white jacket and black bow tie, James carries himself with dignity and greets each arriving guest with great panache. "Evening!" he intones in a hoarse but booming voice, as he pulls back your chair in a grand sweeping motion.

While it has its high spots, the Half Way House's food is not as grand as its atmosphere. Our French onion soup was passable *after* it was sent back to be reheated; the salad, however, could not be redeemed. Totally reliant on iceberg and mealy tomatoes, it was topped with a crumbly mass of Roquefort cheese trying to pass as Roquefort dressing.

Fortunately, the fried chicken entrée represented an upturn

of events. It was an attractive plate with two large breast pieces along with green beans, carrots, half a baked potato au gratin, and three unshelled peanuts (a new garnish for us) on a bright green lettuce leaf. The green beans, usually a disappointment in the South, were effectively spruced up with chopped tomatoes and onions; best of all was the chicken, moist and tender, with a delicate fluffy breading.

At $8.75, fried chicken is actually the lowest-price item on a menu that runs all the way up to $27.50 for Australian lobster tail. Chicken livers with bacon and onions ($9.00), breaded veal cutlet ($12.75), and "San Salvadore 20 Fathom, Blue Water, Fried Shrimp" ($12.75) are a few others.

HOURS Every day, 5:30–10 pm; reservations suggested Fri. and Sat.

SPECS 10301 Jefferson Davis Highway; (804) 275-1760; all cards; beer and wine.

DIRECTIONS **Northbound:** Exit 6W puts you on Route 10 West. In ½ mile, turn right onto US 301 North (Jefferson Davis Highway). Go 2.2 miles; it's on right.

Southbound: From Exit 6A turn right (Willis Rd.). In 0.3 mile, turn left onto US 1/US 301 South (Jefferson Davis Highway). In exactly 1 mile, it's on your left.

GRACE PLACE, *Exits 12 & 13, Richmond*

On a street of lovely 1880s houses across from Virginia Commonwealth University is a building that blends in architecturally but stands out functionally. No longer a residence, 826 West Grace Street is now a natural-foods restaurant specializing in international vegetarian cuisine.

The most delightful place to sit here, we are told, is the tree-shaded brick patio. That was out of the question in February, but we were quite happy inside. The first floor has been converted to a natural-foods bakery/deli. You won't find sugarcoated doughnuts or pastrami, but the likes of tofu cheesecake and "zippy pimento salad" sandwiches. Homemade soups like black bean or Mexican tomato, chili sans carne, pasta salads, sprouty sandwiches, and a display case full of enticing pastries can have you fed quickly and happily. All of it is made here each day, bread included. Drink carrot, spinach, or other vegetable juices; a "health shake"; or any of a half-dozen sodas like ginseng or carob (less exotic drinks also available). Whatever you decide on, you can take it out with you or sit at one of several blond oak tables on the boldly patterned checkerboard floor.

The first-floor café is open only at midday, but the real restaurant, upstairs, serves both lunch and dinner. At least half a dozen salads ($3.75) can be had for either meal. Here's just one example, called "Super Salad": mixed greens and vegetables topped with avocado, cheddar cheese, nuts, and a tasty legume pâté. The featured item is the day's international special, published on a monthly calendar: mushroom moussaka, fettuccine Alfredo, eggplant-almond enchiladas, ratatouille, and Greek spaghetti are a few examples, along with Indian, Oriental, and Ukrainian platters. We'd heard raves about the last, but poor timing prevented our introduction to that cuisine. But our whole-wheat crêpes were delightful, filled with spinach and mushrooms, and doused with a smooth Mornay sauce. These came with soup, salad, bread (need we say whole-wheat?), and coffee for $5.50.

Given the restriction to meatless dishes, few of the "international" specialties are true to their origins, but from what we could see, they are true to the uniquely American cuisine called natural food. Within that genre, the Grace Place is tops.

HOURS   Mon.–Sat. 11 am–9 pm; closed Sun.

SPECS   826 West Grace St.; (804) 353-3680; no cards; beer and wine.

DIRECTIONS   **Northbound:** From Exit 12, turn left onto Chamberlayne. In 0.1 mile, take a gentle right onto North Adams. Go 0.3 mile, crossing Broad St. to West Grace. Right on Grace, go ½ mile, and you'll see it on the right, shortly after you cross Laurel.

Southbound: From Exit 13, turn left at stop sign, go one block to the light, and turn right onto Belvedere. In ¼ mile, go straight through the light at Broad St., and turn right at the next light onto West Grace St. It's in the third block, on the right, shortly after you cross Laurel.

O'BRIENSTEIN'S, *I-64 West Interchange, Richmond*

See page 84 for a description of this rather entertaining restaurant that is not hard to reach from I-95.

DIRECTIONS   About 4 miles north of downtown Richmond, enter I-64 West (signs for Charlottesville). In about 5 miles, take Exit 37A, then follow directions given on page 86.

LA CASITA, *Exits 16 & 17, Richmond*

La Casita means little house, and this thoroughly delightful Mexican restaurant is small indeed. So are its prices, but certainly not its portions.

John and Eva Fadool grew up in Mexico City as part of a Lebanese community that numbers 200,000. Eva visits her family there twice a year and brings back to her restaurant seasonings that are unavailable in the States, along with ideas for new dishes that have not yet entered the Tex-Mex mainstream.

We couldn't resist starting our meal with a mango daiquiri—and we didn't worry about whether or not it was authentically Mexican. From there things got even better. An appetizer called Gina's Bessas Kisses was a Mexican version of a ham and cheese melt, using homemade flour tortillas as bread ($2.10). As an en-trée, a canasta ($3.50/4.50) is a flour tortilla fried crisp in the shape of a basket, filled with beef, melted cheese, lettuce and tomato; the fine flavors were fresh and lively. According to Mr. Fadool, chimichangas are the most popular dish, and so we couldn't go without one—a crisply fried, chicken-stuffed tortilla topped with sour cream and guacamole, it was sort of a cross between nachos and a burrito; delicious, however it is to be classified.

Although tacos and other snacks can be had for as little as $1, most entrées run $4.00–$5.50. They come with Spanish-style rice and beans—not black beans ("They're Cuban," explained Mr. Fadool), but pintos and red beans. Alongside each order you will be presented with three salsas in stoneware cups: red, white, and green. A taste test will determine that the red tingles (jalapeños and tomato); the white stings (jalapeño, sour cream, and spices); and the green scorches (similar to medium without sour cream to douse the fire). Have fun experimenting.

Perhaps overdecorated in an innocent way with sombreros, baskets, dolls, fans, piñatas, and those electric paintings on black backgrounds that are found only in Mexican restaurants, La Casita is nevertheless an unpretentious and fun place that isn't trying to be anything more than the family restaurant it is.

HOURS Tues.–Thurs. 11:30 am–10 pm; Fri. 11:30 am–11 pm; Sat. 4–11 pm; Sun. 4–10 pm; closed Mon.

SPECS 5204 Brook Rd.; (804) 264-9896 & 262-8729; major cards; full license.

DIRECTIONS **Northbound:** From Exit 16, bear right off ramp and then turn left at the light onto US 1 South. In 0.2 mile, it's on your right.

Southbound: Exit 17 puts you on US 301 South. Go about 1 mile to the light at Azalea. Turn right. In 0.1 mile, at the intersection of Brook Rd., you can see **La Casita** across the street, but highway regulations make it impossible (or illegal) to get there the sensible way. What you must do is cross Brook Rd., and turn into the parking lot for Pearle Vision (on the right). At the far end of the lot, turn right and you'll be in **Casita's** backyard.

THE SMOKEY PIG, *Ashland*

The Smokey Pig *(sic)* is a barbecue with the consciousness of a café, a pretty place with brown-and-white-checked tablecloths, ruffly curtains, and copious natural light that comes through large front and side windows. But the Pig's most distinctive feature is its collection of art—pig art.

We can't say for sure, but we doubt you'll ever see in one place so many media applied to the portrayal of swine. On the Smokey Pig's walls and in a glass display case up front can be found representations of its mascot in posters, potholders, photographs, macramé, silk sculpture, carved wood, embroidery, porcelain, glass, stoneware, linen, and God-knows-what-else. There are crayoned pictures sent in by a children's art class, and even a few piggy poems donated by inspired customers. Most remarkable of all, perhaps, is the fact that it is all integrated *into* the tasteful decor rather than actually *becoming* the decor.

After this kind of buildup, you're probably wanting to know, "How's the pork?" And after this buildup, we have to admit it's not quite as good as the art. Still, the pork reveals its hickory- and oak-smoked origins, and you can get it (or pit-cooked beef or chicken) in various sandwiches and full-meal combinations running from $1.95 to $4.10.

Surprisingly enough, the Pig excels in one area that has little to do with pork: hushpuppies. Absolute masterpieces these golf-ball-sized globes of fried cornmeal are. Dark brown and rough outside, they are deeply flavorful within, the moist interior dotted with whole corn kernels and chopped bits of onion. These are hushpuppies to calm the most frenzied canines.

There are many other possibilities on the menu, from chicken salad plates to quiche and tossed salad (both $3.95, less at lunch). Every day there are three soups and three pies, all made from scratch; one of those soups and the day's featured sandwich are available each day as a lunch special for $1.98.

HOURS   Tues.–Sun. 11 am–9 pm; Mon. 11 am–3 pm. Closed major holidays.

SPECS   212 S. Washington Highway; (804) 798-4590; MC/V; full license.

DIRECTIONS   From exit labeled Ashland/Route 54 West, go about ¾ mile to the second traffic light and turn left onto US 1 South (S. Washington Highway). In 0.2 mile, it's on your right.

JARRELL TRUCK PLAZA CAFETERIA, *Exit 40, Doswell*

That old bromide about following the truckers to the good eats is nothing we've ever had much truck with, but gear jammers from Maine to Miami swear by this place. We knew that at a minimum it would be an authentic slice of Americana, and it has the undeniable virtue of never closing. So off we went to check out Jarrell's.

No doubt about it, this is the real McCoy, surrounded by an ocean of asphalt populated by literally hundreds of 18-wheelers that haul everything from Wise Potato Chips to Dodge vans. Here you can take a shower, get your shocks changed, have your rig weighed (free with 40-gallon purchase), and buy a tape deck or a girlie magazine or anything else you'd need to survive out on the open road. And in the cafeteria line, you can load your tray until it sags.

Unfortunately, every item of food must be purchased separately, which turns out to be a rather expensive way to eat. Adding the individual costs for two eggs, toast or biscuits, grits or potatoes, and coffee, we arrived at a sum of $3.00. (If you're a CB-handled "professional driver," deduct 10 percent.) Still, the light and fluffy biscuits, like everything else here, are freshly made by women whose assignment is to do at work exactly what they would do at home in their own kitchens; as far as food goes, one customer told us, Jarrell's is a second home.

We aren't able to exude such enthusiasm, but we did enjoy the fried chicken breast, Jarrell's special pride. We're not sure whether it's the light batter in which it's dipped or the peanut oil in which it's fried ("It's *got* to be fried in peanut oil," says the kitchen manager), but Jarrell's fried chicken puts the Colonel to shame ($1.80 for two pieces). Still, no matter what you order on the hefty menu, there's no escaping the fact that this is truck-stop fare—near the top of its class to be sure, solid stick-to-your-ribs body fuel, but truck-stop fare nonetheless.

What truly distinguishes this from any other truck stop we've seen are the dining room's billboard-sized murals depicting Virginia of yesterday, today, and tomorrow. We especially liked the sleek spaceship cars of the future, and since they were painted in the 1950s, we wondered if the artist had the mid-1980s in mind when he painted them.

HOURS   Always open. *Always.*

SPECS   (804) 876-3361; all cards, no liquor.

DIRECTIONS   From Exit 40, bear right if northbound, turn left if southbound. It's the first thing you'll see on your left. Tunnel through the parked trucks to your left and eventually you'll reach the cafeteria.

ANNE'S GRILL, *Fredericksburg*

When the herring start running up the Rappahannock River, its waters teem with almost as many hip-booted fishermen as fish. Depending on their timing, some anglers will go home empty-handed and others with their baskets full, but one thing is certain: few will leave Fredericksburg without a stop at Anne's Grill. The same can be said for the coon hunters who show up every fall and fill the air with talk about the relative prowess of their canine companions. But not only sportsmen flock to Anne's Grill. In a feature article, the *Fredericksburg Free-Lance Star* reported, "It's said that more political decisions have been made over cups of coffee here at Anne's than in the municipal office buildings down the street."

Now finishing up its 25th year of service to Fredericksburg's workers, villagers, and visitors, Anne's is a downtown institution likely to flourish for at least another quarter-century. That suits us just fine, because it's precisely the kind of place we love to find in our travels: unpretentious but attractive, local but hospitable, low-priced with simple but caringly prepared food.

The hamburger steak, for instance, was well deserving of its esteemed status as Anne's specialty. A huge patty of fresh-ground meat, it came smothered in onions and wading in good, dark gravy. With two vegetables and rolls, it cost a fair $3.65, typical of dinner prices. Liver and onions, roast beef sandwiches, and ham omelettes are also popular; if you're in more of a sandwich mood you probably won't have to pay over $1.50; a regular burger (smaller than the hamburger steak, of course, but also freshly ground) is only 95 cents.

Breakfast is a big meal at Anne's. In addition to all the usual fixin's and superior coffee, Anne serves saltfish on Saturdays. The fish is local herring that she cures herself in salt, brown sugar, and molasses. To prepare it for the plate it's soaked overnight, rinsed, coated with cornmeal, then fried to golden crispness.

The aged knotty pine paneling and well-worn wooden booths of Anne's Grill give it an appropriate lodgelike ambience. Even more important, perhaps, are the waitresses—friendly, patient, and chatty, and they pride themselves in having the coffee on your table the moment you hit the seat.

HOURS   Mon.–Fri. 5 am–9 pm; Sat. 5 am–10 pm; closed Sun.

SPECS   1609 Princess Anne St.; (703) 373-9621; no cards; full license.

DIRECTIONS   See **Carl's Frozen Custard,** page 313.

THE HAPPY CLAM, *Fredericksburg*

The story of the Happy Clam has a happy beginning and a happy ending, but most fascinating of all is what happened in between. We'll tell it just as we heard it over one of the best bowls of Manhattan clam chowder we've seen south of the World Trade Center.

In 1975, Withers Moncure and his son, Buzz, opened a carry-out fish market on the main road into Fredericksburg. Long deprived of first-rate seafood, customers went wild over the Moncures' live lobsters flown in from Portland, their homemade crab cakes packed full of Maryland backfin crabmeat, and their chunky chowders sold by the quart. It was the clientele who suggested that the proprietors add a few seats to the shop and serve hot dishes, and in an effort to please, the Moncures brought in a dozen chairs. On rainy days, the overflow of customers leaned against the walls.

Eventually 12 seats grew to 150, and then the intoxicating smell of success went to the owners' heads. Why limit ourselves to Fredericksburg? they asked and poof!—in no time at all they had 11 Happy Clams in every corner of the state from Roanoke to Winchester to Virginia Beach. And then, like Humpty Dumpty, the Happy Clam had a great fall, and all the boss's consultants and all the boss's men couldn't put it together again. What happened?

"Despite our size, we wanted to keep running it as a Mom and Pop business," said Buzz, as we finished our chowder and moved on to Imperial Flounder. "We didn't want to become a slick, franchised operation and lose all our personality, so we put a lot of trust into our managers." But most importantly, the Moncures didn't want anything to change at the original Fredericksburg shop, so they stayed close to home. Without regimentation, the ten outside managers went off in their own undisciplined directions and within a couple of years the Happy Clam chain was on the brink of disaster.

Ultimately the owners closed every restaurant but the original, which they sold to Bostonians Matt and Joan Howard. The Howards' first action was to hire Buzz as manager. And so, with the same man stirring the chowders as before, the Clam's customers remain as happy as ever.

That Manhattan clam chowder will cost you $1.50 per cup or $2.50 per bowl, a little higher than the average, perhaps, but this isn't an average bowl of soup. Masterfully spiced to tingle but not burn, it is thick with tender chunks of shellfish. Also delicious was the crabmeat-stuffed Imperial Flounder ($9.25 including salad bar, potatoes, and hushpuppies). Other dinners run $6.50–$10.50; meaty—not mealy—crab cakes are a big favorite ($7.75), as is the Clam's Smithfield ham and crab quiche ($8.75). Seafood dominates the lunch menu too, both as an entrée ($3.75–$4.50) and in sandwiches ($1.95–$3.75).

Naturally enough, the Happy Clam's logo depicts a smiling mollusk. We think you'll smile too when you eat here. We smiled twice—once for the restaurant's food and once for the story that verified what we've suspected all along: a scaled-up operation can't keep both its charm and its profits. The history of the Happy Clam was an open-and-shut (ouch!) case.

HOURS Mon.–Sat. 11 am–10 pm (sometimes 9 pm in winter); Sun. noon–10 pm. Closed Thanksgiving, Christmas, New Year's.

SPECS 422 William St.; (703) 371-5590; MC/V; full license.

DIRECTIONS See **Carl's,** next page.

CARL'S FROZEN CUSTARD, *Fredericksburg*

From Buzz Moncure of the Happy Clam we learned about Carl's, and everyone else we met testified to its larger-than-life status in Fredericksburg. But before they said anything else, their eyes went dewy as they gave us the all-critical news: "It's closed." Our eyes went dewy too, as they described with more passion than we could have imagined a thick, semihard, unfathomably creamy kind of ice cream that is related to Dairy Queen only in the same way that a Rolls is related to a Chevy. And then, always, they repeated the fateful words: "It's closed."

But wait a minute, you say Carl's is going to reopen on Valentine's Day? It's closed only for the winter? Aha! We thought you said it was closed forever. Oh, three and a half months without Carl's feels like forever.

Let us know.

HOURS Sun.–Thurs. 11 am–11 pm; Fri. & Sat. 11 am–11:30 pm. Closed November to mid-February.

SPECS 2200 Princess Anne St.; no phone; no cards; no liquor, just ice cream.

DIRECTIONS From exit labeled Route 3/Fredericksburg/Culpeper, head east toward Fredericksburg. Stay on Route 3 and it's 2½ miles to the **Happy Clam,** on right, just past the light at Prince Edward St. For **Anne's** and **Carl's,** continue another 0.2 mile and turn left at Caroline St. (the second light past the **Clam**). Go about ½ mile on Caroline and turn left on Herndon. In 1 block you're at Princess Anne St. For **Anne's** turn left and it's immediately on your left; for **Carl's,** turn right and in 0.4 mile it's on the left at the corner of Hunter St.

ABOUT ALEXANDRIA

If it pains you that I-95 doesn't afford easy access to Washington's marvelous restaurants, despair no longer. Alexandria, Virginia, just ½ mile from the highway, is far more manageable, easier to park in, and gentrified enough to boast an entire United Nations of restaurants. It's also picture-pretty, a sort of mini-

Georgetown with ancient trees, cobblestone streets, and colonial buildings.

Within eight blocks along King Street we uncovered excellent Jewish, Greek, Italian, Vietnamese, and even Ethiopian restaurants, a trendy fish house, and much more. As you descend King Street toward the Potomac, the restaurants get thicker (and the parking harder) until every other renovated building proclaims itself a café, bistro, lounge, or grill.

There was no way we could check all this out, and we urge you to park, walk, peek, and pick (do the parking away from the river). We've written up the well-known **Taverna Cretekou** and the less costly **Fish Market.** But by all means consider **Germanio,** a pricey but excellent Italian place; the Vietnamese **East Winds;** the **Addis,** moderately priced Ethiopian; and **Terlitzky's Jewish Deli.** And check the side streets. Even those that appear to be merely cobblestone alleys usually hide some sort of eatery.

TAVERNA CRETEKOU, *Exit 1N, Alexandria*

If the flavors here seem hearty but the textures light, it's because this Greek chef was trained in France. Those who have experienced only the heavy sort of Greek cooking will marvel at the subtlety he imparts to the tiropita (feta and cream cheese in pastry) or the roast leg of lamb seasoned with lemon and garlic.

Taverna Cretekou offers a large menu that includes the more common Greek dishes as well as appetizers like taramosalata (red caviar whipped to a light, creamy paste, $3.25) and the tempting entrée exohikon (lamb sautéed in butter with spring onions, artichokes, peas, carrots, pine nuts, casseri, and feta, all wrapped in phylo dough and baked to perfection, $9.75).

The atmosphere is as pleasant as the food is delicious. Although the tables are formally set with white and blue tablecloths, the floors are bare, the chairs plain wood, and the windows large. The mood is light and relaxed, and with a patio out back it all adds up to an environment that feels naturally Mediterranean, with nothing overdone.

Dinners are from $8.50 for moussaka to $14.50 for a filet mignon shish kebab. Full lunches run $5 to $7.75, with a meal-sized Greek salad at $4.20. Lighter appetites may want to sample the baby zucchini salad for $2.75. Whatever your choice, we think you'll like Taverna Cretekou. Even the Greek ambassador is rumored to have declared it better than the restaurants of Athens, but we suspect that that was off the record.

HOURS Tues.–Fri. 11:30 am–2:30 pm and 5–10:30 pm; Sat. noon–11 pm; Sun. 11 am–3 pm and 5–9:30 pm; closed Mon.

SPECS 818 King St.; (703) 548-8688; major cards; full license.

DIRECTIONS See Directions for Alexandria Restaurants, below.

THE FISH MARKET, *Exit 1N, Alexandria*

Trendy, noisy, happy, youthful, and spicy—such is the Fish Market in the briefest possible description. Its seven small dining rooms carved out of an old warehouse try to offer "something for everyone"—ragtime entertainment, a piano bar, raw bar, and a nearly free lunch in the main bar at Happy Hour. The tone is set by the rough-hewn wood and brick, and the place is good-naturedly gimmicky.

The Fish Market makes no concessions to beef eaters. It's all seafood, with prices running anywhere from $1.55 for a "swabby Joe" (a fishy sloppy Joe) to $11.50 for Prawns Imperial topped with crabmeat. We tried the house specialty, a chunky, zippy seafood stew full of delicious, tender scallops, chunks of snapper and haddock, clams and oysters ($2.10 for a healthy serving). It's really quite good, but have ice water on hand to put out the fire.

Most entrées are standard seafood items at about $7.50, around $2 less at lunchtime. A wide assortment of appetizers and sandwiches makes for a multitude of inexpensive possibilities.

You'll get your money's worth in any case, and you can see the Potomac for free. The shoreline is two short blocks away.

HOURS Mon.–Sat. 11:15 am–2 am (limited menu after midnight); Sun. 11:15 am–12:30 am.

SPECS 105 King St.; (703) 836-5676; major cards; full license.

DIRECTIONS FOR ALEXANDRIA RESTAURANTS

Exits 1N puts you on US 1 North. In 0.6 mile, turn right on King St. One and a half blocks brings you to **Taverna Cretekou,** on the right. Six and a half more blocks take you to the **Fish Market,** on the left. The other restaurants described (and many others) are also on King St., easily located by street address: **Addis** Restaurant, 702 King; **Germanio,** 724 King; **East Winds,** 809 King; **Terlitzky's** Deli, 1324 King. (Turn left from US 1 onto King St. if you're headed for **Terlitzky's;** all the others require a right turn.)

Florida

TOM NORRIS' PLACE FOR RIBS, *Exit 20, Tamarac*

The Great South Florida Ribs War is on! First Bobby Rubino was undisputed king, then Tony Roma rose to the challenge. Soon Roma's main man, Tom Norris, split off from his boss and opened his own place. And others are getting in on the rush to ribs. Customers pledge undying allegiance to one place or another and then switch loyalty when a newcomer sets up shop. We won't pick a champ because we didn't try them all, but we will say that the others have a long way to go to beat Tom Norris.

It's a big, slickly run, extremely popular place. As manager Marty Schwartz puts it, "We're selling the sizzle as well as the steak." Generally, *we* are more interested in the steak than the sizzle, but this kind of operation seemed to epitomize suburban Miami, so who's to say it isn't genuine? Besides, those baby back ribs were fab. They're addicting, and that's fine because you get a whole slab of them—enough to sate the most voracious addict ($9.95; $5.95 for half a slab at lunchtime).

With your ribs come a baked potato (sweet or regular) and tossed salad or slaw. Should you wish to challenge your digestive capacity you might want to precede your ribs with Tom's appetizer platter: deep-fried zucchini, eggplant, mushrooms, and onion rings ($3.00, and it'll appetize two people nicely).

It's not all ribs at this spacious, rustically appointed barn-style restaurant. Surprisingly brook trout and roast turkey got onto the menu, along with burgers, shrimp scampi, and your typical steak-house fare. There's quite a spread in prices, running $3.95–$13.95 at dinner, $2.95–$9.50 at lunch. Probably the best deal is

Tom's Dinner at Dusk (read "Early Bird") offered from 3–6 pm every day and including everything from soup to dessert for $6.95. Alas, those ribs are not among the dusk dinner entrées.

HOURS Mon.–Sat. 11 am–2 am; Sun. 3 pm–2 am. Likely to be a wait at dinner, especially on weekends; no reservations taken but can call in a takeout order. Closed Thanksgiving Day only.

SPECS 5825 N. University Drive; (305) 722-8380; major cards; full bar.

DIRECTIONS From Exit 20 tollbooth, turn right and go about 2½ miles to the light at University Drive. Right on University, and in 1 block it's on your left.

YE TOWER LUNCH, *Exit 36, Lantana*

It's about 9 miles from the turnpike to this nifty little place in Lantana; see page 251 for a description. The detour will be greatly mitigated if you can continue your travels on I-95 (it runs parallel to the turnpike in this part of the state).

DIRECTIONS From Exit 36, take Lake Worth Rd. (Route 807) east about 7 miles to US 1 (Dixie Highway). Turn right and go about 2 miles to the restaurant on left, at the corner of Central Blvd. (a little past the *National Enquirer* offices which are on the right).

ENRIQO'S MEXICAN KITCHEN, *Exit 56, Fort Pierce*

See page 254 for a description of this quite creditable Mexican restaurant accessible from the Turnpike.

DIRECTIONS From Exit 56, take Route 70 East (Okeechobee Rd.). In 1½ miles you'll pass under I-95; keep going straight on route 70 for 1½ miles, when you will bear right at the fork across from the Orange Blossom Mall. That will put you on Virginia Ave. In 2½ miles, turn right onto US 1 South. Go 1¼ miles to Center West Shopping Center on the right; **Enriqo's** is to the right of the movie theater.

THE FISH MONGER, *Exit 56, Fort Pierce*

Here's a fine seafood place with some interesting meat entrées as well. See the description on page 256.

DIRECTIONS From Exit 56, enter I-95 North for about 2 miles to the first exit, Exit 66A, which puts you on Route 68 East. In about 4 miles turn left onto US 1 North. Go about ¾ miles to the light at Fisherman's Wharf. Turn right, cross the railroad tracks, and in about 500 feet you'll see it on the right.

DESERT INN, *Exit 60, Yeehaw Junction*

It's a package store, a motel, a bar, a gas station, and it's the best little country restaurant between the two coasts of Florida. Best of all, it's a perfect antidote to the misconception that Florida is exclusively suburbs, beach towns, and retirement communities.

For everything that Florida is, it is *not* a desert, but the adobe Desert Inn looks as if it belongs in the Mojave. Inside, you'll find a cowboy-hatted clientele that wouldn't be out of place in the Southwest either, but they work the orange groves and cattle ranches of South Central Florida. You've arrived in Cracker Country, and there's no better vantage from which to view it.

The first characters you're likely to meet are permanent residents of the Desert Inn: wooden Indians who have occupied two of the fifty-odd chairs in the homey, homely room for years. Behind them is a wood-burned sign that reads: "Yeehaw Junction Chamber of Commerce." It seems that a letter addressed that way once arrived from a man inquiring about land purchase. Since there was no Chamber (there isn't even a town government), state troopers off the turnpike made up a sign and proclaimed this particular corner of the Desert Inn to be the Chamber of Commerce; the two famous Indians were designated its executive board. The letter is stuck up underneath the sign. Poor fellow never did get his land.

It's that kind of place. There's also a screened wooden box labeled: MONGOOSE WILL BITE—HANDS OFF. The door is left invitingly ajar. Naturally we had to investigate, and with a loud pop, out sprang a furry beast. It was stuffed and rigged to a spring, of course, but we didn't realize that until *after* we'd jumped six feet.

So you get the picture. What about the food? It's as close to northeastern diner fare as we've come south of the Mason-Dixon. There's something for everyone—all of it homemade and low-priced—not subtle but with plenty of character! Our chili ($1.45) was excellent; the baked chicken dinner ($3.00 complete) was almost as good. Although we never got to try it, we heard raves about the owners' homemade sausage. Doughnuts are also made from scratch, but it's best to ask when.

HOURS   Mon.–Sat. 6 am–10 pm; Sun. 8 am–9 pm.

SPECS   Highways 441 & 60; (305) 436-1054; no cards; full license.

DIRECTIONS   From Exit 60 tollbooth, turn right and in 0.4 miles you'll reach a stop sign at Route 441. It's directly across the junction.

ANGELO'S, *Exit 70, Orlando*

The search for good, inexpensive Italian food in Central Florida ends with a visit to Angelo's, winner of the *Orlando Sentinel's* Favorite Italian Restaurant poll 5 years running. But unlike the typical low-priced Italian place that is filled with chatter, clatter, and frenzy, Angelo's is dark, quiet, and pubby. In fact, from the decor there's nary a clue to the cuisine, but the antipasto buffet that greets you 4 feet inside the door pretty much answers any doubts you may have.

Overflowing with black and green olives, imported peperoncini, cherry peppers, pepperoni, anchovies, spiced jardinière, mozzarella cheese, fresh and marinated mushrooms, and Italian bread sticks as well as salad bar standbys, this buffet costs $4.50 by itself. But—and it's a big "but"—it comes free with all dinners, including the special of the day. Our day's special, lasagna, cost only $3.95! That was on a Tuesday. Monday's special is spaghettini, and it's the same price, as is Wednesday's ravioli. And so on. (More on weekends.) The lasagna was quite creditable, its ricotta creamed with parsley, and its sauce, while not highly spiced, still left a pleasant tingle on the palate.

Of course you can spend a lot more than $3.95. Veal is this restaurant's particular pride, and for it you'll pay as much as $11. In the house specialty, Veal Angelo, a tender cut of meat is first simmered in butter and lemon, then served with mushrooms and peppers in a wine sauce. Other dinner entrées run $5–$10. Lunches are less, of course, and $2.95 sandwiches appear at midday; at that time of day, add $1 for the antipasto bar.

Whatever you start out with, Angelo's snowy, lemony Italian ice leaves you with a sprightly taste that will last many miles.

HOURS Lunch: Mon.–Fri. 11:30 am–2:30 pm. Dinner: Mon.–Thurs. 5–10 pm; Fri. & Sat. 5–11 pm; Sun. 4–10 pm.

SPECS 6223 South Orange Blossom Trail; (305) 855-6223; major cards; full license.

DIRECTIONS From Exit 70 tollbooth, go straight, following signs to Orlando (*not* Orlando International Airport). This will put you on Orange Blossom Trail North. Go about 2¼ miles; it's on the right, just past the light at Lancaster. Under 5 minutes.

BAKERSTREET RESTAURANT, *Exit 70, Orlando*

On page 24 we describe the Bakerstreet Restaurant and Bakerstreet Seafood Grill. The good news for Florida turnpikers is that there's another Bakerstreet in Orlando quite easy for you to reach. The bad news is that this one doesn't have a bubble-enclosed kitchen. But even if you can't watch the chef from your seat, the fish is cooked over mesquite and tastes just as good. All the favorites of the other Bakerstreet Restaurant are served here too.

HOURS   11 am–1 am, every day.

SPECS   7403 Orange Blossom Trail; (305) 851-8811; major cards (except Diners); full license.

DIRECTIONS   From Exit 70, go straight, following signs for Orlando (*not* Orlando International Airport). This will put you on Orange Blossom Trail North, and in 1¾ miles it's on your right.

KIM WU CHINESE RESTAURANT, *Exit 75, Orlando*

This first-rate Chinese restaurant is almost as accessible from Florida's Turnpike as it is from I-4. See page 22 for a description.

DIRECTIONS   From Florida's Turnpike use Exit 75 to enter I-4 West and in half a mile get off at Exit 30B. This puts you on Route 435 North. In about 1½ miles, turn left into Turkey Lake Village. It's at the far left end of the shopping center, hidden behind a hardware store.

INDEX OF RESTAURANTS
AND TOWNS

Abingdon, VA 175
Aiken, SC 37–39
Alexandria, VA 313–316
Alfalfa Restaurant 155
Amy's/Los Amigos 203
Angelo's (Orlando, FL) 320
Angelo's (St. Mary's, GA) 274
Angus Barn, The 74
Ankie's Deli Delights 217
Anne's Grill 310
Annie Oak's 218
Another Thyme 234
Apple Cake Tea Room 144
Archie's 278
Ashland, VA 307
At Lana's, Naturally 216
Athenian, The 257
Athens, TN 141
Atlanta, GA 122–129, 205–209
Augusta, GA 34–37
Aunt Fannie's Cabin 124
Aw Shucks 105

Bakatsias Cuisine 231
Bakerstreet Restaurant 24, 321

Bakerstreet Seafood Grill 24
Baldwin, FL 27
Barnes' Family Restaurant 100
Beacon Drive-In 49
Beall's 1860 117
Beautiful Restaurant, The 123
Beignets 271
Berea, KY 151, 153
Berry's-on-the-Hill 55
Bethea's 137
Black Mountain, NC 64
Black Tulip, The 260
Blacksburg, SC 220
Bluff City, TN 171
Blythewood, SC 159
Boone Tavern Hotel 151
Brett Brett's Sandwich Shop
  98
Brian's Steak House 238
Brickworks, The 130
Bridgetender Inn 265
Bristol, VA/TN 173–175
Brunswick, GA 275, 276
BT's 182
Buddy Burger 186
Buddy Freddy's 19

Buddy's BBQ 146
Burlington, NC 228, 229
Bushnell, FL 100

C. H. Mitchell, the Barbecue
   King 109
Calhoun, GA 134
Camak, GA 33
Canton Restaurant 181
Canton, NC 63
Carl's Frozen Custard 313
Caro-Mi Dining Room 44
Carolina Café 298
Carrie Nation's 40
Cartersville, GA 133
Caryville, TN 147
Center View Inn 69
Central Coffee Shop 290
Chandler's Downtown 211
Charleston, SC 56–59
Charlotte, NC 160–163
Charlottesville, VA 86, 87
Chattanooga, TN 137–139
Cherokee Restaurant 279
Chester, VA 302
Chic-a-Plenty 287
Chrome Plate Cafeteria 138
Claire's 73
Clark's Restaurant 289
Cline's Barbecue 65
Coalie Harry's 201
Cocoa Village, FL 260
Colonial Inn, The
   (Hillsborough, NC) 230
Colonial Inn, The (Vienna,
   GA) 114
Colonnade, The 207
Columbia 51–53
Commerce, GA 211

Concord, TN 144
Continental Corner, The 56
Conyers, GA 29
Corbin, KY 149
Cordele, GA 114
Corky Bell's 258
Couch's Real Pit Barbeque 140
Country Adventures
   Barbecue Barn 68
Country Kettle 121
Country Place, The
   (Cartersville, GA) 137
Country Place, The
   (Chattanooga, TN) 133
Cove Lake State Park
   Restaurant 147
Crab Trap, The 94
Crawfordville, GA 31
Crazy Elliot's 72
Creedmore, NC 235
Cross-Eyed Cricket, The 143
Cutting Board, The 228

D & H Barbeque 290
D & W Cafeteria 149
Dalton, GA 135, 136
Darien, GA 278
Davidson, NC 164
Dayton, VA 191
Daytona, FL 263
Desert Inn 319
Ding's 173
Dixie Cream Restaurant 103
Dobson, NC 167
Don Murray's Barbecue
   Restaurant 78
Doswell, VA 308
Duke's Barbecue 55
Durham, NC 73, 231–234

Elettra's 46
Elite Epicurean, The 52
Elizabeth on 37th 284
Emmeline and Hessie's 276
Enriqo's Mexican Kitchen 254
Everybody's Restaurant 27
Expressions Restaurant 43

Falls View Restaurant 119
Fancy Fox Tearoom and Gift
    Shop 223
Fancy Gap, VA 168
Farmer's Hall Restaurant, The
    214
Fish Market, The 315
Fish Monger, The 256
Flagler Beach, FL 265
Florence, SC 40, 291
Fort Lauderdale, FL 250
Fort Myers, FL 90
Fort Pierce, FL 254, 256
Fredericksburg, VA 310–313
Fresh Air Barbeque 120

Gainesville, FL 103–106
Gastonia, NC 221, 223
Georgia Pig, The 275
Gilbert's Restaurant 37
Grace Place 303
Grandma's 135
Grapevine Pub 250
Green Jacket, The 34
Greensboro, NC 72, 226–228
Greenville, SC 215, 216
Guiseppe's Streets of New
    York Pizza 131
Gypsy Cab Company 268

Half Way House 302
Halfmoon Landing, The 280
Hallandale, FL 248
Ham's Southern Style Deli
    229
Hamburger Heaven 253
Hampton, VA 81
Harborside Restaurant 270
Hardeeville, SC 287
Harold's Kosher Style Deli 60
Harrisonburg, VA 193, 194
Helena Café 93
Henderson, NC 236
Hendersonville, NC 43
Henry's 56
Herb's Grill 51
Heritage Family Restaurant
    194
Hickory, NC 68
High Falls, GA 119
Hillsborough, NC 230
Homeplace, The 183
Huck's 72
Hungry Pioneer, The 148

Irregardless Café 75
Islander, The 280

Jackie's Seafood Kitchen 273
Jackson, GA 120
Jacksonville, FL 271, 273
James Place 92
Jarrell Truck Plaza Cafeteria
    308
Jerry's Menagerie Truck Stop
    290
Jess' Quick Lunch 193
Jim's Ranch 210

Jimmy the Greek's 131
Joe Dale's Cajun House 205
Joe's Home Cooking 91
Joe's Stone Crab Restaurant 242
John's 294

Kannapolis, NC 224
Katz's Deli 208
Keith's Red Barn 288
Kelly's Steak House 220
Kernersville, NC 71
Kim Wu Chinese Restaurant 22
King's Barbeque 240
Klaus' Cuisine 263
Knoxville, TN 60–61, 146

La Casita 305
La Esquina de Tejas 244
La Tache 161
Lake City, FL 107
Landmark Place 165
Lane Street Grill 224
Lankford Manor 112
Lantana, FL 251
Lantern, The 167
Le Café Naturel 35
Le Paris 101
Le Pavillon 267
Left Banque, The 117
Len Berg's Restaurant 116
Lenoir City, TN 143
Lexington Barbeque 225
Lexington, KY 154–158
Lexington, NC 225
Lexington, VA 187
Lincoln Restaurant 17

Lineburger's Fish Camp 221
Little Dutch Restaurant 170
Littlejohn's New York Delicatessen 23
Log House Restaurant, The 178
Love's Catfish Restaurant 281
Lumberton, NC 294

Macon, GA 116, 117
Madison, GA 30
Mae's Country Kitchen 108
Maggie Foster's Restaurant 110
Mammy's Kitchen 283
Manning, SC 290
Mansion at Griffin Gate, The 157
Marietta, GA 130, 131
Marimack Inn 175
Mario the Baker 246
Marion, VA 177
Martinsburg, WV 203
Mary Mac's Tearoom 127
Maurice's Piggy Park 53
McDonough, GA 121
Mel's Hot Dogs 97
Melbourne, FL 257, 258
Melvin's 129
Miami Beach, FL 242
Miami, FL 244
Michael's Restaurant 33
Middleburg Steak House 237
Middletown, VA 198
Midway, GA 279
Millstone Inn, The 62
Miss Pearl's Soul Café 101
Mitch's Cozy Kitchen & Ice Cream Parlor 131

Mocksville, NC 69
Morganton, NC 65–67
Morristown, TN 170
Morrisville, NC 74
Mountain Greenery, The 64
Mountain Top Restaurant 168
Mrs. Bonner's Private Club 31
Mrs. Wilkes' Boarding House 286

Natural Bridge, VA 186
Neal's Barbeque 33
New Market, VA 195
New Perry Hotel 115
New Prospect Seafood 48
New Prospect, SC 48
Newbern, VA 179
Newport, TN 62
Noah's Gallery 47
Norfolk, VA 80
Norlina, NC 237
North Miami, FL 246
Nottoway Restaurant, The 239

O'Brienstein's 84
Oakwood Café (Inc.) 136
Ocala, FL 101, 102
Old Original Barbecue House 162
Old Point Steak and Spaghetti House 81
Olde Bell Restaurant 63
Ooletawah, TN 140
Orangeburg, SC 55
Original Pizza Palace, The 106
Orlando, FL 21–25

Palm Beach, FL 253
Palm Parlor, The 187
Palmetto, FL 94
Palms Restaurant, The 287
Pampered Palate, The 190
Papaleno's 153
Parker's Barbecue 297
Peking Restaurant 300
Pendleton, SC 212–214
Peregrine Fine Food and Spirits 164
Perlis Truck Stop 114
Perry, GA 115
Petersburg, VA 240
Pierce's Pitt Bar-B-Q 83
Pink Restaurant, The 292
Plant City, FL 19
Plaza Restaurant 275
Polly's Luncheonette 37
Poogan's Porch 58
Punta Gorda, FL 91

Rachel's Café 33
Radford, VA 181, 182
Rafter's, The 141
Raleigh, NC 75–79
Ray Lever's Bar-B-Que Hut 159
Read House, The 139
Red's Seafood 212
Regas, The 61
Richmond, VA 84, 303–306
Ridgeland, SC 287
Ridgewood Restaurant 171
Roanoke City Market 185
Roanoke, VA 185
Robert's Dock 107
Rock Hill, SC 160
Rocky Mount, NC 298

Ronnie's Restaurant 23
Rowe's Family Restaurant 189
Rowland, NC 292

Sage Bagel and Appetizer
  Shop 248
Saint Augustine, FL 266–270
Saint Mary's, GA 274
Salem Tavern 70
Sand Point Inn 261
Santee, SC 289
Saratoga, The 154
Savannah, GA 281–286
Shepherd Restaurant 134
Shilling's on the Square 131
Skipper's Barbecue 236
Smithfield Bar-B-Q 296
Smithfield, NC 296
Smokey Pig, The 307
Snook's Old Fashioned
  Barbecue 69
Snow's Good Food 71
Some Thyme 232
South Hill, VA 238
Southern Kitchen 195
Spartanburg, SC 49, 217–218
Spring Garden Bar and Grill
  228
Spring House, The 196
State Farmer's Market
  Restaurant 90
Statesville, NC 165–167
Staunton, VA 189, 190
Sterling Snack Bar 66
Stone House, The 67
Sub-Express 167
Summerville, SC 56
Sunset Café 226
Suwannee, GA 210

Sweetwater, TN 142
Syble's Restaurant 235

T. K. Tripp's 77
Tallent House 177
Tam's Tavern 160
Tamarac, FL 317
Tampa, FL 17–19, 96–99
Taverna Cretekou 314
The Happy Clam 311
Thomas House Restaurant
  and Home Bakery 191
Thompson, GA 33
Thunderbird Motor Inn 291
Tifton, GA 112
Titusville, FL 261
Tom Norris' Place for Ribs 317
Tony's Chuckwagon 86
Trainstation Marketplace 174
Triangle Diner 200
Tryon, NC 44–48
Twin Tops Fish Camp 221

Valdosta, GA 109, 110
Valley Pike Inn 179
Variety Restaurant 38
Varsity, The 126
Venice, FL 92, 93
Victorian House, The 29
Vienna, GA 114
Vince Perone's Restaurant 215

Walt Disney World Village 20
Walterboro, SC 288
Warfield, VA 239
Waterside, The 80
Wayside Inn 198

Weldon, NC 300
West Columbia, SC 53
West Tampa, FL 17
White Springs, FL 108
Williamsburg, KY 148
Williamsburg, VA 83
Wilson's Barbecue 297
Wilson's Drive-In 142
Wilson, NC 297
Winchester, VA 200, 201
Winston-Salem, NC 70

Woodbine, GA 275
Woodstock, VA 196
Wytheville, VA 178

Ybor City, FL 19
Ye Olde Colonial Restaurant
  30
Ye Tower Restaurant 251
Yeehaw Junction, FL 319

Our best source of leads to worthwhile restaurants is you, the traveler who cares. Please tell us of any you know that lie close to the road, and we'll check them out for future editions in THE INTERSTATE GOURMET series.

Send your suggestions to:

Summit Books
Code ISG
1230 Avenue of the Americas
New York, NY 10020

Restaurant name_____

Near Highway_____

Exit_____

City_____ State_____

Directions_____

_____

_____

_____

Comments_____

_____

_____

_____

_____

_____

_____